THE EMPTY

THE
EMPTY PROMISE
OF
GODISM

Peter Sammons

Glory to Glory Publications

*Published in Great Britain by
Glory to Glory Publications, an imprint of Buy Research Ltd.*
Glory to Glory Publications
PO Box 212 SAFFRON WALDEN CB10 2UU

Cover design by Roger Judd

ISBN 978 0 9551790 6 8

*Printed in Great Britain
by Bookmarque Ltd, Croydon*

Contents

FOREWORD

Godism — an empty promise

Let's begin with a game — we'll call it *the oligarch's game*. There are today dozens of men who single-handedly own large slices of industry and commerce — especially, for example, in Russia. They are generally called *the oligarchs*. Their fortunes are measured in billions and they frankly have more money than they can possibly spend. So the game we are about to describe is one that, who knows, an oligarch may one day decide to play for his personal amusement. Think of yourself as a potential player. You are down on your luck. Your mortgage is in arrears. Your bank manager wants to see you. Your job is looking a bit shaky — and it doesn't pay you very well, in any case. You have $250 in the bank. Your car is twelve years old and badly needs a service.

The game goes like this: before you sits an industrial oligarch, with a slight smirk on his face. He is a multi-billionaire. In front of him is a small table and on it are three identical, unmarked and sealed envelopes. One contains a bankers draft made out in the sum of $1M payable to you. The other two envelopes contain IOUs ('I owe you' in English parlance) made out from you to the oligarch in the sum of $5K. The game is simple; you choose between the three envelopes. If you pick the one containing the bankers draft, then you walk away enriched. If you pick one of the other two, then you simply owe the oligarch five thousand dollars, a sum he will ensure you pay, eventually. What gives this game its real zest is that the offer of $1M must be tempting; it will certainly resolve your short term (and perhaps long term) financial problems. But the risk is high: you stand only a one in three chance of picking the right envelope. You don't have to play the game, the choice is yours. What do you do? Readers might want to pause and think through this for a few minutes!

What has the oligarch's game got to do with a religious book? In this world there are many religions. Some people think of God as being like an oligarch and that He plays an elaborate game of hide and seek with us. Most think of God, if they think of Him at all, as being generally both moral and good, and One Who would never place us into an oligarch's game and would not dream of treating us in that way. Unlike an oligarch, God certainly is not seen as One sitting with an imperturbable smirk on His face. Rather, most people seem to believe that God views humans with the love and concern of a good parent, indeed a loving Father Who desires the very best for his children.

The analogy we are making is that there are 'on offer' many religions—rather more, in fact, than the three envelopes sitting on the oligarch's table. It is the author's contention that the choice that a finite human makes about an infinite God will affect their life here in this world. Indeed such a decision must ultimately have a transformational effect both in this world, and for eternity. But getting to know and follow the God revealed in the Holy Bible requires effort on our part. Indeed it requires a choice to be made. Like *the oligarch's game* — if you want the reward, you will need to 'get off the fence' and make a positive decision. If you stay on the fence forever, then in a sense the decision is already made for you — you remain as you are, for better or for worse. If you decide to make a choice, then there is a risk that you will make a wrong choice. Far from being blessed, you may find your condition worse than it was before you chose.

Will people get off the fence and make a choice? If they make the right choice then their future should be secure, although it is uniquely Christianity that candidly tells its followers that to be a true disciple of God will inevitably lead to problems, difficulties and uncertainties in this world. To be more precise, it tells us that to be a follower of Jesus Christ will bring opposition. As Jesus Himself said, in Matthew 10:22 **"all men will hate you because of me"**. Although Jesus was speaking to disciples whom He was sending out to preach the simple message that 'the Kingdom is near', there is no doubt that He meant His words to be understood by His disciples down through history, as we will explore later in this book.

What do people most want in life? Peace; security; loving relationships; a future. These wants and needs will come near the top of the list for most people, irrespective of gender or culture. It may be an inexplicable and unwelcome fact to many people in the West that 'religion' is resurgent in this world. At the time of writing, the Western world is celebrating the 150th anniversary of the publication of Charles Darwin's *On the Origin of Species*. Just thirty years ago plenty of atheists believed that Darwin's theories had sounded the death knell of organised religion. Indeed Darwinism was seen as the prime philosophical engine to marginalise religion and make it irrelevant. The atheists were premature. The Iranian Revolution in 1979 marked the beginning of an assertive form of Islam not experienced for more than 200 years. The rising economies of the East gave their local religions greater confidence. The recycling of petro-dollars from the West and the consequent phenomenal growth of the Arab economies led to 'Shariah compliant banking' becoming a semi-mainstream financial tool. Political correctness led to protections in the Western world for the 'new' religions that had been brought with them by immigrant communities — protections from what had once been considered normal civil discourse, in other words discussion about what people actually believe and the reasons why they believe those things. Only in the West did religion — in the shape of traditional Christianity — suffer broad setback during the late twentieth and early twenty-first centuries, for reasons largely beyond the scope of this book.

The unexpected resurgence of *the religions* coincided with the social and economic factor known as Globalisation. Suddenly religion had taken on a global dynamic never before experienced. Borders seemed to matter for little as migration surged to become a significant economic and political reality. The Western world, in particular, which had for the previous fifty years welcomed immigrant communities (though with varying degrees of warmth) experienced in the 1990s an invasion of new cultures complete with their religions and with no real desire to integrate with their host communities. Western people generally were — and still are — reluctant to confront the sober reality of what all this meant. The West lacked any clear religious certainty of its own but was being forced to make way for, and to make concessions to, a range of non-western religions. Suddenly 'god' mattered in a way that had not been apparent for 100 years or more.

And now today: the fact that *the religions* can be a catalyst for social tension and even for warfare is well understood. Indeed for many people in the West this religious potential for tensions is a prime reason (or excuse?) in their rapid retreat from traditional Christianity. For a long time there has been a gathering hope: a hope that all *the religions*, which many people — even seriously irreligious people — understand can be equally a catalyst for good as much as for harm, will in some way come together in human unity; will put aside their differences and 'see' that they all worship the same deity who loves and values them all. People often hold this rather vague view whether or not they are personally observant of any religion. As noted above, many people have in the Western world retreated from organised Christianity. Predominantly they have opted instead for a halfway-house of religious semi-belief, usually called 'agnosticism' — an agnostic being someone who essentially will not, or cannot, make up their mind about God. From empirical evidence (based largely on surveys) agnostics tend towards a half belief that somehow 'god' if 'he' or 'it' exists at all, will look after them personally — and indeed has an obligation to do so. The traditional understanding of Christianity, that those who knowingly refuse Jesus the Son of God and refuse His substitutionary and propitiatory death on the cross, will find themselves on the wrong side of eternal judgement is, in any case, a notion broadly rejected in the West with its relativist moral framework. It is widely seen as God's 'fault' that competing religions are so different, and so it is His responsibility either to get His message straightened-out so that everyone can see which path is right or, more popularly, to provide for mankind a sort of *package deal* leading to eternal happiness. Providing people are not proactively sinful (although there is little common consensus about what 'sinfulness' actually is) then it is God's responsibility to 'see people alright in the end' — in other words to 'save' them and provide an eternal home for them. In a very real sense people expect God, to use a technical Christian word, to 'justify' them before Himself.

The Evolutionary Theory of Religion

That many ordinary people who would be happy to call themselves irreligious should hold such views is not altogether surprising. These views are in some vague way comforting and put the onus upon 'god' to sort things out. That people who are 'religious' should hold these views is also not altogether surprising, as religious people can often hold quite vague notions about 'god' and their relationship with 'him' – or 'it'. For example, Hindus can quite comfortably hold these underlying assumptions as they believe in many gods, although their views on 'the hereafter' are a long way from the hopes and aspirations of most Western people. It is when we come to people who are church-attending Christians, who hold the view that all religions are essentially the same and that 'we all worship one God', that we frankly should be surprised. The idea or proposition of the gradual confluence and mingling of religions — the evolutionary theory of religions, if you will — is one that is indisputably a departure from broadly 2,000 years of Christian belief and understanding. A question then must be faced, if people have any integrity about this new religious belief. It is simply this: *is this god-focus or god-centric, god-positive and (selectively) religion-negative view of the deity correct*? A subsidiary question might be can you hold this view and still be a mainstream Christian? And perhaps most pertinently of all, is this view about *the religions* one that God Himself has revealed? That, broadly, is the subject of this book.

The one thing that encompasses the Hindu religion

certain other eastern religions, 'syncretistic Christianity', and more generally relativist Western thought on the subject of religion, is this notion of 'god'. I use a small 'g' in describing this idea of deity because at the very best, it is simply a collection of ideas about the Eternal. At its worst it is little more than woolly thinking. A Godist, then, is someone who believes that there are many paths to 'god' and that no one religion holds all the answers. In this politically correct age, in any case, to suggest that one religion is right implies that the others are wrong and this could offend some people. Causing offence — in the Western world, at any rate — is becoming *the* unpardonable sin! Polite people will no longer make any suggestion that there can be serious differences between *the religions*, for fear of causing offence. And nice people generally will make it their business to 'work together' for mutual respect, mutual tolerance, mutual understanding and 'peace'. The words 'respect', 'tolerance', 'understanding' and 'peace' have become almost modern theological terms, to rival the older Christian ones of grace, justification, faith, propitiation and so on.

It must be a profoundly debatable point as to whether our ideas about God can ever be right, especially when they clash with His disclosure of Himself. For those sold on the idea of Godism as a theological belief system, or even flirting with Godism, there are some uncomfortable and difficult questions that, once again, must be faced by anyone with real integrity in this debate. Just what sort of a God do we believe in? Is He good, or bad? And can we logically hold to the notion that all religions, providing they are not 'extreme' (another word that seems to have taken on almost religious overtones!) are sent by God. It is this subject area that we will explore together in this book.

This is not a book about religion in the West. Nor is it a book about comparative religions — although some inevitable comparison must be made if we are honestly and thoroughly to investigate the phenomenon of Godism. It is however a book that is written from a traditional Christian perspective. Accordingly, considerable use is made of the Holy Bible to draw out what Christians generally believe to be what God has revealed about Himself. If the reader is a Christian then hopefully this will be considered a useful place to begin our investigations. If the reader is a non-Christian or a doubter/agnostic, then it may be objected that the Holy Bible must *ipso facto* be biased and to that extent must be an 'unreliable witness'. Such readers are invited not to forget their objection, but simply to lay it to one side whilst reviewing the subject of Godism from a traditional Christian perspective. You can always come back to your objection at a later stage and reconsider the arguments contained in this book from that perspective of objection.

Does all this matter? *So what* if people do have differing notions of 'god' in a modern (or postmodern!) pluralistic, open society? If you don't believe in God, surely it is good that those people who actually do believe should also believe that all *the religions* are essentially the same. At the very least, it's a comfort to them. At the very best, it may help to make the world a nicer place in which to live. This book, however seeks to demonstrate that it *does* matter what people believe about Godism, because there is real evidence that the whole idea is actually repugnant to God Himself, and that belief in Godism takes people further away from God, not closer to Him. And, indeed, that if Godism is as wrong as the author believes it to be, then those who put their faith in this Godist 'god' cannot and will not find true peace in this world. Rather they risk facing an eternity without

God, Who is described in so many magnificent ways in the Holy Bible, but perhaps most profoundly as a God who is love. Is it worth risking eternal injury simply to placate the notions of a culturally acceptable, politically correct, relativist, post modern theological *theory of religions*? And, moreover, a belief system that may itself become outmoded in a few years and be replaced by some other belief system yet to be devised — and indeed replaced by something far, far worse?

Readers will, it is hoped, forgive frequent reference to the British Broadcasting Corporation (BBC) as a sort of shorthand or metaphor for basic Godist beliefs. The Corporation, which was set up in 1922 under the chairmanship of an avowed Christian (John Charles Walsham Reith, later Lord Reith) has morphed over the years to become an organisation dominated by what may be considered as 'liberal left' social values which include a strong disdain for organised, traditional Christianity. Surprisingly, even the BBC itself has expressed concern about its skewed political and cultural leanings. This is demonstrated by the fact that an internal BBC summit attended by senior executives and broadcasters was held in September 2006 to review the whole subject. This summit was reported, on the basis of leaked documents, by a range of UK newspapers, notably in the London *Evening Standard* and in its online version *This is London* (October 2006) from which these extracts are taken:

WE ARE BIASED, ADMIT
THE STARS OF BBC NEWS

It was the day that a host of BBC executives and star presenters admitted what critics have been telling them for years: the BBC is dominated by trendy, Left-leaning liberals who are biased against Christianity and in favour of multiculturalism.

A leaked account of an 'impartiality summit' called by BBC chairman Michael Grade, ... reveals that executives would let the Bible be thrown into a dustbin on a TV comedy show, but not the Koran, and that they would broadcast an interview with Osama Bin Laden if given the opportunity. Further, it discloses that the BBC's 'diversity tsar', wants Muslim women newsreaders to be allowed to wear veils when on air.

At the secret meeting in London last month .... BBC executives admitted the corporation is dominated by homosexuals and people from ethnic minorities, deliberately promotes multiculturalism, is anti-American, anti-countryside and more sensitive to the feelings of Muslims than Christians. One veteran BBC executive said: 'There was widespread acknowledgement that we may have gone too far in the direction of political correctness. Unfortunately, much of it is so deeply embedded in the BBC's culture, that it is very hard to change it.'

In one of a series of discussions, executives were asked to rule on how they would react if the controversial comedian Sacha Baron Cohen — known for his offensive characters Ali G and Borat — was a guest on the programme *Room 101*. On the show, celebrities are invited to throw their pet hates into a dustbin and it was imagined that Baron Cohen chose some kosher food, the Archbishop of Canterbury, a Bible and the Koran. Nearly everyone at the summit, including the show's actual producer and the BBC's head of drama, Alan Yentob, agreed they could all be thrown into the bin, except the Koran for fear of offending Muslims.

The full account of the meeting shows how senior BBC figures queued up to lambast their employer. Political pundit Andrew Marr said: 'The BBC is not impartial or neutral. It's a publicly funded, urban organisation with an abnormally large number of young people, ethnic minorities and gay people. It has a liberal bias — not so much a party-political bias. It is better expressed as a *cultural liberal* bias.'

Former BBC business editor Jeff Randall said he complained to a 'very senior news executive', about the BBC's pro-multicultural stance but was given the reply: 'The BBC is not neutral in multiculturalism: it believes in it and promotes it.'

Andrew Marr told The Mail on Sunday last night: 'The BBC must always try to reflect Britain, which is mostly a provincial, middle-of-the-road country. Britain is not a mirror image of the BBC or the people who work for it.'[1]

Its easy to bash the BBC and there can be no doubt that it does try to exercise at least a measure of fairness and impartiality in its output. Yet it does at the same time articulate a worldview that, where it intersects with religion, is Godist in its overall complexion. True, the BBC at the time

---

[1] www.thisislondon.co.uk/news/article-23371617-details/We are biased, admits the stars BBC News/article.do

of writing continues to provide a *daily service* broadcast on Radio 4, as well as occasional TV presentations such as the broadly Christian *Songs of Praise*. But beyond these nods to religious conventionality, its light entertainment output reflects its true ethos in being very often blasphemous and dismissive as regards Christianity — and sadly this is no exaggeration. The Rev. David Holloway wrote a useful book first published in 2000 called *Church and State in the New Millennium* and sub-titled 'Issues of Belief and Morality for the 21st Century'. In it he makes the point that Britain, most of Europe and the US are in practice secular *theistic* societies — not secular *atheistic* societies. He notes that, if 'secular' is defined by an absence of public reference to God, then we are secular. There is, he notes, little said about God, Jesus Christ and His purposes for the world (apart from blasphemously) in the mainstream media or in education. But Holloway notes that social surveys continue to show that approx 70% of people regard themselves as Christian, while roughly 4% regard themselves as belonging to another faith, whilst only 20% are of 'no faith'.

That the BBC (as a case in point, but the same comment can be made of the media generally) can heavily promote such a one-sided, secular and Godist agenda means that it is simply non-representative of its core constituency. Indeed it could now be considered, without much exaggeration, as the propaganda arm of the secularist movement! So readers will find a number of references to the BBC in this book as illustrative of a broadly Godist media agenda, and often as a sort of metaphor for heavily secularised belief systems.

David Holloway makes one other key point in the Foreword to his book: although it concerns *political* developments in the UK, Holloway's observation actually helps to articulate a general reality within British society at large (which will inevitably be reflected in other Western societies — though often in a less exaggerated form). Holloway notes that in the UK Labour Party there are, on the one hand 'ethical socialists'. Sadly, notes Holloway, their numbers are in decline, but they used to reflect a strong sense of personal responsibility, strong social conscience and strong working class roots. They would often include traditional Roman Catholics and Methodists in their number. But these are being replaced on the other hand by 'egoistic socialists'. These are often university educated, middle class, former student protesters. Many will have tried drugs, most support cohabitation and seem to vote in favour of relaxation of curbs on homosexual practice. They are socialist only in the sense that they call for the state — which in practice means other people — to pick up the bill for their folly.

This is matched, continues Holloway, on the right wing of politics by, on the one hand 'ethical capitalists' or classic liberals. The heart of a free society for these is personal responsibility guided by conscience. With a strong attachment to marriage and the family, a good number traditionally held allegiance to the orthodox Church of England. But on the other hand there are 'egoistic capitalists', or libertarians. Some of these, notes Holloway, can be brutal, playing little attention to human need, and morally decadent, therefore supporting the broad immoral agenda as much as the 'egoistic socialists'. Although Holloway does not so comment, it is a fact that 'egoistic capitalists' also expect the state to pick up the bill for the casualties of their policies as, for example, some right-wing media argue for a complete relaxation of anti narcotics legislation and accept, with a shrug, that there will be an increase in the numbers of serious drug abusers. But they simultaneously argue that state sponsored health services should simply be geared-up to deal with these additional drug victims.

With the media and political classes increasingly of a like-minded approach to moral issues, there seems to be a growing willingness to promote a Godist agenda in the interests of social cohesion. Or perhaps more pertinently, to co-opt *the religions* to become an extension of the state's apparatus to manage society's casualties. If *the religions* can be persuaded to partner with the state in this way, then the state increasingly offers them financing to undertake 'good works'.

This book will explore, then, the promise that Godism appears to hold out. To politicians Godism is seen as a useful prop to their plans for social cohesion in a world of rapid and potentially vast future population migrations. To some religiously minded people, Godism seems to promise a new 'understanding' between *the religions*, enabling them to worship 'god' in their various ways whilst discovering a joy in each other's diverse and differing beliefs — and indeed celebrating those beliefs. In this way mankind will build and discover an elusive peace that this world has never before enjoyed. We may indeed not only improve the world immeasurably, but save it from the self destruction that is today re-emerging as a real existential threat. These are lofty visions indeed to build on what is actually a perilously narrow theological base. Further, there remains the awkward reality of God and what are His plans for this World. Are His plans in any way furthered by Godism? It is all these questions that we are about to explore together as we discover whether Godism is a pregnant promise, with much to deliver to the world, or an empty promise, that merely confuses and distracts.

One word used in this book that may require explanation is the word *identikit*. Most British readers will know that this is a device used by police services that need to speedily build a picture of a wanted suspect based upon one or more eye witness accounts of his or her facial features. To quote from the Oxford dictionary, an identikit picture is 'a constructed picture of a person assembled from transparent strips showing typical facial features according to witnesses' descriptions.' *Identikit* is used as a metaphor in this book for the idea that people think very little of assembling bits and pieces from *the religions* and from their own assumptions to build a picture of the sort of deity that they would like to see — and then call this 'god'. It might also be referred to as a sort of 'DIY god' (from 'do it yourself'). Whether these same people truly understand the various beliefs and shibboleths that they so casually borrow from *the religions* is a moot point — generally, it would appear, they do not. But the word *identikit* does seem to capture some of the flavour of the way that many, particularly in the relativistic Western world, seem to approach religion. For the record, identikit pictures more often than not fail to provide a good, recognisable, likeness of a wanted criminal — the success rate is put as low as 20% in some studies. It is perhaps superfluous to query: is the Godists' 'DIY god' likewise one with an 80% probability of being an incorrect image of the Divine?

Throughout this book we quote from the Holy Scriptures. Readers are invited to judge this book and in a sense its author, on the basis of whether the extracts taken are true to the spirit of the Bible as a whole, and true to the context in which the verses taken were originally given. It has been rightly said that *a verse taken out of context is a pretext*.

In other words there are people who will take parts of the Bible and use them in ways never intended by God, Whom the Scriptures tell us, is their ultimate author. People may take verses right out of context and use them as a pretext to support some factional viewpoint. In this regard then, the author of this book does wherever possible and where it does not interrupt the flow of the argument being developed, try to give a sense of the context in which the Scripture portion as used in this book was originally understood by its first readers, back in biblical times. The nomenclature of Bible references — book, chapter and verse — will be in the following format: *Psalm 34, verse 8* is rendered *Psalm 34:8*. In this book, direct quotations from the Holy Bible are taken from the New International Version (NIV) unless otherwise stated. Reference to the GNB in parentheses is to the Good News Bible ©American Bible Society 1966. Reference to the RSV means the Revised Standard Version. Reference to NRSV means the New Revised Standard Version (pub. Zondervan 1993). Reference to NKJV means the New King James Version Version©. Where no version is acknowledged in the text in this book, it is generally because the wording is identical in more than one English translation. Bible version acknowledgements appear on the title verso page, opposite the Contents page.

1

THE PROMISE

Imagine a world . . . .

Times move on. It shows that we truly are living in a new century and a rapidly changing world when a writer considers it necessary to explain who *The Beatles* were, but for those who don't know or have forgotten, *The Beatles* were one of Britain's major rock and pop successes of the 1960s, a band of four singing artistes and widely seen as symbols of a revolutionary new age — the *swinging sixties*. The group consisted of John Lennon, Paul McCartney, George Harrison and Ringo Starr. It broke up in 1970 and the artistes went their separate ways. Separated from *The Beatles* John Lennon now wrote what was to become his personal 'hymn' in praise of his own anti-religion, anti-nationalist view of the world. Remember, these were the years of 'flower power'! Called *Imagine*, his song (recorded and released in 1971 in his second solo album — also called *Imagine*) invited people to imagine a world where there was no hell below us, and above us, only sky. Imagine, sang Lennon, a world where there was no religion and all the people lived life in peace. A world where there were no countries — so nothing to kill or die for. The song was, in Lennon's words, 'chocolate-coated' for public consumption. By this he apparently meant he wanted the *Imagine* album to be a commercial success, rather than a critical success, as had been his first solo album, *Plastic Ono Band*. But the song struck a chord, in more ways than one. At the height of the cold war people were very frightened of the prospect of total annihilation, and had vivid memories of the Second World War, just a generation earlier. Besides, the Western world was throwing off the yoke of Christianity (as many saw it) and had not 100 years of Darwinism proved that there is no God and that we are all here by chance? So, better make the most of life — it's short, in any case — and find a way to co-exist peacefully and live happily ever after.

Superficially, *Imagine* is attractive. It invites us to find a way to live together, to build an elusive peace and to focus on the here and now. It sees religion as the primary culprit in mankind's woes, and wants to replace God with . . . Man. As religion, in the shape of Christianity, has always sought to make people consider the effects of their actions, and to lead a happily sober and upright life before a holy God, those children of the swinging sixties were bound to be on a direct collision course with Christianity as the established faith, if not with 'religion' as a whole. Perhaps this begins to explain the popularity of Lennon's hymn. Sadly we will never know just how Lennon's own life and beliefs might have developed. He was assassinated in New York in December 1980. It may be that *Imagine* was unduly naïve. Few still talk with any real sense of conviction of a building a totally peaceful world, although it remains the holy grail of the intellectual political classes. The Lord Jesus was rather more realistic and honest when he affirmed quite simply that wars and rumours of wars will persist — right up until the end of human history (see Matthew 24:6).

There is today, however, a growing interest in the idea of the benefits of a confluence of religions. Mankind is troubled by the world that we have built for ourselves. Globalisation means that individual people are more intimately aware than they ever have been, of the belief systems of *other* peoples and races, right across the world. We live in an age when the concept of 'diversity' has been thrust upon us, and many now promote that idea as a means to demonstrate how people of all religious persuasions can live together in 'peace' and harmony. The exclusive claims of Christianity as providing the sole means to peace with the Divine — of salvation — are considered by many – both within and outside of the Christian church, to be simply wrong. How could a Deity, God, allow religions to develop when only one of them is authentic? It is just plain unfair of Him to do so. So the idea must be wrong. Most people do not consider God to be unfair or indeed capricious, so there must be something wrong with the traditional claims of Christianity and it is time that they were changed. Again, there must be a superficial attractiveness to the idea that all religions are acceptable to God and that it does not really matter what you believe so long as you are sincere and tolerant. But the fact that something is popular does not make it right. And the more important question, surely, is this: just how *has* God revealed Himself to His world? As a righteous and loving Saviour, or as a sort of Chief Executive Officer of a religious conglomerate with multiple brands but one (loose) unifying theme? It is these questions that we are embarked upon to explore in this book.

There are many religions and many philosophies in this world. There always have been, and always will be. Because of this extraordinary juxtaposition of ideas and ideals, a veritable religious-collage making up a sort of identikit picture of a god-like figure, this book will *not* attempt to analyse all *the religions* in depth. The task would be quite impossible in a short book. Comparative religion is the task of a lifetime's study — perhaps — although this author would argue that an undue emphasis on *the religions* is actually injurious to people and is not what God wants. Far from it, in fact! Nevertheless we will look at specific beliefs of *the religions* where it is helpful to compare and contrast them with traditional Christianity. Already we have hit a problem: in defining Christianity we must acknowledge that there are a huge range of people that would call themselves 'Christian' but who do not in practice believe its basic tenets. Whilst Christianity has rightly been called a 'broad church', the question must be faced and answered — just how broad can it become and still be true to its core beliefs? An analogy may help: in the UK if a member of parliament ('MP') representing the Labour Party happens to believe in and votes for all the policies of the Conservative Party and only a few, if any, policies of his own party, is he truly a Labour MP? He may say he is. He may think he is and be able to rationalize his 'distance' from what Labour actually stands for. But any objective observer from outside Parliament will conclude, with no difficulty, that he is not truly a Labour man, no matter what he was when he first became an MP. The author will develop this theme further in this book because, if people are prepared to be honest with themselves, and with others, and with God, they will recognize and acknowledge that there are an increasing number within the Church who would find it difficult to put their hand on their heart and say 'I am a Christian.' And it is true that a growing band within the umbrella of the Church are beginning to openly acknowledge that they are not in fact Christians by any biblical definition. There are probably others who *would* so acknowledge, if they were being totally honest with themselves. This reality of non-believers within the Church must be of more than a passing interest to non-Christians who may actively be searching for truth. They have a right to know whether those who claim to be Christians are in fact, something different. As total honesty in this regard is (sadly) not always to be expected, this book will explore some simple biblical yardsticks by which an enquirer should measure where people actually stand. The dangers of division within the Church are acknowledged and it is not the desire of this author to create new ones. Also acknowledged is Christ's call for unity amongst His followers — something that is championed in this book. But we are not called by the Lord Jesus to find unity at *any* price. Indeed He warns us of wolves disguised in sheep's clothing and of false teachers invading the Church (e.g. Matthew 7:13–23).

This question about the nature of God (and ultimately that is what this whole subject really boils down to) is just too important to ignore. If God is as the pantheists or religious-syncretists want us to believe 'He' or 'It' is, then 'He' or 'It' has a lot of questions to answer. If, on the other hand God is as the Holy Bible clearly states He is, then *we* have a lot of questions to answer!

Who is likely to be reading this book? There are perhaps three broad types who will have a real interest in this whole area:

(1) Those who are of what the author later defines as '*the religions*'.[1] In other words, those who follow a faith system that is not Christianity, but who, nevertheless, are still interested in the biblical claims of Christianity and how they compare with their own beliefs. These might be described as people who are willing to undertake a religious self-audit.

(2) People of no religion and/or agnostics, but who remain

---

[1] See chapter 11

interested in knowing what Christianity has to say about the nature of God.

(3) Church attending Christians who want to remind themselves in a (hopefully) humble and expect manner, of what the Holy Bible has to say about the nature of God and the nature of Jesus the Messiah.

What precisely, then, is the 'promise' held out by pantheists, or syncretists (and are these two groups the same as what we will later define as Godists?) A pantheist in this context is one who believes in more than one 'god'. Hinduism is perhaps the archetypal pantheist religion although some Hindus believe that their various gods are part of a greater god. A syncretist, according to the Oxford dictionary, is one who tries to reconcile differing schools of thought. In the context of this book it is someone who wants (and believes in) the melding of *the religions* so that in some way — a way that is perhaps not defined, or is ill-defined — they should increasingly become one. Syncretistic religion in its current fashion seeks to encourage the so-called 'higher religions' (another term that is ill-defined!) to recognize that they all worship the same deity/ deities and will increasingly rejoice in each others' separate 'revelations' of deity. The most obvious outworking of this belief-system at the time of the writing this book is the so-called 'multi-faith service' where different religions come together under one roof, ostensibly to 'worship' one or more gods. We will delay defining Godism whilst we review the multi-faith agenda.

The Multi-Faith Agenda
Because in the West we live in open societies, and because those societies have for more than a century been the primary engine of global economic growth and societal

development, we have seen a steadily increasing extent of migration from developing countries to the West. Because of the West's generally exponential economic growth and improvement in living standards and living expectations, there has been a perceived need to invite people from other cultures to take on many of the more basic jobs. This in turn has led to the development of expatriate populations of immigrants, who either cannot or will not meld with their host communities. A form of physical and societal ghettoisation of immigrant communities has developed in many Western countries. Sometimes those of new cultures live in separate areas, in other cases they live close to the host community but decline to integrate with them. Immigrant populations in most Western countries have been sufficient in number to make a reality of the idea of a multi-cultural society. There has been little or no debate about the long term consequences of these societal developments, and indeed until the 2001 Islamist attack on the New York World Trade Centre in what has universally become known as 9/11, Western middle and governing classes tended to see multi-culturalism as an unalloyed positive and welcome development. In the words of one UK Labour politician, Britain had become a collection of different cultures unified by a common language. The same ideas were in vogue around the rest of the Western world at the turn of the twenty first century. Living within a multi-culture society of different but equal citizens, what could be more natural than the idea of a multi-faith society of different but equal religions? To suggest that one religion is right implies that others are wrong and this in turn runs the risk of committing the unpardonable modern sin — the risk of causing offence! If God is the Deity of the whole world, then all of the 'higher' religions must in their own

29

various ways be right, although some would say perhaps not equally right. In other words some people hold the private view that some religions are 'higher' than others! There is also the vague concept of the *divine spark*, to be found in all humans, being some reflection of the Deity, a spark that must also therefore be present in all of these 'higher' religions as they seek to bring us closer to that Deity.

The muti-faith agenda is now pursued vigorously by Western politicians, as one plank in their cohesiveness policies. That is to say, those policies aimed at developing and maintaining a sense of togetherness within society, in an attempt to resist what could otherwise easily become the real and emphatic 'balkanisation' of Western countries. In a generally post-modern and therefore post-Christian society, there is some reason for the populace at large also to consider that *multi-faith* as opposed to *competing-faith* is generally a good thing, and therefore to be welcomed. At the time of writing the former UK Prime Minister Tony Blair had created the Tony Blair Faith Foundation which shared its values in its online mission statement. We consider it briefly, as a clear statement of the multi-faith agenda: *'The Tony Blair Faith Foundation aims to promote respect and understanding about the world's major religions and show how faith is a powerful force for good in the modern world.'* Most right thinking people would consider that 'respect' is a good thing. But it means very different things to different people. The Oxford dictionary talks of respect as being deferential regard, esteem, heed, reference and good wishes. Most Western people would respect the right of others to maintain their belief systems providing those same beliefs do not threaten others. But should, for example, Christians (or indeed any Westerners) be expected to respect Hindu temple prostitution or the Islamic concept of Dar-al-Harb?

'Faith is vitally important to hundreds of millions of people. It underpins systems of thought and of behaviour. It underpins many of the world's great movements for change or reform, including many charities. And the values of respect, justice and compassion that our great religions share have never been more relevant or import-ant to bring people together to build a better world.' Again the word 'values' is one that needs consideration. Western politicians and especially British ones, speak of 'values' in almost hushed tones, as they try to establish 'values' that will unite people in social cohesiveness. So we are told we need to value 'respect', without being clear about just what respect is and to what extent it must be applied. We are to value 'justice', which again can be defined in very diverse ways. And finally we must value 'compassion'. In a UK context (and probably in a Western context generally) all these words appear at first glance to be very reasonable and unobjectionable. But the question then must be asked (*and answered*!) as to whether the 'great religions' have the same concept of, for example, compassion. Again in the Hindu context, what *do* we understand of respect in terms of the *devadasi system*? Its roots go deep into Hindu history — but to most Western eyes the devadasi system is simply the exploitation of the lower castes. Are we really to respect this, and to consider this to be justice? *'But religious faith can also be used to divide. We have seen throughout history and today we still see how it can be distorted to fan the flames of hatred and extremism.'* Most people can recognise this statement as true, especially today, in the twenty-first century. If 'religious extremism' can be successfully tackled by Tony Blair's Foundation and similar initiatives, then most people would be happy enough. But the question has to be asked (and again honestly answered)

are the so-called 'extreme' beliefs actually mainstream beliefs? Is it only the West — and Western politicians in particular — that are in denial about the true and mainstream beliefs of at least some of the 'great religions'? *'The Tony Blair Faith Foundation is a response to these opportunities and challenges. We will use the full power of modern communications to support and step up efforts at every level to educate, inform and develop understanding about the different faiths and between them.'* Will the multi-faith agenda promote true 'understanding' or will it promote an apparently benign form of politico-religious propaganda? Already we see that so-called 'religious education' appears increasingly to be simply a servant to Western politicians' social cohesiveness objectives. Current religious education, rather than comparing and contrasting religious beliefs in any systematic and scientific way, is yielding to superficially well-meaning attempts to evolve new ways to think about old religions. Rather than gaining systematic instruction, Western children are being taught what well-intentioned but non-expert politicians, aided and abetted by the religious education establishment, think that *'the religions'* ought to believe! *'At the same time, the Foundation will use its profile and resources to encourage people of faith to work together more closely to tackle global poverty and conflict. By supporting such inter-faith initiatives, the Foundation will help underline the religion's relevance and positive contribution.'*

Whether inter-faith initiatives truly represent the will of Almighty God is a key theme of this book. Plainly, where mutual understanding can help avoid suspicions and therefore break down barriers, then in principle most people would probably think of inter-faith 'dialogue' in positive terms. But is the multi-faith agenda truly honouring to Almighty

God? There seems to be a secular assumption that multi-faith is *ipso facto* a good thing. But is it? What dangers does it entail? Has anyone troubled to undertake a religious risk-audit of where multi-faithism might lead? As expressed by the Tony Blair Foundation, the underlying objective seems to be to co-opt religions to become (inexpensive) delivery systems for government social programmes, such as 'tackling' global poverty. The slightly arrogant objective as expressed by the Blair Foundation seems to be to keep religious people away from their religions and help them to 'see' that, with Government support, they can become doers of good works — which presumably is considered to be honouring to 'god' — if 'he' or 'it' exists at all! Even more arrogantly, all this government inspired religious busyness will help to make *the religions* appear 'relevant' to the world at large. The Blair Foundation mission statement finally went on to ask for people's support in realizing its objectives, vague those these were. And it concluded with an inevitable plea for financial donations!

At the time of writing this book, one Karen Armstrong,[2] a UK based religious author and well known campaigner for the multi-faith agenda was chairing an internet based campaign aimed at developing a multi-faith 'Charter' that would call for the universal upholding of a 'Golden Rule' that was said to exist in all religions (although precisely which religions were covered was not made entirely clear). According to early press-releases, the proposed Charter would be based on 'the universal principles' of compassion and respect, which were seen as being the Golden Rule at the heart of *the religions*. On the official website Armstrong stated that 'the chief task of our time is to build a global

---

[2] Karen Armstrong, an ex-Catholic, now describes herself as a 'freelance mono-theist – Public Affairs Television (PBS), interview with Bill Moyers, Jan 2002.

society where people of all persuasions can live together in peace and harmony. If we do not achieve this, it seems unlikely that we will have a viable world to hand on to the next generation. Instead of being seen as part of the problem, *the religions* could make a vital contribution to this urgent undertaking.' Various contributors on the website stated that *a militant kind of aggressive religiosity*, or *fundamentalism*, had grown in all the major 'world traditions' as a rebellion against an imbalanced world: people were rebelling against powerlessness and against humiliation, whilst religion itself focused more and more on 'a narrow definition of religious dogma'. Every religion, said one contributor, had a history of intolerance. Armstrong herself said that she wanted people to 'hear the compassionate voice of religion — to bring compassion to the forefront'. Noticeably absent from the initial video contributions was any mention of God!

The idea of a Golden Rule, as a sort of *religion outside of the religions*, was always likely to find support among ordinary people. It sounded so kind, so reasonable and so compassionate, as it aimed to make people forget their differences and live together gladly in peace. At a superficial level this was bound to be attractive. And it was music to the ears of politicians, who ultimately wanted their general populace to live peaceably and productively, serving society as a whole. Both the so-called Golden Rule and its attendant muti-faith Charter were, at the time of writing this book, being overseen and coordinated by a group called, with absolutely no sense of irony, *The Council of Sages*. These 'Sages' were well known religious types from various religions. Once the Golden Rule was crystallised and codified, it would be affirmed that:

- Compassion is celebrated in all major religious, spiritual and ethical traditions.

- The Golden Rule is our prime duty and cannot be limited to our own political, religious or ethnic group.[3]
- Therefore, in our divided world, compassion can build common ground.

It seemed likely that, in the UK at any rate, the Golden Rule would become part of the curriculum in the so-called religious education establishment. It also seemed likely that the Tony Blair Foundation would find itself in complete agreement with the concept of a religious Golden Rule. As noted in the Foreword to this book, the UK British Broadcasting Corporation (BBC) actively promotes multiculturalism. Increasingly the BBC's output in the early 2000s favored multi-faith initiatives and multi-faith reporting. In this regard it was seen by many in the UK as a foregone conclusion that the BBC's attitude to organized, traditional Christianity would become increasingly shrill and intolerant. At the time of writing this book the BBC had recently screened a drama depicting 'Christian terrorists' murdering a child in support of their anti-abortion campaign. Although completely fictional, the BBC insisted the drama was 'realistic' and 'well researched'. But the drama let slip the mask on how the BBC intended to treat Christianity in the early years of the twenty-first century. In the same spirit of muli-faithism, the BBC simultaneously screened series called *Around the World in Eighty Faiths* and *Extreme Pilgrim*, both hosted by Peter Owen Jones, a Church of England vicar. Both these television series sought to confirm that 'god' may be sought in many places in a veritable *sea of faiths*.

---

[3] Interesting to compare this so-called 'Rule' with the Holy Bible, Matthew 22:37, when Jesus was asked what is the greatest commandment. His answer is instructive.

The 'promise' of Godism

Even before fully defining Godism we begin get a sense of its overall thrust and objective in the discussions above. According to Godist philosophy: 'god' (whoever 'he' or 'it' is) wants us all to live in harmony; our individual beliefs matter far less than the way we live our lives; old fashioned concepts such as sin and salvation, if they are to be accepted at all, need to be reinterpreted and constantly updated to fit with the complex and diverse world in which we live; and by recognizing that all religions are essentially the same, no matter what 'superficial' differences there may be, we can generate a feeling of the brotherhood of man — or perhaps in these days, the brotherhood and sisterhood of humankind! — and so find a way to a peaceful future of human harmony.

The need for a change of heart — some fundamental change in the individual leading to a totally new outlook on life and conduct of life — if it is acknowledged at all by the multi-faith creed, is seen only as a need to create a heart of compassion (or 'love') for our fellows. Providing we are compassionate, then our little peccadillos (we dare not call them sins!) actually do not matter very much, and 'god', in 'his' or 'its' various manifestations, will ultimately find a way to overlook any such shortcomings. Only serious misdemeanors, offences against our fellows when we should observe the Golden Rule and be compassionate, are categories of offences which really matter. For good measure, many Godists would add that offences against the environment are also likely to bring about the displeasure of 'god', as these offences show that we do not have compassion. In Godist philosophy the question of our eternal destiny is very much up to the preferences or 'understanding' of each individual. For some people there will be a hell to fear, although this notion is considered rather passé to most Godists ('how could a god of love send people to hell'?) [4] The idea of hell is alright for those who need to believe in it, but it is a concept not for those of greater sophistication (in their eyes!) Nirvana and reincarnation are probably more comfortable options than hell, in any case, especially to those Westerners who do not understand the true nature of the Hindu caste system! In the Godist philosophy, 'heaven', however it may be understood, awaits virtually all people at some point — *if*, that is, there *is* such a thing as a hereafter!

So the promise of Godism, such as it is, is that *all will be well in the end* and we need to live our lives here on earth as considerately as we can, *showing compassion to all*. 'Love' is the keynote in all this, although love in the Godist sense has about it a rather sentimental quality and is more akin to the human emotion we think of as romantic 'love', rather than the more complex derivations found in the Holy Bible.

So we find ourselves back with *The Beatles*, who in 1967 released their song *All You Need is Love* which in its simple lyrical form managed to include the word 'love' 36 times! The song was written by John Lennon (with contributions from Paul McCartney) in response to a request from the BBC to compose a song that would be the UK's contribution to an international pop broadcast called *Our World*, to be beamed to 26 countries and watched by an estimated 400 million people. Lennon's song contained a simple 'message' aimed to be understood by all nationalities. 'It was an inspired song and they really wanted to give the

---

[4] See the readily available book *The Road to Hell* by David Pawson (reprinted Terra Nova, ISBN 978-1-90194-952-0), and another short book on this theme: *How Can A God of Love Send People To Hell?*, John Benton (1985, Evangelical Press ISBN 0-85234-216-0).

world a message,' said Brian Epstein, then *The Beatles*' business Manager. 'The nice thing about it is that it cannot be misinterpreted. It is a clear message saying that love is everything.' Lennon, never afraid to create propaganda out of art, was apparently fascinated by the power of slogans to inspire and unite people. When asked in 1971 whether songs like *Give Peace a Chance* and *Power to the People* were propaganda songs, he answered, "Sure. So was *All You Need Is Love*. I'm a revolutionary artist. My art is dedicated to change."

So to many people all you need is love; and if 'god' can be co-opted to provide religious imprimatur to the idea (never John Lennon's intention!) then so much the better. But *we* must ask ourselves once again *if we are being honest*, is the Godist philosophy in its various and diverse guises, honoring to the Deity we call God? Is the Godist philosophy consistent with the way (or ways) that God has chosen to reveal Himself? Of equal importance, is the Godist philosophy just a man-made religion with an identikit 'god'? And if it is just a man made religion, how does adherence to Godism affect the eternal destiny of those who hold these beliefs and teach others to do so, no matter how sincerely they may hold such views? These are big questions indeed!

We move now to look, with a due sense of reverence, more closely at the self-revelation of Almighty God in the pages of the Holy Bible.

2

THE NATURE OF GOD

A Contract . . . .

Throughout this book we aim to explore the nature of God with special reference to what the Holy Bible reveals about His nature. This should not be thought of simply as an academic exercise, where we put God under a microscope, twist Him around a few times and see what He looks like from different angles. We are embarked upon a study of Almighty God, and how He has chosen to reveal Himself to the human race that He has made. This, then, is a subject that should be approached with genuine reverence, a sense of awe and in a spirit of expectation, *if* we really want to see and experience God in a new way. God *does* want us to know Him, and to know Him intimately, but we must always remember that ultimately we are but dust, as created beings, whilst He is holy and majestic. Ultimately He will judge us, not the other way around! In preparing this book, the author was struck by the willingness and casualness with which humans are prepared to judge God, and to try to recast Him in ways that they find comfortable. If the reader is a Christian, then they might want to pray (if they have not already done so) that God will bless them in some new way as they reverently and diligently look into His nature and at who He truly is. If the reader is not a Christian, or is unsure of what he or she is (perhaps as an 'agnostic', or someone belonging to one of the various religions) you may also want to pray at this early stage that *if* God exists, then He will graciously reveal Himself to you through the pages that follow. If you already have fixed views about the nature of God, you may want to pray that He will graciously reveal to you any errors that there may be in your present understanding, for we all have limited understanding of God. That is quite inevitable — we are finite and He is infinite. The author would make no special pleading to be an 'expert' in the study of God, but only to be one who is willing to talk about God on the terms that God has clearly set down in Holy Scripture. In other words, in this book we seek to look at God on His terms, and with the clarity already set out in those Scriptures, rather than to try to construct an indentikit image of 'god' from various philosophical viewpoints.

Readers will note that in this book we do not set out to defend the Holy Scriptures as the definitive word of God. There are many good books that examine the Holy Bible in that context and no doubt someone who is genuinely interested in this subject will readily find what they need without having to look too hard. If the reader comes to this study with the objection that the Bible *is not*, or *may not be*, the sole revelation of God then he or she is invited simply to 'park' that objection for the time being. There surely can be no great problem in looking closely at what the Scriptures have to say about God so as to acquire a clear understanding of the argument being put forward in this book. In a court of law a witness is called and a judge or a jury will form an opinion as to the trustworthiness of that particular person, and the validity of the testimony they offer. The author invites the reader to adopt the same attitude towards the

Bible. Readers can always 'call more witnesses' at a later stage if they feel that the witness of Scripture is incomplete or invalid. The key suggestion made by this author is that a doubter holds on to his or her doubts but proceeds from this point onwards with the basic working assumption that the Scriptures *are* valid and trustworthy. If at the conclusion of these studies the reader finds the testimony is finally un-compelling, then he or she is free to take up their doubts once more. Maybe we should consider this as being a sort of 'contract' between the reader and the author: the contract may be considered as discharged once the reader turns the last page of this book! Until then, let us use those Scriptures as the platform from which to review what Almighty God has revealed about Himself. Allowing that many readers will be Westerners, then we might as well also 'park' the gender issue: some may feel that reference to God as 'Him' and 'He' represents some form of gender aggression. If so, you too are simply invited to park that objection for the time being. We use those terms because the Holy Bible uses those terms. You can always return to your objection later if you feel that the gender issue remains a challenge for you personally.

But God does invite us to examine Him in minute detail. Only by so doing can we hope to begin to understand Him and to draw closer to Him, closeness being the ultimate objective, logically, of any such study of the Almighty. *Taste and see that the Lord is good* it says in Psalm 34:8. We *are* invited to taste, to sample God. That the Lord is good is a basic tenet of the whole of Scripture, both Old and New Testaments. So why not take God at His word and, in a sense, sample Him? The foolish thing in this life, surely, would be to reach its end and have to say, 'I never even bothered to sample God, let alone to draw close to

Him.' That would be an absolute tragedy, especially when there could be an eternal blessing, or indeed an eternal curse, that finally depends on the decision we make about God in this life.

Inherent Characteristics of God

The normative Christian view of God, held by Roman Catholics, Protestants and Eastern Orthodox traditions — and that means by the vast majority in this world who call themselves Christian — is that God is revealed as being three co-eternal Persons — Father, Son and Holy Spirit — in One God. This is known as the doctrine of the *Holy Trinity*, or the *Trinitarian* doctrine. We get a strong sense of this from the following Bible texts which are suggested as a starting point in understanding this doctrine, *although they should not be taken as proof-positive of this doctrine*. Readers may want to check them out in the Bible itself and if so, possibly to read a little around those key verses, so as to get a sense of the context in which they are written.

Key attributes of God

One and only — Isaiah 44:6 (and Galatians 3:15–20)
Unchangeable — James 1:17
Invisible — Colossians 1:15
Infinite — 1 Kings 8:27
Holy — 1 Peter 1:15-16
Spirit — John 4:24

His unity

Deuteronomy 6:4
Galatians 3:20 (see also verse 16)
1 Timothy 2:5
James 2:19

Father, Son and Holy Spirit
Matthew 28:19 (name, not names!)
2 Corinthians 13:14
Hebrews 1:8
1 Peter 1:2

"I AM"
Exodus 3:13–15 God reveals His name to Moses

The inherent characteristics of God as displayed throughout the Scriptures are characteristics equally, it is argued, of the three Persons of the Holy Trinity: Father, Son and Holy Spirit. And they are characteristics *always* displayed in the way that God acts in biblical history. According to the Bible, the whole of creation displays God's glory, His eternal power and His deity:

> **The heavens declare the glory of God;**
> **and the firmament shows His handiwork.**
> **Day unto day utters speech,**
> **and night unto night reveals knowledge.**
> **There is no speech nor language**
> **where their voice is not heard.**
> **Their line has gone out through all the earth,**
> **and their words to the end of the world.**
> **In them He has set a tabernacle for the sun,**
> **Which is like a bridegroom coming out of his**
> **   chamber,**
> **and rejoices like a strong man to run its race.**
> **Its rising is from one end of heaven,**
> **and its circuit to the other end;**
> **and there is nothing hidden from its heat.**
>   (Psalm 19:1 – 6, NKJV)

For since the creation of the world His invisible *attributes* are clearly seen, being understood by the things that are made, *even* His eternal power and Godhead, so that they are without excuse. (Romans 1:20, NKJV)

Both passages suggest that we can obtain a clear sense of God simply from looking at what He has created — the world in which we all live. The Scriptures similarly tell us that God's 'providence', in other words the way that He deals with the human race on a day to day basis, also displays the consistency of His nature. So we read:

. . . that you may be sons of your Father in heaven; for He makes His sun rise on the evil and on the good, and sends rain on the just and on the unjust (Matthew 5:45 NKJV).

But love your enemies, do good, and lend, hoping for nothing in return; and your reward will be great, and you will be sons of the Most High. For He is kind to the unthankful and evil. (Luke 6:35, NKJV)

. . . who in bygone generations allowed all nations to walk in their own ways. Nevertheless He did not leave Himself without witness, in that He did good, gave us rain from heaven and fruitful seasons, filling our hearts with food and gladness. (Acts 14:16 – 17, NKJV)

Then Paul stood in the midst of the Areopagus and said, "Men of Athens, I perceive that in all things you are very religious; for as I was passing through and considering the objects of your worship, I even found an altar with this inscription:

TO THE UNKNOWN GOD.

Therefore, the One whom you worship without knowing, Him I proclaim to you: God, who made the world and everything in it, since He is Lord of heaven and earth, does not dwell in temples made with hands. Nor is He worshiped with men's hands, as though He needed anything, since He gives to all life, breath, and all things. And He has made from one blood every nation of men to dwell on all the face of the earth, and has determined their preappointed times and the boundaries of their dwellings, so that they should seek the Lord, in the hope that they might grope for Him and find Him, though He is not far from each one of us; for in Him we live and move and have our being, as also some of your own poets have said, 'For we are also His offspring.' Therefore, since we are the offspring of God, we ought not to think that the Divine Nature is like gold or silver or stone, something shaped by art and man's devising. Truly, these times of ignorance God overlooked, but now commands all men everywhere to repent, because He has appointed a day on which He will judge the world in righteousness by the Man whom He has ordained. He has given assurance of this to all by raising Him from the dead." (Acts 17:22 – 31)

God's Attributes

These texts begin to suggest to us the consistency of God in His dealing with people, as well as His love and mercy to all mankind. The attributes of God are today understood by scholars as focusing around attributes that are His alone, as well as attributes that He shares with those people who become His followers. Inevitably there is some debate and variance of views around these questions, but the following can be considered as a normative Christian understanding:

There are things that we can say of God alone. He is Spirit; He is: sovereign; eternal; infinite; immutable (or unchangeable); omnipotent; He is One in three persons. There are also characteristics which He may impart to His adopted children. Thus we may grow in knowledge of Him; we may grow in wisdom; holiness; love; truthfulness. We are meant to be transformed by the renewing of our minds as we study His Word; we are to be bearing fruit — the fruit of the Spirit — and so we are to grow more and more in the likeness of Christ, displaying more of the character of the one who is the only-begotten Son of the Father. It goes without saying that not all His children display these characteristics, all the time, or in equal consistency. And sadly even some professing Christians will stray far from the character that God would impart, in which we should be growing. That is a sad reflection of the sort of people that we often are, but to share some of the character of their Lord is the expectation of a Christian and their general desire. It is also a fact in the author's experience of observing Christians over many years that, as those years roll by, faithful followers of the Lord Jesus do seem to display more and more of the character of Christ, who they love and worship.

By now, of course, readers will have a sense of the sheer magnitude of the subject that we are investigating. If God exists at all, then logically He will be well out of our ability to comprehend in a natural and unaided way, and that is before you take into account our nature as sinners who 'naturally' live blind to God! Readers are encouraged to persist, however, as God *does* make it possible to know Him, and to know Him indeed as Abba — or Father, and

THE NATURE OF GOD

this is more correctly translated as 'daddy'.

How do the Scriptures express the characteristics of God? We can look first and briefly at the divine names by which God revealed Himself. In Genesis 1:1 we hear the name of 'God'. In Genesis 2:4 he is described as the 'Lord God'. In Genesis 17:1, simply as 'the Lord'. In Exodus 3:6, as God calls Moses for the first time, He describes himself in the following way. **"I am the God of your father, the God of Abraham, the God of Isaac and the God of Jacob."** The Bible goes on to tell us that Moses hid his face because he was afraid to look at God. In the same chapter of Genesis, as this foundational encounter between Almighty God and Moses takes place, God also reveals Himself as **"I Am"** (verse 14). Readers may want to pause to read the whole of Exodus chapter 3 as it is so key to the Christian understanding of how God dealt with his chosen people, the Hebrews, and how in turn He introduced Himself to Moses who was to become the godly and God-fearing leader of the Jewish nation.

Some of God's attributes are seen implicitly in the biblical accounts of the creation, the fall, the flood and the exodus. And these attributes are emphasised in the 'covenants' that he made with His chosen people. By the time that the Hebrew people had reached Mount Sinai, as part of their long and drawn-out escape from slavery in Egypt, God's self revelation had become more explicit. In Exodus 34:6–7, **I the Lord, am a God who is full of compassion and pity, who is not easily angered and who shows great love and faithfulness. I keep my promise for thousands of generations and forgive evil and sin; but I will not fail to punish children and grandchildren to the third and fourth generation for the sins of their parents**. (GNB)

To the 'liberal' and post-modern West, this idea of a

God who punishes children for the sins of their parents may immediately seem unfairly harsh and indeed the very opposite of forgiving! However we need to take God at His word on this: He is honest about the effects of sin and of how He deals with it. Taken in context with the nature of God as revealed in other places in the Scriptures, we need to understand this apparent harshness in the light of His other attributes. But there is perhaps a more straightforward way to understand this apparently harsh promise of God. It is not so much that He sends the punishment, but rather that we humans create the awful reality of sin seeping from generation to generation. In the UK for many years we suffered in the province of Northern Ireland what became universally known as 'The Troubles'. This was the political conflict between the left wing (culturally 'Catholic') and the right wing (culturally 'Protestant') that outworked itself in 30 years of political turmoil and terrorist outrage.[1] Whilst not wishing to over-simplify this sad and difficult period in UK history, it must be noted that one vital component of the problem was the willingness of the protagonists to hate their neighbours with a venom that defied rational explanation. Men and women, fathers and mothers, were too willing to pass on their antagonisms to the next generation. The history of Ireland, if it suggests nothing else, shows that hatreds can so easily be 'visited' from one generation to the next. Each generation must take its share of responsibility for stoking the fires of hatred, which in turn pollutes the chances of the next generation to live in peace. So we should, perhaps, reflect upon God's candour about the reality of cross-generational punishment with the understanding that we

---

[1] Sadly, within 48 hours of writing these lines, two British soldiers were murdered in Ulster after a dozen years of 'peace' which had followed an exacting political process aimed at securing a lasting settlement in Ulster.

humans are wholly the problem. The 'Troubles' of Ulster are sadly replicated right across this planet, perhaps with different labels, but always with the same self-justification, the same self-righteousness, the same desire to get even with our assumed enemies. Not for nothing did the Lord Jesus tell His followers to love their enemies and to do good to those who abuse them (Matthew 5:43). So God does indeed reluctantly allow us to pass from generation to generation the sin that so easily pollutes — and in this we begin to see the practical outworking of that clear statement in Exodus. And it must be read in the context of the preceding clause, that God is in practice full of compassion, where all too often we are full of hatred. He is full of pity, where we are full of venom. He is not easily angered, where we have very thin skins! God shows great love and faithfulness, where we show a capacity for hatred. It might be added, God knows that we need God!

We must bear in mind our inability to fully understand God as mere humans. Reading this book will not lead to a full and complete understanding of Almighty God, however much the author may wish otherwise! But through His revelation God is truly known through faith, even though no creature can fully understand Him. To Christian believers, Scripture presents God's attributes as being *the* standard for living. So, we are to be holy because God is holy. We are to be loving because God is loving (see for examples Leviticus 19:2 and 1 John 4:8, 11). A sober acknowledgement that we cannot fully understand God in this life should lead us to a certain sense of humility every time we consider God and His attributes. As the Psalmist said in Psalm 139:6, such knowledge **is too wonderful for me, too lofty for me to attain**. This is emphasised again in 145:3 **Great is the LORD and most worthy of praise; his greatness no one**

can fathom. And again by the major prophet Isaiah:

> **Have you not known?**
> **Have you not heard?**
> **The everlasting God, the LORD,**
> **The Creator of the ends of the earth,**
> **Neither faints nor is weary.**
> **His understanding is unsearchable**.
>
> (Isaiah 40:28, NKJV)

Readers who want to follow this idea through the Scriptures are directed to Isaiah 55:8–9; Matthew 11:25–27; Romans 11:33–36; 1 Corinthians 2:6–16; and 1 Corinthians 13:8–13. The incomprehensibility of God is a fact known throughout the Old and New Testaments of the Holy Bible, as the above Bible verses demonstrate. And yet, as noted earlier, God has indeed invited us to know Him. *Taste and see that the Lord is good* says God (Psalm 34:8), and of this we need to remind ourselves constantly as we look at His nature and His attributes in this book.

God's unity is the key expression of Christian monotheism — the fact that the God of the Scriptures is the only, living and true God. From the biblical perspective, therefore, all other 'gods' are figments of imagination. This attribute of unity is reflected in the first of the Ten Commandments — **"You shall have no other God before me"** (Exodus 20:3 — confirmed by the Lord Jesus Himself in Matthew 4:10). These Bible verses emphasise the same point: **"Hear, O Israel: The LORD our God, the LORD *is* one! You shall love the LORD your God with all your heart, with all your soul, and with all your strength."** (Deuteronomy 6:4–5, NKJV)

Having affirmed that God is One (as above), He

immediately commands that we should love Him— unstintingly. When Jesus was asked which of the Commandments was the most important, He replied: **"The first of all the commandments is: 'Hear, O Israel, the LORD our God, the LORD is one. And you shall love the LORD your God with all your heart, with all your soul, with all your mind, and with all your strength.'"** (Mark 12:29–30, NKJV). And Jesus went on to add the supplementary requirement for men to love their neighbours as themselves. We note especially in verse 29 that Jesus acknowledged the unity of God. Jesus prayed for His future Church shortly before His crucifixion. He said: **"........ this is eternal life: that they may know you, the only true God, and Jesus Christ, whom you have sent."** (John 17:3, NKJV). We note again Jesus' teaching that God the Almighty is the only true God.

The fact that God is Spirit reminds us that He is not a physical being and He is invisible. God is shown to be personal, living, self-conscious and self-determining. The invisible God, it must be clearly understood, cannot be seen by human eyes (Ex 33:20) and the second of the Ten Commandments forbids every visible representation of God (Ex 20:4). From the Godist viewpoint, this must be a particular challenge, as so many of the world's religions do have physical representations of 'god'. It really is for the Godist to show why God gives one instruction in the Holy Scriptures and then countermands it by allowing and approving of physical images of 'god' by *the religions*. Inconsistency is certainly not an attribute of God indicated in Scripture! Because God is Spirit He must be worshipped in spirit and truth, said Jesus in John 4:24. This is a helpful and valuable passage in John's Gospel, telling us about the Lord Jesus' conversation with a Samaritan woman as they discussed together the need for a spring of 'living water' to well-up from within a person and how such a spring could provide ultimate and life-giving sustenance. Jesus confirmed that a time was coming when *true worshippers* will not worship in particular geographical locations, but rather they will worship God anywhere, *in spirit and in truth*. (See John 4:1–26 for the full context in which this statement was made by Jesus).

God's immutability or constancy demonstrates His faithfulness to Himself, to His holy laws, to His promises, and to His works. God remains forever the same God who undergoes no change in Himself either from within or from outside of Himself. So it is in that we read: **Every good gift and every perfect gift is from above, and comes down from the Father of lights, with whom there is no variation or shadow of turning.** (James 1:17, NKJV)

God's promises made to Abraham express His immutability – or changelessness – so that His covenant people (the Hebrews) could be sure of the unchanging nature of His purpose (Hebrews 6:17, NIV). King Saul in the Old Testament was told by the prophet Samuel that "**He who is the glory of Israel does not lie or change his mind; for he is not a man, that he should change his mind**" (1 Sam 15:29, NIV — see also Numbers 23:19). In Malachi 3:6 we read "**For I *am* the LORD; I do not change. Therefore you are not consumed, O sons of Jacob**" (NKJV). This message is reinforced in the New Testament in regard to the Lord Jesus as we read in Hebrews 13:8 — **Jesus Christ is the same yesterday, today, and forever**. Accordingly, Christians were warned not to be led astray by 'strange doctrines'. This again, it is suggested, must be a challenge to the Godist position, especially where the Godist is someone who considers themselves also to be a Christian.

God's immutability or constancy does not in any manner suggest that He is static or immobile. The God of the Scriptures is seen as being one Who is constantly working (John 5:17) and Who is dynamic. Sometimes God is described in the Bible as being sorry, of 'repenting' or changing His mind (see Genesis 6: 6–7, 1 Samuel 15:11 and Jonah 3:10). Read within context these figurative expressions show the constancy of God who, in holiness and righteousness, always hates sin and responds in outright opposition to it. But in His mercy and grace He actively forgives those who repent (that is, have a complete change of heart and turn to Him for forgiveness). God carries out His stated purposes and His promises, without fail. So we read:
"The instant I speak concerning a nation and concerning a kingdom, to pluck up, to pull down, and to destroy it, [8] **if that nation against whom I have spoken turns from its evil, I will relent of the disaster that I thought to bring upon it. And the instant I speak concerning a nation and concerning a kingdom, to build and to plant it, if it does evil in My sight so that it does not obey My voice, then I will relent concerning the good with which I said I would benefit it."** (Jeremiah 18:7–10, NKJV)

Plainly this text suggests that we should try to deal as consistently with God as He deals with us. Promises to God should not be made lightly, especially if we are in two minds about whether we will fulfil them.

"I make known the end from the beginning, from ancient times, what is still to come. I say: My purpose will stand, and I will do all that I please." (Isaiah 46:10)

In him we were also chosen, having been predestined according to the plan of him who works out everything in conformity with the purpose of his will. (Ephesians 1:11)

This final verse, from Ephesians, is found in the apostle Paul's great letter to the early church located at Ephesus (in modern Turkey). Paul's letter is concerned first and foremost with: **God's plan ..... to bring all creation together, everything in heaven and on earth, with Christ as head"** (Ephesians 1:10, as above). In the first part of the letter, Paul explores how God has chosen His people, how they are forgiven and set free from their sins through Jesus Christ, God's Son. Paul reminds us (again from the GNB version) that **even before the World was made, God had already chosen us to be his through our union with Christ, so that we would be holy and without fault before him**. Another amazing statement that speaks of God's immutability and His constancy of purpose.

We have begun to explore in this second chapter, then, the nature of God. Whether the Godist's vision of 'god' matches the sheer majesty of God as revealed from the pages of Holy Scripture is a constant theme throughout this book. Whether the Godist position, that 'god' can be found in a range of manifestations and worshipped in a range of ways, can be reconciled with what God has so consistently revealed about Himself in the Holy Bible is, it is suggested, problematic at the very least! Readers will by now recognize what a huge task that we are undertaking, but they should feel encouraged that the Holy Spirit of God can and will enable them to achieve the understanding that they need. For it is the Spirit who provides both wisdom and knowledge (1 Corinthians 4:8).

Up to this point we have looked at certain facets of the nature of God. It must be said that we have not exhausted these by any means, but we should now have some sense of God's sovereignty, His unity, independence and immutability. We will explore at a later stage the centrality of His attribute of holiness to the whole of our argument. In the next chapter we shall begin to explore how God revealed Himself with progressively greater clarity through His dealings with His chosen race, the Hebrews.

3

GETTING TO KNOW YOU

How the Holy Bible reveals God
In the 1956 Rogers and Hammerstein's musical film *The King and I* we are treated to a memorable song with one of those tunes that it is difficult to get out of your head, once it is in there! In the story, an English governess travels to Siam (now Thailand) to become a teacher for the king's many children. As there are so many children, it will be a real challenge for the governess to truly get to know them, as she explains to them in her song. Its all very twee, and fits so very well in this very entertaining tragic-comic musical, in which we encounter both pain and pathos, in addition to a growing love between governess and her royal charges, as well as her growing platonic love for the irascible king. But it is the chorus of the song that most people can remember best. Its memorable words run:

> *Getting to know you,*
> *Getting to know all about you.*
> *Getting to like you,*
> *Getting to hope you like me.*

Do human beings gain an instant knowledge of God, even when they yield their lives to Him and become

His followers? Indeed, can human beings gain such a knowledge — are they capable of such knowledge? In the context of this book this is a question that we do need to explore, as we review the often vague interpretations of the Godist philosophy of what the nature of 'god' may be and how 'he' or 'it' can in some sense become all things to all men. From a specifically Christian viewpoint it might be added that there must be a sense of suspicion about any idea of an 'instant' and all inclusive revelation of God, because this seems to be precisely the way that He did NOT make Himself known to people as revealed by the Scriptures. These Scriptures were written and compiled, in the case of the Old Testament, over a period of circa 2,000 years, but they concern events that date back in some cases much further. We must look, then, at the overall quality and thrust of the message of the *whole* Bible in order to achieve a good understanding of Who God is, and what He requires of us. But in saying this we also need to keep firmly in mind that most profound statement of Jesus — that anyone who has seen Jesus has seen the Father (John 14:9). Jesus is the perfect revelation of the nature of God. So the apostle Paul wrote in his letter to the early church at Colossae (in modern Greece) that Jesus is the **image of the invisible God** (Colossians 1:15) and that in Jesus **all the fullness of the deity lives** (Colossians 2:9). If readers have the time they may want to follow up for themselves the full scope of Paul's argument by reading Colossians 1:1 through to 2:15.

The Torah

We will consult the first five books of the Old Testament for this initial review of the manner in which God began to disclose His Divine nature to the world through the Hebrew people. The first five books of the Old Testament

(Genesis, Exodus, Leviticus, Numbers and Deuteronomy) are variously known as the 'Torah' (from the Hebrew word meaning 'instruction', as this collection is known in Jewish tradition), or the Pentateuch in Christian tradition, from the Greek, meaning 'five books'

If readers are looking for a basic introduction to the Bible, then they may be interested in the author's earlier book, *The Birth of Christ*[1] which contains a short appendix looking at the Holy Bible and why Christians consider it both truthful and dependable. However there are plenty of good books that look at the veracity of the Holy Bible, so genuine searchers will not have to look too hard for excellent research articles on this subject. Although we speak of an 'Old' and a 'New' Testament, these terms are used in this book solely because they are universally understood and recognized. In some ways it is helpful to think of the *Old Testament* as *'The Promise'* and the *New Testament* as *'The Fulfilment of the Promise'*, as so much of the Old consists of 'signposts' pointing towards the future Messiah, whilst the New is the record of the birth, life, death and resurrection of that same Messiah, as well as other promises as yet unfulfilled, concerning the bodily return of the Lord Jesus to this world.

So just how did Almighty God make Himself known through history, as recorded in the Holy Scriptures? And how has He disclosed Himself through those same Scriptures? It seems that He chose to introduce Himself to His world gradually and to have used the Hebrew people, His chosen people, to be the foundation on which He would build His superstructure of self-revelation. It needs to be said straight away, that the Hebrew people were themselves

---

[1] Peter Sammons *The Birth of Christ* – Glory to Glory Publications, 2006 ISBN 0-9551790-1-7, and see Appendix 4

double-minded and often rebellious in their attitude to God, and were repeatedly unfaithful to Him. No religiously observant Jew would today deny this, and indeed some Jews attribute the ultimate reason for their nation's many periods of wandering and subjugation to their serial sins against God, as He was forced time and time again to withdraw His blessing from them.

This book avoids straying into the rather sterile debates about creation, evolution and the 'how' of the building of this physical world in which we find ourselves. Readers are also invited to put that particular philosophical cul-de-sac to one side — it's a debate for a different sort of book! We acknowledge there can be two legitimate but in many ways opposed views about how these creation accounts are meant to be understood — as either literal or as allegorical accounts that lead to the same broad conclusion — that *God created this world and created it as a totally fit dwelling place for humans*. The author of this book would simply state his own view that the Holy Bible is to be interpreted as literal where style and context make it obvious that this is the intention of the writer and should be read in the plainest sense possible, unless the context is clearly demanding a different interpretation. We proceed now to look at how God interacted with the key figures of the Old Testament and within the history of Israel, as both these are foundational to the way that God has made Himself known to the world at large.

It is in Genesis chapter 2 that we encounter the creation and naming of mankind. Having created the heavens and the earth, as well as living creatures, God created what this author thinks of as *homo spiritualis*, that first man to whom He would disclose Himself and with whom God would build a relationship of love and trust. So we read: **When the**

LORD God made the earth and the heavens (Genesis 4a) .... the LORD God formed the man from the dust of the ground and breathed into his nostrils the breath of life, and the man became a living being. (Genesis 7)

God's relationship with man, then as now, is one of initiative: God created men and women in his own spiritual image (Genesis 1:27). Later in chapter 2 God 'formed' the man and gave to him the role of carer of the Garden which the Bible calls Eden. God's first instruction to Man was to warn of the dangers of knowledge of good and evil. There's an old saying in the English language that 'a little knowledge is dangerous' and perhaps there was something of this thought in God's heart as He considered the pain and sorrow and waste entailed in rebellion ('sin') against God, which pain and sorrow and waste will inevitably be entailed in that 'knowledge of good and evil'. Some time later God took the initiative in calling Abraham to leave the place where he was living, Haran, and to travel to the land that He, God, would show to Abraham. God makes His key promise to Abraham, to make him into a 'great nation' in chapter 12:22. In chapter 22 God reminds Abraham that **"through your offspring all nations on earth will be blessed"** (v.18). Already we see that blessing is in God's heart, and we find that this urge to bless — to bring good outcomes — is foundational to all that God does.

For the time being we bypass the account of God's dealings with the Hebrews through Genesis and Exodus and rejoin them in their wanderings between the time when they were slaves in Egypt, and the time that they take control of the land of Canaan — their 'promised land'. God demands obedience from the Hebrews as in a very real sense, He demands it from all people today. Deuteronomy 4:2 gives us **"Do not add to what I command you and do not subtract**

from it, but keep the commands of the LORD your God that I give you." It's a recurring thought in this book, that Godism entails both adding to what God has said and surreptitiously deleting or downplaying (subtracting) other things. Godism then, reformulates God's revelation so as to make it fit with the Godist 'theology'. In Deuteronomy 5 the *Ten Commandments* are repeated (they had already been given in Exodus 20). These Commandments are worth looking at in detail, as they reflect the heart of all God's commands. In the text immediately below, sequential Commandment numbering is added by the editor, for ease of reference:

"I am the LORD your God, who brought you out of Egypt, out of the land of slavery.

"You shall have no other gods before me. [1]

"You shall not make for yourself an idol in the form of anything in heaven above or on the earth beneath or in the waters below. You shall not bow down to them or worship them; for I, the LORD your God, am a jealous God, punishing the children for the sin of the fathers to the third and fourth generation of those who hate me, but showing love to a thousand generations of those who love me and keep my commandments. [2]

"You shall not misuse the name of the LORD your God, for the LORD will not hold anyone guiltless who misuses his name. [3]

"Observe the Sabbath day by keeping it holy, as the LORD your God has commanded you. Six days you shall labor and do all your work, but the seventh day is a Sabbath to the LORD your God. On it you shall not do any work, neither you, nor your son or daughter, nor your manservant or maidservant, nor your ox, your donkey or any of your animals, nor the alien within

your gates, so that your manservant and maidservant may rest, as you do. Remember that you were slaves in Egypt and that the LORD your God brought you out of there with a mighty hand and an outstretched arm. Therefore the LORD your God has commanded you to observe the Sabbath day. [4]

"Honor your father and your mother, as the LORD your God has commanded you, so that you may live long and that it may go well with you in the land the LORD your God is giving you. [5]

"You shall not murder. [6]

"You shall not commit adultery. [7]

"You shall not steal. [8]

"You shall not give false testimony against your neighbor. [9]

"You shall not covet your neighbor's wife. You shall not set your desire on your neighbor's house or land, his manservant or maidservant, his ox or donkey, or anything that belongs to your neighbor." [10]

These are the commandments the LORD proclaimed in a loud voice to your whole assembly there on the mountain from out of the fire, the cloud and the deep darkness; and he added nothing more. Then he wrote them on two stone tablets and gave them to me.

Let's now briefly unpack a little of these Commandments, given by God to Moses, and see what they reveal about the true heart of God.

The Ten Commandments
That God is good is a foundational theme running right through the Bible, both Old and New Testaments — which

as we said earlier, can be thought of as the *promise* and the *fulfilment of the promise* of the Messiah — or the Saviour. When addressed as 'good teacher' by the rich young man in Mark 10:17, Jesus' immediate response is to say **"Why do you call me good? No one is good except God alone"**, after which Jesus recounted several of the Ten Commandments. Later we will look again at this encounter between the Lord Jesus and the wealthy and powerful young man, but for now we revert to Deuteronomy chapter 5 as we unpack the essence of the Commandments one by one.

"You shall have no other gods before me." [1]
Because God is holy and is light, only He can redeem us and sanctify us. If we elevate anything else or anyone else to the position of 'god' in our lives, then ultimately that thing or person will bring us to ruin, precisely because it or they will have replaced the position in our hearts that should be reserved for God alone. God knows what is good for us, and desires to give us what is good for us. If we have 'gods' before Him, then ultimately we must suffer (and suffer terribly) and this is something God desperately desires to avoid.

"You shall not make for yourself an idol in the form of anything in heaven above or on the earth beneath or in the waters below. You shall not bow down to them or worship them; for I, the LORD your God, am a jealous God, punishing the children for the sin of the fathers to the third and fourth generation of those who hate me, but showing love to a thousand generations of those who love me and keep my commandments." [2]
This command again must be a challenge to the Godist philosophy, as many of the world's religions do indeed create

idols and images. The Godist needs to explain whether God has forgotten Commandment No 2! We have seen in the previous chapter that one of the inherent characteristics of God is his immutability (or unchangeability). To assume that Commandment No 2 no longer applies suggests that God is untrue to Himself. It is for the Godist to explain this away, especially where they consider themselves to be 'Christian' in addition to Godist, as some do. The phrase jealous God is one that sits uncomfortably with modern westerners. We invest that word 'jealous' with all that's cheap and nasty in the ugly human emotion that we call jealousy. But this is not what God means when he describes Himself as a jealous God. What He means is that the place that should belong to Him alone, in our hearts, will bring us pain and disaster if it is given to someone or something else. That is something that God will not tolerate. He loves those who have put their trust and faith in His Son and who will therefore be with Him forever as they go on believing. When this lovely outcome is threatened by 'gods' and idols, God is quite simply angered. In this way He jealously guards His own position. Other references to the holy jealousy of God are found in Exodus 20:5; Exodus 34:14; Deuteronomy 4:24; 6:15 and Joshua 24:19. Readers may want to follow these up in their own Bible.

"You shall not misuse the name of the LORD your God, for the LORD will not hold anyone guiltless who misuses his name." [3]
This is a particularly serious sin, in God's eyes. Our reference to God should be in the context of His holiness, and our ultimate unworthiness. It is in this context that we have to view the profane ways in which God's name is used and abused by the world at large. Some seek to co-opt God

to support their narrow factional viewpoints. That in itself is to cheapen God's name. But even worse, possibly, is the jocular and dismissive manner in which His holy Name is used and abused in the commonest of every day talk. We use again as a metaphor for this attitude the BBC's light entertainment industry, where most sitcoms and most dramas seem to find ways of sneering at God's holy name. Of course it is not just the BBC! Abuse of God's name is something that is prevalent throughout (certainly) the western world, although such use and abuse does seem to be noticeably less prevalent in US TV output, a sign perhaps of the greater religiosity of that nation. But God warns quite straightforwardly that this attitude of irreverence will face its day of reckoning.

"Observe the Sabbath day by keeping it holy, as the LORD your God has commanded you. Six days you shall labor and do all your work, but the seventh day is a Sabbath to the LORD your God. On it you shall not do any work, neither you, nor your son or daughter, nor your manservant or maidservant, nor your ox, your donkey or any of your animals, nor the alien within your gates, so that your manservant and maidservant may rest, as you do. Remember that you were slaves in Egypt and that the LORD your God brought you out of there with a mighty hand and an outstretched arm. Therefore the LORD your God has commanded you to observe the Sabbath day." [4]

God demands a weekly period of rest and reflection, firstly so that men, women and children will have the opportunity to draw close to Him and to recharge their spiritual batteries, but secondly because the rhythm of life that God has Himself created demands that we rest. God is angered when the poor are exploited and forcing people to work on days that should be dedicated to rest and worship is, quite simply, forbidden. Societies that flout this divine Law find themselves with increasing social problems. It was the UK that in 1994 finally decided to legalise Sunday trading and thus removing, at a stroke, the last vestige of effective protection for ordinary shop workers and attendant support services. One cannot help but wonder whether this is a powerful contributory factor to the intractable problems of the UK's social underclass, as well as some of the wider problems that affect all of UK society. People who cannot find time to be with and enjoy their families will ultimately find it harder to hold those families together.

"Honour your father and your mother, as the LORD your God has commanded you, so that you may live long and that it may go well with you in the land the LORD your God is giving you." [5]

Again God's interest in families is underlined. Respect for parents is an aspect of love. When families stay together, it seems that longevity really is increased.

"You shall not murder." [6]

Human life, which is created by God in His own image, is sacred. For the avoidance of doubt, God has stated clearly that the unlawful and premeditated taking of life is sinful. Murderers will be held to account. It is unclear that all *the religions* hold this high ethic of the sacredness of human life — another challenge to Godism.

"You shall not commit adultery." [7]

Marriage, which is ordained by God (surely a subject for a different sort of book!) and which is sacred, is not to be broken by adultery — extramarital sexual relations — whether in a casual context or in the context of an 'affair'. Adultery attacks families, and ruins both relationships and lives. God cares deeply about this and is angered by it. Once again there are key differences in the attitude of *the religions* to the sacredness of marriage, another challenge to the Godist philosophy, if they claim that we all worship a single 'god'. If they believe in multiple 'gods' then the problem remains, why the difference in presentation of this most foundational of all human relationships?

"You shall not steal." [8]
Taking from others, almost always from people who are weaker, damages people's most basic interests. What people work for or are lawfully given should not be unlawfully appropriated by anyone else. Breaking this Commandment strikes at the foundation of the laws of most countries. When stealing happens, people get hurt in all sorts of ways — including, ultimately, the thieves themselves.

"You shall not give false testimony against your neighbour." [9]
If people cannot believe 'testimony' as given then many aspects of normal social and economic life become quite impossible. Where the false witness brings direct trouble to an innocent person, then this is doubly reprehensible. A Godist will need to explain in this regard the Islamic doctrine of *taqiyya* (or dissimulation) and explain how this doctrine meshes with the ninth Commandment of the Holy Bible.

"You shall not covet your neighbor's wife. You shall not set your desire on your neighbor's house or land,

his manservant or maidservant, his ox or donkey, or anything that belongs to your neighbor." [10]

Covetousness is close to stealing in a moral sense. By wanting what is not yours you can come to idolize that thing that you covet. This takes us back to Commandments Nos 1 and 2. Covetousness eats away at the soul and at the mind. It can lead to theft, to murder, to adultery and to lying. Covetousness undermines relationships — and relationships of love and integrity are closest to the heart of Almighty God.

In summary the Ten Commandments give a clear indication of the practical outworkings in daily life demanded by a God Whose heart is set on those things that are best for humankind. The Ten Commandments show us a God Who is good as well as demanding. A parent who loves their child will often be very demanding as they seek to bring out the best, to bring out the fullest potential of that child and to set them up for a good life. So too, God is demanding because He knows that only by helping us to tread a narrow path, which is ultimately required by these Commandments, can we hope to live out life as He wants us to, with a measure of security and certainty. In Deuteronomy chapter 8 God reminds His children not to forget Him, especially when life is pleasant: be careful (verse 11) **". . . that you do not forget the LORD your God, failing to observe his commands, his laws and his decrees that I am giving you this day."** Once they forget, and life becomes good for them in this new promised land, (verse 14) **"then your heart will become proud and you will forget the LORD your God, who brought you out of Egypt, out of the land of slavery."** And, God warns, rather than attributing peace and security to Him, they will begin to think that they have secured their own destiny (verse 17) **You may say to yourself, 'My power and the strength of my hands have produced this wealth for me.'** Finally God gives a solemn warning to His chosen people, one to be repeated so many times through Scripture (verse 19) that **"If you ever forget the LORD your God and follow other 'gods' and worship and bow down to them, I testify against you today that you will surely be destroyed."** Idol worship would not be tolerated by God. Will it be today? The Hebrews flirted with idolatry throughout the Old Testament period and *time and time again* this was the sinful act that caused God to remove His blessing from them. This was not so much intolerance on the part of God, although God does of course have the absolute and sovereign right to be intolerant! Rather, idol worship brought in its train many evils, the chief of which was the sacrifice of children to these false 'gods'.

God warned the Israelites not to take their possession of Canaan for granted. Deuteronomy 9:4 shows the real reason why God oversaw and planned the complete defeat and complete subjugation of the Canaanites: **After the LORD your God has driven them out before you, do not say to yourself, "The LORD has brought me here to take possession of this land because of my righteousness." No, it is on account of the wickedness of these nations that the LORD is going to drive them out before you.** The evils entailed in extreme idolatry were deeply offensive to God — especially, once again, the reality of child sacrifice.

Whilst some Bible critics like to characterize the books of Deuteronomy and Leviticus as depicting an 'angry' Old Testament God and compare this unfavourably with a loving New Testament God, these same books give us a good insight into God's primary motivations. So in Deuteronomy

10:17–19 we read. **For the LORD your God is God of gods and Lord of lords, the great God, mighty and awesome, who shows no partiality and accepts no bribes. He defends the cause of the fatherless and the widow, and loves the alien, giving him food and clothing. And you are to love those who are aliens, for you yourselves were aliens in Egypt.** We begin to get a sense of the Lord's social priorities in these verses. He accepts no bribes. Nor should we. It does seem to be highly relevant how political and commercial corruption holds back and retards social development in what we today call the 'developing world'. There is a growing realization today that corruption in all its forms acts as a brake on social progress. What God condemned three millennia ago remains a scourge today. Similarly, God's heart is inclined towards the weak and social outcasts, for whom He demands special concern. So the fatherless and widows are defended by God. Woe betide those who seek to injure these most vulnerable people. And those who are refugees are to be loved, in the way that Jesus would reiterate some 1,500 years later. Jesus then told a parable about a 'good Samaritan' who acted as a loving neighbour to an injured traveler, assaulted by robbers and left for dead.

So in Deuteronomy 11, God reminds the Israelites to love Him so that He in turn will provide for them. But He warns them once more of the prospect of His anger where they are enticed away by false 'gods':

Love the LORD your God and keep his requirements, his decrees, his laws and his commands always.

"So if you faithfully obey the commands I am giving you today—to love the LORD your God and to serve

him with all your heart and with all your soul—then I will send rain on your land in its season, both autumn and spring rains, so that you may gather in your grain, new wine and oil."

Be careful, or you will be enticed to turn away and worship other gods and bow down to them. Then the LORD's anger will burn against you, and he will shut the heavens so that it will not rain and the ground will yield no produce, and you will soon perish from the good land the LORD is giving you.

Once again these commands may seem harsh to modern eyes, but the underlying principle is consistent with a God of love who physically drives out from His promised land the scourge of evil religion — and we need to continually remind ourselves of that evil, involving the sacrifice of children and of shrine prostitution. Promise and warning go together in Deuteronomy:

"If you carefully observe all these commands I am giving you to follow—to love the LORD your God, to walk in all his ways and to hold fast to him — then the LORD will drive out all these nations before you, and you will dispossess nations larger and stronger than you." (Deuteronomy 11:22 – 23)

"See, I am setting before you today a blessing and a curse — the blessing if you obey the commands of the LORD your God that I am giving you today; the curse if you disobey the commands of the LORD your God and turn from the way that I command you today by following other gods, which you have not known." (Deuteronomy 11:26 – 28)

More than this, God demands a complete and permanent break with the false religions of Canaan and the surrounding countries. And so he commands: **"Destroy completely all the places on the high mountains and on the hills and under every spreading tree where the nations you are dispossessing worship their gods. Break down their altars, smash their sacred stones and burn their Asherah poles in the fire; cut down the idols of their gods and wipe out their names from those places."** (Deuteronomy 12:2–3)

Knowing the weakness and duplicity of the human heart, God warns the Israelites very clearly of the dangers that lie ahead and of the real evils entailed in the worship of false gods — which He will not tolerate in any way, shape or form. Again what follows sounds harsh but we need to remember two clear things: first that all these commands were given to a particular people at a particular time in history. Their detailed outworkings are no longer required of humans today. So critics cannot legitimately argue (as some try to) that the Christian Bible is much the same as the other sacred writings used by the various religions which contain bellicose rules that remain applicable today. And second, we must remember that without an absolute determination to remain pure, the Israelites would soon be sucked into the evils of *the religions* around them — and sadly they were. The following verses are selected from Deuteronomy chapter 13. Readers should note the verse numbers, which are not consecutive, and read the entire chapter to get a clearer grasp of God's clear instructions:

[1]**If a prophet or one who foretells dreams ....
says, "Let us follow other gods and let us worship them,"**
[3]**you must not listen to the words of that prophet or**

dreamer. The LORD your God is testing you to find out whether you love him with all your heart and with all your soul .... [5] That prophet or dreamer must be put to death, because he preached rebellion against the LORD your God, who brought you out of Egypt and redeemed you from the land of slavery; he has tried to turn you from the way the LORD your God commanded you to follow. You must purge the evil from among you. [6] If your very own brother, or your son or daughter, or the wife you love, or your closest friend secretly entices you, saying, "Let us go and worship other gods" (gods that neither you nor your fathers have known, [7] gods of the peoples around you, whether near or far, from one end of the land to the other), [8] do not yield to him or listen to him. Show him no pity. Do not spare him or shield him. [9] You must certainly put him to death. Your hand must be the first in putting him to death, and then the hands of all the people.

We are bound to repeat, these rules were time-limited in their application, in the sense that they applied to the Hebrew people entering into and then defending their promised land. It is unclear if these commands were ever carried out in practice. Indeed the cyclical rebellion of the Hebrews against God, by intermittently chasing after other 'gods' suggests that these rules were honoured more in the breach than in the observance! But even here in these undoubtedly harsh commands there is no sign that God was seeking a sort of knee jerk reaction in these situations. In Deuteronomy 13:14, God tells the Israelites that, before taking any action, they are to **enquire, probe and investigate thoroughly** and that only if true that **a detestable thing has been done among you** may they then apply the death penalty. Once again we have a sense of God making provision for the application of true justice in an otherwise unjust world.

We need to remember, as God clearly understood, that these were primitive times when Deuteronomy was given to the Hebrew people. This was the late bronze age, prior even to the iron age. There was no social insurance. The economies of the time could not support any of the ideals that we today think so important. There were no hospitals, schools or infrastructure in any way that we would recognize. The need for justice to be enshrined for the ordinary people was an important objective in God's laws. Warfare was never far away, in these times of petty kings who often led petty kingdoms. Kings, it might be added, whose word or whim was law. Israel was qualitatively different from any of the other nations, in its monotheism and in its laws that were designed to protect the weak and to yield true justice. Warfare was never far away as pagan kings all too often sought to resolve their problems through the sword. God's commands, as far as they referred to the evil of war, were concerned with the protection of the weak. So we have the inevitable situation of what happens when women are captured by a victorious Hebrew army. Only marriage was contemplated by God and the restriction on Hebrew military victors (men) was telling:

When you go to war against your enemies and the LORD your God delivers them into your hands and you take captives, if you notice among the captives a beautiful woman and are attracted to her, you may take her as your wife. Bring her into your home and have her shave her head, trim her nails and put aside the clothes she was wearing when captured. After she has lived in your house and mourned her father and mother for a full month, then you may go to her and be her husband

and she shall be your wife. If you are not pleased with her, let her go wherever she wishes. You must not sell her or treat her as a slave, since you have dishonored her. (Deuteronomy 21:10–14)

This was a powerful disincentive, indeed, to any desire to forcibly take and then discard captive women. In the context of the day, these commands were exceptional. In today's parlance, we might say that God had demanded a cooling off period — there was to be no immediate gratification, and no treatment of the captive as a slave. No, she was to be taken — if at all — as a wife. This immediately implies offspring, responsibility to offspring and to inheritance rights. Furthermore, if a man decided later that he was no longer interested in this woman — for whatever reason — then she must be allowed to go 'wherever she pleases' because she has been dishonoured by the man. This implies she might return to her own kith and kin, or go anywhere else. And the man may not sell her or treat her as a slave. With the inevitable drain on family resources entailed in taking on wives, these were powerful disincentives to the enticements of casual fancies. We may presume that many women were saved from much heartache by the simple existence of this command, a command that it would be difficult for a soldier to circumvent under the witness of his compatriots.

So God's focus here is on protection of the weak and defenceless. It remains for the Godist to explain how this command ties in with the teachings of the various religions on use and abuse of captives in war. The fact that Western history in particular and Christian history in general shows that people who call themselves Christian have become involved in warfare, cannot be counter-argued to the effect that Christianity is as 'guilty' as *the religions* in this regard. That some people who have called themselves Christian and have thought that they were fighting on God's 'side' may be a fact of history — that those same people attempted to use this as some sort of 'justification' for their actions may also be true but it is difficult (with integrity) to sustain as a counter-argument — or a side-stepping *argument of convenience*! Those who plan and conduct temporal warfare cannot use the Bible either as a general or as a specific justification for that warfare. It is readily acknowledged however that the Bible might be appealed to by some genuine Christians in developing an argument that warfare can in some circumstances represent *the lesser of two evils*.

If a man has two wives, and he loves one but not the other, and both bear him sons but the firstborn is the son of the wife he does not love, when he wills his property to his sons, he must not give the rights of the firstborn to the son of the wife he loves in preference to his actual firstborn, the son of the wife he does not love. He must acknowledge the son of his unloved wife as the firstborn by giving him a double share of all he has. That son is the first sign of his father's strength. The right of the firstborn belongs to him. (Deuteronomy 21:15–17)

The first thing to say in looking at this passage is that the Hebrew tradition was in bronze age times, has remained since (and has been inherited by the Church), that a man can marry only one wife. Here God seems to recognize the unhappy reality that there will be circumstances where a man actually has, for whatever reason, more than one wife. How, in these circumstances, must he behave? Again God's first thought and primary thought, is to the defence of the weak. The prohibition on favouring children of one wife over another, would have been a powerful disincentive

(a) to take more than one wife in the first place and (b) to discriminate against children of the unfavoured (or 'unloved') wife. It should be added that, again, such a circumstance of unhappy marriage would have been under the observation of the Hebrew community as a whole, so it would have been difficult for a man to circumvent this command. We may presume that many real day to day family problems were avoided in the first place by this command in Deuteronomy.

In exactly the same way, God commands protection for the weak and marginalized (and that always meant women) in marriage violations — see Deuteronomy 22:13 through 30. And God commands the use of fair and accurate measures in trading (Deuteronomy 25:13 through 16). Plainly there will always be a disparity in bargaining power between people who are trading. God's heart is for justice to be done in such situations, but again with an emphasis on protecting the weak. We will close this chapter on 'getting to know' God and the way that He progressively began to disclose His true nature through Deuteronomy with a few final thoughts on that book.

Deuteronomy

More than 80 Old Testament quotations found in the New Testament are from Deuteronomy. The Lord Jesus focused attention on Deuteronomy when he summarized the essence of the Old Testament Law (Matthew 22:37) in the two great commandments of love for God and love for neighbour. Jesus also quoted Deuteronomy (actually 6:13 and 16, and 8:3) in responding to the devil's temptations — see Matthew 4:4–10. The primary need for love toward God and neighbour were to become the basic belief and ethic of the early church and has remained so ever since. The book of Deuteronomy is thus one of vital importance to the Lord and should be for His followers today.

To think of Deuteonomy as a 'second law' is misleading. The author, Moses, is primarily concerned with Israel's relationship with God and their determination to maintain that relationship in their own and their children's lives. Although the Ten Commandments are repeated, the focus is placed very much on the first Commandment which explicitly requires exclusive devotion to God. Moses' emphasis is not legalistic. Although he did warn of the need to keep all of God's laws (Deuteronomy 28:1, 58) his message as a whole is clear that he is not concerned solely about legalistic compliance. Rather, the key message of Deuteronomy is the unique relationship that has been established between a unique God with His unique people, the Israelites. Love is the key word in that relationship. Moses boldly asserted that **The Lord our God is one Lord; you shall love the Lord your God with all your heart, and with all your soul and with all your might.**[2] All the other commandments as set out in chapters 5 through 11 depend on this foundational 'Law'. The Israelites were never to forget that God had chosen them to be His people, not the other way around! So in Chapter 7 and verses 7 though 9 we read: **The LORD did not set his affection on you and choose you because you were more numerous than other peoples, for you were the fewest of all peoples. But it was because the LORD loved you and kept the oath he swore to your forefathers that he brought you out with a mighty hand and redeemed you from the land of slavery, from the power of Pharaoh king of Egypt. Know therefore**

[2] chapter 6:4,5 — and taken from the *Revised Standard Version* which seems to capture the essence more accurately than most English language translations

that the LORD your God is God; he is the faithful God, keeping his covenant of love to a thousand generations of those who love him and keep his commands. They were to fulfil God's judgment on the Canaanites, who had been spared from judgment since Abraham's time (Genesis 15:16). Although the Israelites did not themselves merit God's love, it was in love and mercy that He had rescued them out of Egypt.

Love of the 'alien' is second in importance to undivided love for God. Love for the neighbour or traveller is basic to all other human obligations and so the Israelites were commanded in Leviticus 19:9–18

When you reap the harvest of your land, do not reap to the very edges of your field or gather the gleanings of your harvest. Do not go over your vineyard a second time or pick up the grapes that have fallen. Leave them for the poor and the alien. I am the LORD your God.

Do not steal.

Do not lie.

Do not deceive one another.

Do not swear falsely by my name and so profane the name of your God. I am the LORD.

Do not defraud your neighbor or rob him.

Do not hold back the wages of a hired man overnight.

Do not curse the deaf or put a stumbling block in front of the blind, but fear your God. I am the LORD.

Do not pervert justice; do not show partiality to the poor or favoritism to the great, but judge your neighbor fairly.

Do not go about spreading slander among your people.

Do not do anything that endangers your neighbor's

life. I am the LORD.

Do not hate your brother in your heart. Rebuke your neighbor frankly so you will not share in his guilt.

Do not seek revenge or bear a grudge against one of your people, but love your neighbor as yourself. I am the LORD.

Social obligations were rooted in a person's relationship with God. As a people who had benefited from God's love, the Israelites were to show that love to others. God loves the stranger, the widow and the orphan: if anyone claims to love God, therefore, they are under an obligation to display that love to other people. God is concerned about justice and righteousness. Someone who professes to love God will share and display those same concerns. So, the Hebrew people were to be known for their concern for people whose social position exposed them to exploitation and oppression. Readers who want to get a good appreciation of the whole scope of Deuteronomy are directed to the article on that subject in the *Baker Encyclopaedia of the Bible*[3] which makes this interesting observation: the profound humanitarian spirit of the Mosaic law stands in unique contrast to the approximately contemporary Babylonian *Code of Hammurabi* and the Assyrian and Hittite legal codes, which contained no vital consciousness of a love relationship with the deity. The deeply humanitarian spirit of Deuteronomy is reflected again in these extracts which readers may want to follow up separately:

Canaan's abundant blessings should be shared with neighbours (Dt 14:22 – 15:23

In human relationships justice was to prevail among the Hebrews (Dt 16:18 – 21:23)

---

[3] Baker Encyclopedia of the Bible, ISBN 8010 2139 1 (4 volume set).

In domestic and social relationships the law of love was to prevail (Dt 22:1 – 26:19)

It only needs to be added, as we draw to a conclusion, that the Lord Jesus would come into conflict with the religious leaders of His day because they had replaced the essence of the Law with a maze of legalism. For Jesus, the greatest commandment was to love God, and the second was to love one's neighbour. Those two commandments, if kept perfectly, provide the basis for eternal life (see Matthew 22:37–39, also Mark 12:29–31, and finally Luke 10:27–28). Christians believe that the climax of God's self-disclosure of love came in the man, Jesus Christ. For Christians, then, responding to God's love means to accept Jesus in wholehearted devotion; to become, in other words, His disciples. And in addition, to love one's neighbour as Jesus so clearly demonstrated in His life.

The moral perfection and moral precision of God's law, as revealed in the Old Testament (and later as we shall see, consummated in the New Testament) must inevitably be compared to the precise moral requirements of the laws of *the religions*. It is simply a straightforward side-stepping of the problem (and it *is* a problem, though Godists try to avoid it) to say that the essence of *the religions* and of the Holy Bible are much the same. The Godist also side-steps the problem of how devout followers of *the religions* work out their devotion to their religious laws in practice, as compared with the absolute moral requirements clearly laid down in the Holy Scriptures. Finally, we repeat, the detailed and sometimes legalistic requirements of the Old Testament Law, whilst they *do* provide to modern people at least clear guidance as to how to order our priorities and direct our concerns for the poor and oppressed, they are no longer legal requirements for a true child of God, for that same Law has now been fulfilled (completed) in Jesus. We will explore this theme later in this book,[4] but we finish with the words of Jesus on this matter: **"Do not think that I have come to abolish the Law or the Prophets; I have not come to abolish them but to fulfill them."** (Matthew 5:17)

---

[4] See Chapter 12

4

GOD SPEAKS TO
HIS PEOPLE

Promises and Warnings

Hopefully by now we are developing some real sense of the
heart of this God who has chosen to reveal Himself — to
make Himself known — to the world that He made. From
the very earliest of times and then into the Bronze and Iron
Ages, God progressively disclosed His nature. Readers may
feel that they now have some clarity as to this nature but,
at the risk of labouring the point, more should be said. One
early objection needs to be cleared away: some people may
accuse the author of focusing attention on the 'nice' bits of
the Bible, whilst ignoring the 'nasty' bits. This objection
can be repudiated relatively straightforwardly: the nature
of God revealed so far in our studies is His nature as it
has always been and always will be. Whilst 'love' is a key
facet of His self disclosure, there are other facets of equal
importance; His holiness and righteousness are two[1]. In
this book we choose to focus on those attributes of God's
nature that show His recognizable beauty, because these

---

[1] In chapter 2 we looked at the key 'communicable attributes' of God. A purist
might observe that love, along with holiness, righteousness, wisdom, truthfulness etc are not facets, or expressions of God. These things run rather deeper
than that! God is not loving, therefore: God *is* love. However for the point we
are making in this chapter, we are merely noting that the attributes or 'facets' of
God are held in holy tension with each other.

attributes of His nature are so clearly revealed as being immutable — or unchanging. Where God appears to us to be 'harsh' we need to remember that His punishments were exacted on particular people at particular times. *Those punishments were discharged in a historical setting that has now passed.* So when, for example, God in His sovereignty commands the Israelites to totally destroy the city of Jericho we know that that was done in an historical context which will not recur.[2] No one can say that because God allowed the destruction of Jericho, that we can order the destruction of Birmingham (with apologies to the people of Birmingham, but no doubt readers will see the point we are making) whether in God's name or in anyone else's! God's social concern, however, His concern for the weak, the marginalized, the downtrodden, and the vulnerable remains of relevance today and will always remain relevant so long as there are humans in *this* world. The 'nasty' bits, then, if they exist at all (and many people seem to assume that the Old Testament is full of bellicosity) are now dealt with — they are history. It should be added, moreover, that it is unwise to the point of folly for modern people to 'judge' God on these issues. Whatever punishments He has exacted, He has exacted with a heavy heart. For example, in Ezekiel 33:11 God says, **"As surely as I live," declares the Sovereign LORD, "I take no pleasure in the death of the wicked, but rather that they turn from their ways and live. Turn! Turn from your evil ways"**! Again in Matthew 23:37 Jesus lamented over the unbelieving Jews

---

[2] It is important to add that, in spite of the fact that these events are now passed and therefore not to be replicated today, they nevertheless contain deep spiritual truths and lessons that are still of great value today. The Old Testament is not therefore some dusty ancient history book. It is the foundation upon which God's self disclosure in Jesus must be understood. See 1 Corinthians 10 for a biblical perspective on this.

of His day, **"O Jerusalem, Jerusalem, you who kill the prophets and stone those sent to you, how often I have longed to gather your children together, as a hen gathers her chicks under her wings, but you were not willing."** In both these verses we see a clear desire on the part of God that the lost turn from their wicked ways and be saved from destruction. Since God has given humans free will, in some ways the most precious gift of all, it is true that those who have rebelled in the most grievous ways (and the sins of the Canaanites were absolutely appalling) have done so with their eyes open.

By the end of the book of Joshua, the Israelites are installed in their promised land. No matter how aggressive it may seem to modern eyes, it was God's sovereign choice to drive out the Canaanites and to give the land to His chosen people, in exactly the same way that it was His sovereign choice to choose the Israelites to be His covenant people in the first place. In the light of Old Testament history — as this author likes to call it, the *history of the promise*, and in the light of New Testament history (as this author calls it, the *fulfilment of the promise*) we can see real theological sense and continuity in God's great plan of salvation to be worked out first through a chosen covenant people, and later through a chosen people living under a new covenant. At the end of the book of Joshua, therefore, the Israelites are at the threshold of a new age, and age of self-sovereignty in their own promised land. But God, through Joshua (now a very old man) issues warnings about what the future may hold. We continue to see God's self-revelation in these passages (Joshua 23:3, 5 and 7):

You yourselves have seen everything the LORD your God has done to all these nations for your sake; it was the LORD your God who fought for you.

[5] **The LORD your God himself will drive them out of your way. He will push them out before you, and you will take possession of their land, as the LORD your God promised you**.

[7] **Do not associate with these nations that remain among you; do not invoke the names of their gods or swear by them. You must not serve them or bow down to them**.

The warning could not be clearer. God had given the Israelites their promised land. Those who 'remained among' them were peoples with which they could not safely mingle. And just as important, their 'gods' were ones that absolutely must not be allowed to entice the Israelites away from the one, true God. These warnings are continued below (Joshua 23:11–13 and 15–16):

[11] **So be very careful to love the LORD your God.** [12] **But if you turn away and ally yourselves with the survivors of these nations that remain among you and if you intermarry with them and associate with them,** [13] **then you may be sure that the LORD your God will no longer drive out these nations before you. Instead, they will become snares and traps for you, whips on your backs and thorns in your eyes, until you perish from this good land, which the LORD your God has given you**.

[15] **But just as every good promise of the LORD your God has come true, so the LORD will bring on you all the evil he has threatened, until he has destroyed you from this good land he has given you.** [16] **If you violate the covenant of the LORD your God, which he commanded you, and go and serve other gods and bow down to them, the LORD's anger will burn against you, and you will quickly perish from the good land he has given you**.

Now fear the LORD and serve him with all faithfulness. Throw away the gods your forefathers worshiped beyond the River and in Egypt, and serve the LORD. But if serving the LORD seems undesirable to you, then choose for yourselves this day whom you will serve, whether the gods your forefathers served beyond the River, or the gods of the Amorites, in whose land you are living. But as for me and my household, we will serve the LORD. (Joshua 24:14–15)

Joshua said to the people, "You are not able to serve the LORD. He is a holy God; he is a jealous God. He will not forgive your rebellion and your sins. [20]If you forsake the LORD and serve foreign gods, he will turn and bring disaster on you and make an end of you, after he has been good to you." (Joshua 24:19–20)

"Now then," said Joshua, "throw away the foreign gods that are among you and yield your hearts to the LORD, the God of Israel." (Joshua 24:19–20)

With all these warnings, we see the heart of God deeply concerned at the prospect of His chosen people following other 'gods'. In the light of these warnings, we need to understand to what extent they continue to apply to God's people today. It seems difficult to argue that God has somehow changed His mind in allowing the 'worship' of other gods, or indeed that the true God has masqueraded Himself in a number of different guises. Once again it is for the Godist to explain or refute this, because this seems to be the position that they have adopted.

Judges

Immediately after the book of Joshua we find the book of Judges, as the Israelites were to be governed by men raised up by God as prominent leaders who governed on a day to day basis in His place. Sadly, the beginning of this book reads almost as a reversal of the close of Joshua. Although commanded by God to drive out completely all the indigenous Canaanite peoples, we very quickly see that this Command is breached. In 1:27 we read that Mannaseh did not drive out the people of Beth Shan. In v. 28 the Israelites choose to put some Canaanites to work for them as forced labourers (presumably little better than slaves). In v. 29 Ephraim failed to drive out the indigenous peoples from Gezer, and Zebulun failed to drive out the Canaanites from Kitron or Nahalol. In verse 31 Asher fails to drive out those living in Acco, Sidon and several other villages. In verse 33 Naphtali committed the same sin in relation to the Canaanites of Beth Shemesh and Beth Anath. The stage is set. In chapter 2:10 the inevitable flirtation with foreign 'gods' begins: **After that whole generation had been gathered to their fathers, another generation grew up, who knew neither the LORD nor what he had done for Israel. Then the Israelites did evil in the eyes of the LORD and served the Baals. They forsook the LORD, the God of their fathers, who had brought them out of Egypt. They followed and worshiped various gods of the peoples around them. They provoked the LORD to anger because they forsook him and served Baal and the Ashtoreths. In his anger against Israel the LORD handed them over to raiders who plundered them. He sold them to their enemies all around, whom they were no longer able to resist.**

Yet they would not listen to their judges but prostituted

themselves to other gods and worshiped them. Unlike their fathers, they quickly turned from the way in which their fathers had walked, the way of obedience to the LORD's commands.

But when the judge died, the people returned to ways even more corrupt than those of their fathers, following other gods and serving and worshiping them. They refused to give up their evil practices and stubborn ways.

The people are determined to go their own way and this leads to reduction of security and to social decay. By chapter 6 of Judges, the sins of the people have brought Israel to such a low point that once again they cry out to the LORD. God sends them a prophet (v. 7) and reminds them they must not worship other 'gods'. Gideon is raised up by God to tear down the shrines to false 'gods' that the Israelites have worshipped. In v. 27 he chooses to do this by night — presumably first and foremost as by doing it in this way he will encounter less opposition from the Baalites, but we are left to wonder whether in some way this night action was cowardly or demeaning. Brought right up to date we need to challenge ourselves, are there people in the Churches who should speak out more openly about the ever bolder syncretism that is presently being introduced by Godists into the Church? Is opposition to this syncretism a task for the daylight, or for the night?

Immediately following Judges comes the book of Ruth. Although we inevitably tend to read this as a sort of romantic love story, where the faithful and lovely widow Ruth eventually is married by the honourable and kind Boaz, the account tells us two clear things about God. Firstly what is His concern is for the 'alien' in His promised land, and secondly that God rewards the faithfulness of Ruth, in exactly the same way that He rewards the faithfulness of His followers in all ages. Following the book of Ruth we find the first book of Samuel. It is not long before the familiar problem of the Israelites *wanting to behave like other nations* once again rears its ugly head. So in 1 Samuel 8:6, the Hebrews are demanding a 'king' rather than judges, so that they can be governed like other nations. God warns them as to precisely what possession by a king will mean in practice, but still they persist in their demand. God tells the prophet Samuel, however, that the rejection by the Hebrew people is not of him, Samuel, or even so much of the rule by Judges — it is a much more fundamental rejection: **But when they said, "Give us a king to lead us," this displeased Samuel; so he prayed to the LORD. And the LORD told him: "Listen to all that the people are saying to you; it is not you they have rejected, but they have rejected me as their king. As they have done from the day I brought them up out of Egypt until this day, forsaking me and serving other gods, so they are doing to you. Now listen to them; but warn them solemnly and let them know what the king who will reign over them will do."** (1 Samuel 8:6–9)

Chasing after false 'gods' will bring disaster for Israel. To rescue Israel from the travails of King Saul, God raises up a future King, the shepherd boy David. Now the promises of the future Saviour Messiah become more overt. So in 2 Samuel 7:10, God rekindles His special covenant with Israel: **And I will provide a place for my people Israel and will plant them so that they can have a home of their own and no longer be disturbed. Wicked people will not oppress them anymore, as they did at the beginning . . . .** But the promise goes further. Now God promises to provide, through the line of David, a King who will have a kingdom that will endure forever: **"... I will raise up your offspring to succeed you, who will come from your own body, and I will establish his kingdom. He is the one who will build a house for my Name, and I will establish the throne of his kingdom forever. I will be his father, and he will be my son. When he does wrong, I will punish him with the rod of men, with floggings inflicted by men. But my love will never be taken away from him, as I took it away from Saul, whom I removed from before you. Your house and your kingdom will endure forever before me; your throne will be established forever.** (2 Samuel 7:12–16)

That David's line would be established and would pass down to Jesus of Nazareth is a fact of history.[3] God's promise immediately above seems to have both a near-term and a long-term future outworking. So, we know that David's son Solomon did actually build the first great Temple to God in Jerusalem. But the *throne* that has been established forever is the throne of King Jesus, and his Kingdom goes down through the ages to the end of time. In all generations since the resurrection of Christ, countless people have put their faith in Him and become His subjects, living in His Kingdom and acknowledging Him as King. Verse 14 above alludes to the fact that Jesus is acknowledged by God to be His Son (see Matthew 4:17). We know that Jesus is without sin — see for example 2 Corinthians 5:21, which would be written nearly a thousand years after the second book of Samuel — **God made him who had no sin to be sin for us, so that in him we might become the righteousness of God**. This is a subject that we will follow up later, but for the time being the reader is asked to note

---

[3] Readers who want to follow this up in greater detail may want to refer to *The Birth of Christ* by Peter Sammons (ISBN 0-9551790-1-7 Glory to Glory Publications, 2006)

the clarity of the Messianic prophecy in 2 Samuel 12ff. As it says in verse 14 **"when he does wrong, I will punish him with the rod of men, with floggings inflicted by men."** This may seem puzzling. As Jesus did no wrong, how and why could God punish Him with the floggings of men? The answer came a thousand years later in Paul's second letter to the Corinthian church. Jesus *was* flogged (see for example John 19:1) because *Jesus had been made sin* on our behalf. We are straying now into some deeply theological material, but hopefully the reader begins to see the consistency and the purity of God's revelation. David's response to God's promise which has been unveiled in 2 Samuel 7 is given from verse 18 onwards. It is summarized in verse 25f: **And now, LORD God, keep forever the promise you have made concerning your servant and his house. Do as you promised, [26] so that your name will be great forever. Then men will say, 'The LORD Almighty is God over Israel!' And the house of your servant David will be established before you.**

In King David we begin to see God's deep love for His people reciprocated. In spite of being a King who sinned, David can still receive God's forgiveness and restoration which leads him to offer this prayer of love, to God.[4]

> **For I have kept the ways of the LORD;**
> **I have not done evil by turning from my God.**
> **All his laws are before me;**
> **I have not turned away from his decrees.**
> **I have been blameless before him**
> **and have kept myself from sin.**

---

[4] See also Psalm 51. The wonder remains that despite the enormity of David's sin, it is overshadowed by God's mercy. In this there must be an encouragement for all sinners, everywhere!

> **The LORD has rewarded me**
> **according to my righteousness,**
> **according to my cleanness in his sight**.
> **To the faithful you show yourself faithful,**
> **to the blameless you show yourself blameless,**
> **to the pure you show yourself pure,**
> **but to the crooked you show yourself shrewd**.
> **You save the humble,**
> **but your eyes are on the haughty to bring them low.**
> **You are my lamp, O LORD;**
> **the LORD turns my darkness into light**.
>
> (2 Samuel 22:22–29)

A love relationship?

In King David we begin to see the possibility for all people, everywhere, of a personal love relationship with God, where God knows the penitent sinner and knows him (or her) intimately, but in spite of this He is *still prepared* to acknowledge them before men — and it might be added, before the devil as well — as His beloved and as His child. As Godists tell us that humans worship one God no matter how 'he' or 'it' has revealed 'himself' or 'itself', the absence of this great love relationship at a personal level in the main religions is something that the Godist needs to explain. Is it that the Judeo-Christian experience is 'higher' than those of the other religions? Indeed, is there a heierarchy of 'higher religions' — and if so is this not simply unfair of God in His dealings with these religions?

It was not just David who experienced and enjoyed this love relationship with God. David's son Solomon was like his father in being a sad mixture of righteousness and purity, and rebellion and sinfulness. But he was still as a penitent sinner able to draw close to God and express his deep love to God. So in 1 Kings 8:23–27 we read this: **O LORD, God of Israel, there is no God like you in heaven above or on earth below — *you who keep your covenant of love with your servants who continue wholeheartedly in your way*. You have kept your promise to your servant David my father; with your mouth you have promised and with your hand you have fulfilled it — as it is today.**

Now LORD, God of Israel, keep for your servant David my father the promises you made to him when you said, 'You shall never fail to have a man to sit before me on the throne of Israel, if only your sons are careful in all they do to walk before me as you have done.' And now, O God of Israel, let your word that you promised your servant David my father come true.

But will God really dwell on earth? The heavens, even the highest heaven, cannot contain you. How much less this temple I have built! Yet give attention to your servant's prayer and his plea for mercy, O LORD my God. Hear the cry and the prayer that your servant is praying in your presence this day.

It should be noted in verse 23 above that God's covenant of love continues with those *who continue wholeheartedly to follow Him* — that clause is italicized above by this author so as to emphasize it for the reader. This is an important point and one that often seems to be missed by preachers today. When God expresses His love, it is almost always in the context of His love to His disciples, and those same disciples are to continue wholeheartedly to follow Him. Unconditional love, as so often preached from Western pulpits, is at best only a partially true theology. If readers are surprised by this then it is recommended that they begin over a period of time to read their Bible and to try to note all those references to God's love, whether in the Old Testament or the New, where it is *not* clearly stated as being lavished upon His disciples — i.e. those who wholeheartedly follow Him. Once again there seems to be something here that challenges the Godist viewpoint. In the author's experience, many of those who call themselves Godist (by whatever label) have simultaneously chosen *not* to follow Him, but instead to build a theology around what they call the essence of 'god's' teachings wheresoever these may be found and in whatever guise. Will they continue to find themselves at the centre of God's loving attention, or will they see a slow diminution of their relationship with 'god' as they try to discern 'him' or 'it' in the teachings of so many religions?

Solomon continues his prayer of praise as he blesses all the people in God's name: **Praise be to the LORD, who has given rest to his people Israel just as he promised. Not one word has failed of all the good promises he gave through his servant Moses. May the LORD our God be with us as he was with our fathers; may he never leave us nor forsake us. May he turn our hearts to him, to walk in all his ways and to keep the commands, decrees and regulations he gave our fathers. And may these words of mine, which I have prayed before the LORD, be near to the LORD our God day and night, that he may uphold the cause of his servant and the cause of his people Israel according to each day's need.** (1 Kings 8:56–59)

God responds, as He so often does, with a wonderful, affirmative promise which is coupled with a warning: **"I *will* establish your royal throne over Israel forever, as I promised David your father when I said, 'You shall never fail to have a man on the throne of Israel.'**

"But if you or your sons turn away from me and do not observe the commands and decrees I have given you and go off to serve other gods and worship them,

then I will cut off Israel from the land I have given them and will reject this temple I have consecrated for my Name. Israel will then become a byword and an object of ridicule among all peoples. And though this temple is now imposing, all who pass by will be appalled and will scoff and say, 'Why has the LORD done such a thing to this land and to this temple?' People will answer, 'Because they have forsaken the LORD their God, who brought their fathers out of Egypt, and have embraced other gods, worshiping and serving them—that is why the LORD brought all this disaster on them.'" (1 Kings 9:5–10)

Once again the stage seems to be set for that sad cycle of *restoration* followed by *rebellion*, followed by *retribution*. Solomon himself rebelled against God by marrying foreign wives and then following foreign 'gods'. All so sad, and so predictable: so in 11:1–4 we see Solomon's sin unfolding. In verse 14 God's response is both swift and direct: **Then the LORD raised up against Solomon an adversary, Hadad the Edomite, from the royal line of Edom**. This sad cycle is repeated by King Jeroboam who re-establishes the worship of golden calves — chiefly because it is politically expedient for him to do so. There is a high price to be paid for deliberately ignoring God's clear instruction, as the remainder of Jeroboam's life seems to indicate. In 1 Kings 22 we encounter the idea that 'religious' men will tell their political rulers what they want to hear. This is to be contrasted with true prophets, who generally told their political masters what they did not want to hear! We need to wonder, then, in the early years of the twenty first century, whether the rush towards multi-faith dialogue by some 'religious' leaders is exactly that — a desire to tell their 'king' what he wants to hear. It is noteworthy that, at the time of writing this book, politicians in the UK and the US are offering state funding to those 'religions' or 'faith communities' that are prepared to get involved in 'good works' as directed by the state. We have to wonder, then, whether the temptation of state cash and the public recognition and public applaud that multi-faithism today inevitably brings, is not a powerful incentive to sway people towards the Godist agenda and away from the normative interpretation of Christianity. And indeed perhaps, from the normative interpretations of other religions as well.

In 2 Kings 1 we see the continuation of the pursuit by Israel's Kings of false 'gods'. Verse 6 is instructive in this regard. **"Is it because there is no God in Israel that you are sending men to consult Baal-Zebub, the god of Ekron?"** Again the comparison with twenty first century Britain seems stark. A country with 1,500 years of active Christian influence and, without too much mind-stretching, 1,500 years of intervention by God at key points in Britain's history, today seeks the blessing of other 'gods', where it is politically expedient. We echo God's question in 2 Kings 1:6 as we ask the rhetorical question of our leaders; *is it because there is no God in the UK (or US or the various formerly Christian influenced countries) that our leaders feel the necessity to consult other 'gods' under the guise of multi-faithism?* Although it does not logically follow on from our rhetorical question, the slightly depressing account in 2 Kings 5 of Naaman's healing from leprosy, and of the true prophet Elisha's unfaithful servant Gehazi trying to gain financially from Naaman's healing does, nevertheless, surely have a modern resonance. Those who cheat God by effectively taking His name in vain will unquestionably face God's judgement.

By the time we reach 2 Kings 17, Israel's serial rebellions

against their covenant relationship with God leads to their first exile from the Holy Land. God's malediction against Israel is summarized in 2 Kings 17:14 – 15: **...they would not listen and were as stiff-necked as their fathers, who did not trust in the LORD their God. They rejected his decrees and the covenant he had made with their fathers and the warnings he had given them. They followed worthless idols and themselves became worthless. They imitated the nations around them although the LORD had ordered them, "Do not do as they do," and they did the things the LORD had forbidden them to do**.

In 2 Kings 17:17, we find that child sacrifice was again being practiced in the land as the Hebrews had, by imitation, become as bad as the nations they had driven out. It seems so sad that this chosen people, this especial beloved of God, should so rebel and go on rebelling without flagging, until God acts decisively against them.

In 1 and 2 Chronicles we find that some of Israel's kings are faithful to God and others are rebellious. They are certainly a mixed bunch! Among the faithful was Jehoshaphat, who oversaw a general reorientation towards the LORD. As the Israelites return to God, so He grants them success once more against their persecutors (in this case an axis of the Moabites, Ammonites and Meunites) who have come to make war against them. Israel survives and prospers, but still has a divided heart. So we read this, from 2 Chronicles 20:20 – 21: **Early in the morning they left for the Desert of Tekoa. As they set out, Jehoshaphat stood and said, "Listen to me, Judah and people of Jerusalem! Have faith in the LORD your God and you will be upheld; have faith in his prophets and you will be successful." After consulting the people, Jehoshaphat appointed men to sing to the LORD and to praise him**

for the splendor of his holiness as they went out at the head of the army, saying: "Give thanks to the LORD, for his love endures forever."

This latter we might think as a strange battle cry — 'his love endures forever' — but the record is that the invaders were defeated. The summary of the reign of Jehoshaphat is given in the same chapter and vv. 32 – 3. Note that the 'high places', those places on hilltops and remote regions where false 'gods' were worshipped, remained intact: [Jehoshaphat] **walked in the ways of his father Asa and did not stray from them; he did what was right in the eyes of the LORD. The high places, however, were not removed, and the people still had not set their hearts on the God of their fathers**.

The next good Israelite King is Hezekiah, who encourages his people to return to their true worship of the LORD. Hezekiah reflects the passion of God for forgiveness and for restoration of the covenant relationship (2 Chronicles 30:6 – 9): **At the king's command, couriers went throughout Israel and Judah with letters from the king and from his officials, which read: "People of Israel, return to the LORD, the God of Abraham, Isaac and Israel, that he may return to you who are left, who have escaped from the hand of the kings of Assyria. Do not be like your fathers and brothers, who were unfaithful to the LORD, the God of their fathers, so that he made them an object of horror, as you see. Do not be stiff-necked, as your fathers were; submit to the LORD. Come to the sanctuary, which he has consecrated forever. Serve the LORD your God, so that his fierce anger will turn away from you. If you return to the LORD, then your brothers and your children will be shown compassion by their captors and will come back to this land, for the**

LORD your God is gracious and compassionate. He will not turn his face from you if you return to him."

Hezekiah makes a profound statement in the same chapter about the goodness of God. That God is good is a basic tenet running throughout the entire Bible. Hezekiah asks for God's forgiveness for everyone who sets his heart on seeking God. The forgiveness then, will be specific to those who are genuinely penitent. **Although most of the many people who came from Ephraim, Manasseh, Issachar and Zebulun had not purified themselves, yet they ate the Passover, contrary to what was written. But Hezekiah prayed for them, saying, "May the LORD, who is good, pardon everyone who sets his heart on seeking God—the LORD, the God of his fathers—even if he is not clean according to the rules of the sanctuary." And the LORD heard Hezekiah and healed the people.** (vv. 18–20.)

God is good

So, God is good. About that the Holy Bible is adamant. But today we tend to forget what 'good' truly means — in fact we have devalued the word and robbed it of its majesty. The world's appreciation of 'good' is, for example, a rock star who decides to take up some 'good cause'. *That* man, we are told, is fundamentally good no matter what other peccadilloes his life may entail! The idea is that in some way God should be grateful to him, for all his selfless work. In other words the world thinks that it can 'earn' at least a portion of its salvation from God. Salvation, then, becomes a right rather than a gift freely given to those whose hearts are changed and who totally re-orient their lives towards Jesus. It was Jesus who said, 'Why call me good? No one is good but God alone' (in paraphrase — see actual references being Matthew 19:16–17, Mark 10:17 and Luke 18:18). We should be wary then, in one sense, about how we use this common word 'good' for in reality it has a very profound biblical meaning, and should in truth be reserved for God alone. When the Godist talks about discerning 'good' in all *the religions* (besides what they are reticent to call 'bad' in relation to some of the teachings of those same religions) they are in danger of demeaning God unless they are prepared to say honestly that He has revealed Himself in both good and bad. But if they say this, they must then contradict the Lord Jesus who has declared God, and God alone, to be good. They must also contradict the Holy Bible which also is also emphatic throughout that God is good. It is (faithful) King Hezekiah in 2 Chronicles 30:18 who prays for his countrymen when he says **"May the LORD, who is good, pardon everyone who sets his heart on seeking God — the LORD, the God of his fathers — even if he is not clean according to the rules of the sanctuary."** Because God is good, and delights to restore the truly penitent, He hears Hezekiah's prayer. The verse concludes simply **And the LORD heard Hezekiah and healed the people.**

The cyclical record of Israel's faithful and unfaithful Kings continues to the end of 2 Chronicles. We take our leave of this Old Testament book with faithful King Josiah, who originally assumed the throne as a minor (at eight years old). As we are told in chapter 34, Josiah did what was right in the eyes of the LORD. On the rediscovery of the Torah or 'books of the Law' in some dusty corner of the Temple (which we assume had been somehow lost in the many upheavals encountered by Israel throughout the long period covered by Kings and Chronicles in the Bible) Josiah seeks to reinstate it at the centre of Israel's life and worship. 2 Chronicles comments in relation to King Josiah: **Josiah removed all the detestable idols from all the territory**

belonging to the Israelites, and he had all who were present in Israel serve the LORD their God. As long as he lived, they did not fail to follow the LORD, the God of their fathers. (2 Chronicles 34:33). Josiah's reign was notable for its success in reorienting Israel to follow the true path to God. But notable, also, for demonstrating the truth of God's forgiveness and restitution. Sadly this otherwise faithful King died in a battle largely of his own making, or so the Bible seems to indicate.

We conclude this chapter on God speaking to His people through the earlier books of the Old Testament, with a few thoughts from the book of Ezra, which follows 2 Chronicles. These thoughts again have resonance with our consideration of what Godism means and how Godist thinking relates to the Holy God revealed in Scripture. Ezra was a prophet at the time that Israel was exiled within the Persian Empire. The book that bears his name has been described as a compilation of autobiography, official documents, edicts and other material. The book is a straightforward account of one of the most important events in Israel's history — the restoration of the Jewish people to their homeland following the Babylonian dispersion.

As the former exiles return to Jerusalem they begin to rebuild the Temple, which has fallen into great disrepair. They begin the work with praise to their loving God (Ezra 3:11) **With praise and thanksgiving they sang to the LORD : "He is good; his love to Israel endures forever." And all the people gave a great shout of praise to the LORD, because the foundation of the house of the LORD was laid.** Inevitably, in a political world, there is opposition to this rebuilding work, although it is quite clear from the Bible that the root cause of this opposition is demonic. The sound of Israel's rejoicing was heard far away, both literally and metaphorically and it attracted unwelcome attention. So we read in Ezra 4:1–5, **When the enemies of Judah and Benjamin heard that the exiles were building a temple for the LORD, the God of Israel, they came to Zerubbabel and to the heads of the families and said, "Let us help you build because, like you, we seek your God and have been sacrificing to him since the time of Esarhaddon king of Assyria, who brought us here."**

But Zerubbabel, Jeshua and the rest of the heads of the families of Israel answered, "You have no part with us in building a temple to our God. We alone will build it for the LORD, the God of Israel, as King Cyrus, the king of Persia, commanded us."

Then the peoples around them set out to discourage the people of Judah and make them afraid to go on building. They hired counselors to work against them and frustrate their plans during the entire reign of Cyrus king of Persia and down to the reign of Darius king of Persia. We are bound once again to explore whether there is some resonance to the modern Godist agenda in this. Whilst Christians have for two millennia understood, and rightly understood, the exclusive claims of their Lord Jesus in relation to God His Father, and sought to distance themselves from *the religions*, in much the same way that the Hebrews of the Old Testament were commanded to remain strictly separate from *the religions* of surrounding peoples, do we today see at the beginning of the twenty-first century the offer of 'help' in building a new and different 'temple' to God? Our politicians and at least some religious leaders offer us the 'help' of state funding and of state recognition, in return for interfaith 'dialogue'. We are offered the assistance of the state and of the media in order to help us to remain 'relevant' to society at large through funding to assist 'good works' and media air time. It seems that God is no longer dead, but some politicians think He should be on income support. The book of Ezra goes on to describe the oppositions faced in restoring the Promised Land. Some of those who return to Israel and some in Israel itself have intermarried and, inevitably, followed false 'gods'. Again the Godist position seems to be exposed in this: are we today being offered the prospect of 'religious intermarriage' by some of our religious leaders? And is this to be a marriage made in heaven, or a marriage of convenience?

5

GODISM
— A NEW PHENOMENON?

Godism Defined

To this point in the book we have focused on the early revelation of God to His world through His chosen people. We should by now have a sense that God, as revealed in the Holy Bible and in personal experience, is consistent. He has made Himself known, and on His attributes we can depend. He means business — both with His chosen people and with the wider world. His attitude is not laissez faire. We have begun to see that this is the God Who takes the initiative; in principle we do not so much have to 'discover' Him as to respond to His self-disclosure. And we have begun to understand, it is hoped, that God does indeed have an absolute claim to that vast title of 'good' in spite of some genuine difficulties in our understanding of the way that He has sometimes chosen to act in history — what some people (wrongly) consider to be the 'bad' bits in the Holy Bible. Up to this point we have studiously avoided attempting to make a final definition of Godism although we have made a few clear observations about the phenomenon as well as posing some specific questions:

- Is the Godists' god–focus or god–centric, god–positive but (selectively) religion–negative view of the deity correct?

- We use a small 'g' in speaking of the Godist 'god' because at its best it is simply a collection of ideas about the Eternal — and at its worst is inexcusably woolly thinking on the subject.

- A Godist is someone who believes that there are many paths to god and that no one religion holds all the answers.

- It is a debatable point as to whether human philosophies about God can ever be right, especially when they clash with His disclosure of Himself.

- For those sold on the idea of Godism, or even flirting with Godism, there are some uncomfortable and difficult questions that must be faced by anyone with any real integrity in this debate.

- There is real evidence that the whole idea of Godism is actually repugnant to God Himself, and that belief in Godism takes people further away from God, not closer to Him.

- According to Godist philosophy 'god', whoever 'he' or 'it' is, wants us all to live in harmony: our individual beliefs matter far less than the way that we conduct our lives. Concepts such as sin and salvation, if they are to be accepted at all, need to be reinterpreted and constantly updated to fit with the complex and diverse world in which we live.

- Only serious misdemeanours, offences against our fellows when we should observe a 'Golden Rule' of compassion, will achieve God's displeasure.

On this latter point about a 'Golden Rule' it is unlikely that all Godists would agree simply because at this stage in the early 21st century the concept remains relatively novel. Godism, as with so many aspects of religion, defies easy definition to the extent that there will be many variances and many differing interpretations of the same basic theological data. That is why theology can never be a science in the deterministic and empirical sense that we understand the concept of science. We regularly think of science as a mechanism for achieving a thorough and truthful — and therefore exclusive — understanding of 'natural' mechanisms. Despite this there are enough similarities within the broad Godist approach that mean we can posit a definition that should be robust enough to withstand the inevitable changes and evolutions in this overall rather vague concept — a concept that can indeed accommodate diverse and even opposed views. In this overall attempt at a definition we find ourselves having first to define Godism by defining what it is not, because there are other theological concepts that are close to and overlap with Godism:

Theism is a belief in the existence of God and gods and especially the idea that this God or 'gods' reveals Himself to His creatures. Theism represents a philosophical position not to be identified with any particular religion. But theistic lines of thought do develop within the established 'religions' — so some people speak of Hindu or Christian Theists.

Deism is a belief in the existence of a supreme being arising from reason rather than revelation. Deism is both a religious and philosophical belief that a supreme 'god' exists which created the physical universe and that religious truths can be arrived at by the application of reason and observation of the natural world. Deists generally reject the notion of supernatural revelation as a basis of truth or religious dogma.

These views contrast with the focus on divine revelation found in Christian, Islamic and Judaic teachings. Deists typically reject supernatural events (prophecy, miracles) and tend to assert that 'god' has a plan for the universe which 'he' or 'it' does not alter either by intervening in the affairs of human life or suspending the natural laws of the universe. What organized religions see as divine revelation and holy books, Deists see as interpretations made by other humans, rather than as authoritative sources.

Monism is any philosophical view which holds that there is unity in a given field of inquiry, where this is not to be expected. So, some philosophers hold that theology may support the view that there is one God, with many manifestations in different religions.

Holistic Gnoseology holds that only a global approach to reality, by means of a global knowledge, are people able to understand the truth. Holistic gnoseology is therefore a general way to achieve a supposed deeper and comprehensive reality.

It will be seen immediately that there are far too many 'isms' in this world! In the study of religions (or theology) there are a bewildering range of and ultimately innumerable number of belief systems. We mention the above simply as being the more prominent among them. Since Godism shares beliefs with each of the above philosophies, we spend a short moment now to explain why none of the above completely coincides with Godism. So, with Theism there is a belief in a 'god' or 'gods' and the comforting idea that this 'god' is involved in some emotional way in 'his' or 'its' creation. The idea of creation in Theism is a rather vague one. A Godist would hold these views but add that God in not holy and not completely moral in the sense that we understand those concepts.[1] Theism would not necessarily be so bold.

A Godist would share with a Deist that God can be discovered through reason, although the Godist would add that this is not the sole means of an authentic encounter with the Eternal. And of course Godists, like Theists, believe that God is (by and large) actively involved in 'his' or 'its' creation project whereas Deists do not.

The idea of unity as espoused by Monism is one that is certainly shared by Godists but Monism alone does not cover all the beliefs of Godists. Godists do believe in a unity among *the religions*, in spite of powerful evidence to the contrary, and to that extent their beliefs may be described as containing elements of Monism. Global Gnoseology is also similar to Godism in that Godism rejects the absolute superiority in any of the 'scriptures' of any religion — in other words 'god' is to be discovered in all the religious writings of the so-called higher religions (and some of the lower ones, too). Godism therefore depends to some extent on Gnoseology — in other words Godists have a knowledge of these matters which is hidden from the singular adherents of the higher religions. Godists have gone further and faster than the devout of *the religions* and they have a special knowledge of these matters. It should be added that Godists do not believe in the total veracity of any of the 'scriptures' all of which they believe have been corrupted by humans, so again Godists have 'seen' a greater truth than that acknowledged by singular adherents of *the religions*.

Hopefully readers are following the argument so far! We will return to that unfortunate word Gnoseology at a later stage as Godism, when practiced by people who attend

---

[1] The Godist idea of a good/evil god is explored in detail in chapters 6 and 7

Christian churches, does bear alarming resemblance to Gnosticism, which was the earliest and most destructive of the heresies encountered by the First and Second century churches. Indeed it is probably true to say that Gnostic beliefs have infected the church like a virus all through its 2,000 year history in more — and less — virulent strains.

Godism, then, is a belief system that is not systematic! As with much of theology, what it actually means varies with its audience. Some will have more developed ideas of their beliefs towards 'god' and their relationship to 'him' or 'it'. Godism shares or borrows beliefs of all the religious philosophies. It is God-centric, to the extent that it believes in a deity or deities which have an emotional interest in the mortal. Some Godists are adherents of particular religions but they are *religion–negative* to the extent that where religion gets in the way of the overall thrust of Godism (and it frequently does!) then the Godist is happy to bypass or trample the religion, which is not allowed to stand in the way of the overall belief.

Godism then sits happily with the Western politically correct idea that all religions are essentially the same and it does not matter what you believe providing (a) you are sincere and (b) you do not hold your belief with excessive conviction. That Godism itself is intolerant of exclusionary beliefs that *are* held with conviction does not as yet seem to have made any inroad into the self-confidence and self-belief (not to mention self-justification) of Godism as a philosophy. Godists in point of fact are just as intolerant as any religion, but they purport to be otherwise.

It is important to add, however, that Godism is not itself a religion. It is more a series of beliefs that can be highly developed and well thought-through, or just vague notions about 'god' and *the religions*. Godism seeks to draw out and amplify a theme that is seen by Godists to run through all the (higher) religions. A Godist then is someone who believes that 'god' exists, that 'he' or 'it' cares in some way about this world (which 'he' or 'it' may also have created) and that 'he' or 'it' has established religions to help humans to encounter 'him' or 'it'. All religions contain good and all contain bad: it is up to the individual to discern what is good and to 'follow' that. Sin and salvation are aspects of belief that may or may not be held, but the Godist believes that it is 'god's' responsibility to 'save' or 'justify' people and that the vast majority will be so justified. They will be justified because this life is perplexing and 'god' has allowed it to be so, to the extent that it seems impossible to fully live the lifestyle called for by *any* religion. God, although loving in nature, brought sin into this world either by acts of commission or by acts of omission,[2] so 'god' is ultimately to blame for all the woes of this world. To that extent Godists hold their 'god' culpable and answerable, even if 'he' or 'it' in turn has the power and the authority also to hold us responsible. Godist belief is, therefore, in a sort of mutual accountability but where 'god' will have the final say. Although not all Godists would fully concur with every aspect of the foregoing, they remain god–positive and (selectively) religion–negative in the sense that they see 'god' as the 'deity' who is to be followed in order to make sense of this life and to live it as well as possible. The best way of doing that is by selecting one of 'his' or 'its' religions and following that as faithfully as we can. Where the religion is seen to promote views that sit unhappily with the Godist's idea of what is right and wrong, then the religion must give way. This supposed situation of religion

---

[2] We return to this idea in chapter 13.

interfering with 'god's' wishes is seen as being pollution of the divine by the mortal — in other words, men have messed around with the revelations of the divine.

As a belief, this philosophy can be 'systemised' more or less at the whim of the individual. In other words the Godist belief may be held and modified pretty much at will. Providing there is an acknowledgement of the deity and an attempt to live by what is seen as being the *good revelations* contained in 'god's' various self-disclosures, then all will be well. Godism borrows from other religious philosophies, and seeks to unify them overall. Whilst some Godists see themselves as having reached this series of conclusions by the application of reason, others would simply say that all religions lead to 'god' because it would be unfair if they did not. So, to varying degrees Godists hold the slightly arrogant view that they can 'see' more perceptively than those of no faith (agnostics or atheists) as well as more clearly than those of *the religions*, who are limited only perceive the 'truths' within their own dogma. Whether Godists consider this special knowledge that they have as being a gift from their 'god' is unclear. Again it probably boils down to the whim of the individual.

In this book we deliberately avoid engaging in too much philosophy, or in trying to describe the higher religions and their associated philosophies. Readers who want to look more deeply into this will find material on the internet (generally not quality controlled, so be careful!) and in other types of religious study material. The author finds the later printed editions of the *Encyclopedia Britannica* useful as a high quality overview — with at least the knowledge that the overall *Britannica* enterprise is rigorously quality controlled in a scholarly sense. But philosophy and theology are ultimately dead-ends. If God is moral then we have a right to assume that He will have disclosed Himself in ways that we can comprehend and in ways that do not mislead. If God is not moral, even when measured against man's faulty standards of morality, then it is questionable whether further philosophical study of Him will yield good or valuable results for humankind. As, in this book, we work through the issues raised by Godism, we will inevitably posit challenging questions to its philosophy as well as highlight its inconsistencies. We will also continue to review God's self disclosure as revealed in the Christian Scriptures — what we continue to call the Old and New Testaments, or as the author increasingly prefers, *the promise* and *the promise fulfilled*. As we look at these Scriptures and highlight from their perspective God's holiness, His righteousness and His love as expressed through Jesus His Son, *the apparent promise offered by Godism* — of 'peace' between *the religions* and the benefits that are thought to flow from this, *may be found to be wanting*.

It does not matter what you believe — so long as you are sincere

It is a default position of the Godist philosophy that belief is less important than action. Sincerity is a word that conjures images of kindly people doing kindly things. The fact that the Nazi guards at Auschwitz and Dachau death camps sincerely believed they were serving *the Volk* in their day to day work and that this was an honourable duty perhaps begins to belie the idea that sincerity is *ipso facto* a good thing. I may sincerely believe that 2 and 2 make 5 but that does not make my belief either right or valuable in any effort to discern truth. We need to tease out and examine this idea that sincerity in beliefs held is of more importance than *what* you actually believe, and by this people usually mean dogma. Again the word dogma seems to engender in most people almost the opposite of the word sincerity. If people are dogmatic they are failing to acknowledge diversity and are narrow minded. If I believe that 2 and 2 make 4 however, and maintain this position rigidly in spite of suggestions and even evidence that the sum might be 3 or 5, I am being dogmatic. When Winston Churchill decided to fight on, alone, in 1940 after the military defeat at Dunkirk, there were plenty of people who thought his dogmatism was just plain wrong. Its interesting to wonder how different the world might today have been if Churchill had not been dogmatic on this matter in the face of very real opposition in 1940.

A Godist therefore seems to echo the debate encountered by the very early church about the necessity of both faith *and* works. In preparing this book the author encountered Christians — or at least people who claimed to be Christians — who openly doubted the veracity of the Scriptures and who even claim that God is both good and evil (the broad Godist position). But they seemed to think that *if* they are wrong on the theological questions, God will still see them alright in the end because 'You have faith; I have deeds.' What they seemed to mean was that they acknowledged the danger inherent in their philosophy (which might be called heretical) but think that if they are wrong, then God will weight more heavily their investment in 'service' to mankind — so deeds, they think, 'trumps' faith. Some 'Christian Godists' will be aware that this is addressed by the apostle James (widely assumed to be the Lord Jesus' earthly sibling — in other words one of Mary and Joseph's naturally born children after Jesus their first born) in his letter *to the twelve tribes scattered among the nations* — a coded phrase denoting the entire early church. It seems that even in the early church there were some who considered that good deeds were more important than faith in Jesus, which suggests that (a) they were attempting to earn some of their salvation and (b) in fact they may have been engaged in some known but un-repented sin in which they thought they could continue, and buy-off God's wrath by their good works. This debate was conclusively resolved in James chapter 2, and readers may want to pause to read it in its entirety. In summary we can say that the New Testament position is that *it is possible to have a dead faith in Jesus*. In other words to 'believe' in Him in a conventional intellectual way, and even in an orthodox scriptural sense, but still to have a heart that is far away from Him, as evidenced by a lack of practical service in His name (works). If one loves Jesus as Lord and as Saviour, then good works are bound to follow. Conversely, it is possible to have a lack of faith in Jesus — or perhaps more pertinently to have a vague faith which one does not want to solidify — and so to offer to God the compensation of 'good works' in lieu of faith. As mentioned earlier, such a mindset seems typically to be motivated by some known sin that the 'Christian' concerned is unwilling to renounce. Churchgoers who are in this particular mindset need to acknowledge that **God is not mocked** (Galatians 6:7) and that we reap what we sow. To summarise the scriptural position on this subject for Christians we can say emphatically that justification is by grace through faith alone, so readers may want to read Romans 3:24, Romans 5:1 and Ephesians 2:8 — but, as always, read around these verses to ensure you get a grasp on the context. These verses were penned by the apostle Paul and are fully in agreement with James, who points out that true faith will inevitably lead to true deeds/good works. Godism, then, tends to elevate behaviour above belief. In practice this may often be a smokescreen for continued sin. Again in the author's direct experience, when Godism is expounded by churchgoers specifically, one often becomes aware that there are other inconsistencies in that person's life.

Another facet of Godism is its willingness to make excuses for behaviour that the Bible calls, quite simply, sinful. We find, then, that sexual sin is often claimed to be caused by orientation — so a person cannot be held fully accountable (or according to *some* Godists, held accountable at all!) for their sexual behaviour. Violent behaviour may be 'caused' by social circumstances or upbringing, so once again a person cannot be held fully accountable. Financial cheating may well be caused by the 'selfish gene' which itself is part of the evolutionary psychological make-up of individuals, so once again a person cannot be fully accountable for their financial shennanigans. In fact it is difficult to find peccadilloes or sins for which anyone is fully accountable! Because 'god' allowed these things to develop or evolve, the Godist will explain that 'god' must assume some of the blame. One avowed Godist who happens to be involved with a Christian church told the author that his son might in the future sin (actual words 'go wrong') and that if so he, as father, would be partly to blame for not bringing him up the right way. He seemed to be pre-positioning or pre-conditioning his friends for a probable active rejection by his son of Christianity with the obvious possibilities that this might entail for questionable moral behaviour thereafter. Now of course there may have been an element of truth in the assertion: perhaps the gentleman concerned had been less than perfect in his upbringing of his children (no parent is perfect, after all!) but it was the author's strong impression that there was a critical sub-text at play in this comment: since 'god' is both good and evil simultaneously, ultimately 'he' or 'it' is partly responsible for children going off the rails. The key point being that the parent had (selflessly and honestly, as they would see it) acknowledged their own fault, and silently nominated God as co-defendant, so his children would bear only one third of the guilt for any sins that they may subsequently commit! Most authentic Christians would view this as being a reflection of the moral relativism now common in the post-Christian culture in which today we live. No one is truly to blame for anything anymore, although God is being increasingly cited as carrying a share of the guilt!

That some Godists would repudiate this view is almost unnecessary to state. Some would say that 'god' is indeed guiltless, but would still maintain that humans can 'argue' a case for clemency because of what an economist might call the moral 'hygiene factors' at play in their lives — all those things in their personal environment and personal experience that keep them away from the truth and beauty of 'god'. However, the above does seem to be the logical conclusion of the overall Godist philosophy, so it cannot easily be swept under the carpet.

Does Godism matter?

At one level we are bound to say that Godism matters little. Its adherents generally consider that their beliefs represent and unify the claims of the 'higher religions', but in practice they achieve nothing of the sort. So it is unlikely that millions will leave *the religions* in order to become Godist in one of Godism's various philosophical guises. Godism is patently false in the sense that it must at key points deny, holding as false, major planks of belief in all *the religions*.

Godism is also primarily a Western phenomenon, borne out of the greater (boasted, but more apparent than real) educational advancement of westerners who believe they today have oversights and insights of all the major religions and indeed have encountered them all in some limited way through the medium of foreign travel. Godists in that sense exhibit the tourist's mentality to religion, sampling a little here and there on a fortnight's vacation, and returning home declaring themselves as 'A Traveller'! Its like the old idea of the 1950s American whistlestop tour of Europe: 'Its Tuesday so it must be Brussels!' Some westerners are apt to read a pamphlet about a religion, visit a temple and then believe they have a meaningful insight into its teachings! In these ways Godism frankly matters little. As a Western preoccupation it may decline along with the Western population which is shrinking in absolute terms, as well as in proportion to the populations of the rest of the world.

But Godism also holds out at least the prospect that it is wrong and injurious to the spiritual needs of those who find comfort in it. If God is good (and Godists seem to believe 'he' or 'it' is good, in spite of the 'bad' or 'evil' that they also detect) then one might think they would hope that He would provide us with a good and fully dependable means of forming an eternal union with Himself. If God has provided multiple paths to peace with Himself, as Godists unquestionably do believe, and yet has done so in the knowledge that these multiple paths will bring tension and even conflict between religions, as well as confusion among humans as to which path (or paths) to choose for their own life, then even by our faulty human understanding of morality, we can readily see that such a God would have to 'answer' for the woes, wars and sins that inevitably flow from this multiplicity of belief systems. The Godist in particular, but with the wholehearted agreement of much of the wider world, has decided to put God into the dock. When the vague beliefs of Godism are expressed by the wider world, in other words by plain ordinary people who have not much troubled themselves with religion, one detects a certain desire to attempt to lock God into a box. If all religions lead to God and God has a 'duty' to 'save' all, then it does not matter too much how you live because this sugar-daddy God will see you alright in the end! If God *cuts up rough* and tries to lay any moral charges at our door, we will quite simply say that we tried to live in broad agreement with *the religions*. We were confused by the multiplicity of choices that God gave to us so we cherry picked what we thought were the best 'bits' of each. And we certainly could not be expected to choose one to the exclusion of others because each of them had 'bad' or even 'evil' facets and we could not in good conscience ally ourselves wholeheartedly to *any* such Faith system. Rather we tried to do our best — and if that's not good enough, then we know whose fault it is!

To prepare, as many people seem to, what they consider to be such a 'legal defence' against (a) the Judgement that we all suspect may one day happen and (b) any uncomfortable moral requirements that God may place upon us and which in turn we do not want or intend to fulfil, may indeed appear to get us 'off the hook' as regards our relationship (or lack of it) with God. To recap, the mentality seems to be: 'I'm sorry God if I did not choose the right path. I did my best. It was your fault that there were so many paths — so I simply cannot be held responsible.' Meaning, in turn, that God is responsible. Such a thought process may be superficially comforting but is unlikely to bring lasting peace because many such people will also suspect that, in practice, it is a rather weak excuse for sitting on the religious fence. What is more important, such a legalistic defence may not cut any ice with a Holy God.

Godism also seems to many people to hold out the comfort of safety in numbers. If, as humans, we can all agree with the basic Godist position and genuinely try to be respectful of all religions and cherry pick the best bits of all of them, then God will not be able to condemn all of us, because if He does then there will be virtually nobody left to 'save'! We have, we think, painted God into a corner and the only way that He can judge us and pronounce us guilty, is by finding his 'heaven' just about empty! Some have called this the *failure of God's great experiment in creation* — if most are lost then God is in some sense a failure.[3]

If Godism matters at all, then, it is in the manner in which it tries to create what must be pronounced a false sense of security as regards God, and His requirements of those He has created. Since most of *the religions*, not just Christianity, have some idea of a hell or an awful judgement for those who transgress, then we must at the very least take seriously the real prospect that *the religions* are NOT all equal, and that conversely just one may represent the true path to peace with God. This immediately sets hackles rising as it is politically *extremely* incorrect, but since people's eternal destinies may be at stake it seems not unreasonable that people may want to 'test' this Godist position — if necessary to destruction — in order to ascertain whether it is a right and a safe path for the individual to take.

Readers will sense where this argument is heading and may immediately object: 'if you say that Christianity is the right path then God must be held accountable for all

---

[3] Nowhere in the Christian Bible do we find any idea of an 'experiment in creation'.

of Christianity's wars!' Ironically the one 'war' (or series of wars) that most people see as being 'Christian' are the so-called crusades of mediaeval times. In the UK some will speak of the Irish Troubles also as being a 'Christian war'. And there may be other conflicts cited depending on the historical knowledge and/or prejudice of the individual commentator. Whilst it is impossible to deal with these objections definitively in a short book (and it is rather beyond the scope of this book in any case) a few pointers may be given. In relation to the mediaeval crusades, critics often forget or choose to ignore that the crusades themselves were preceded by nearly 400 years of aggressive westward Muslim military expansion that had seen many formerly Christian kingdoms destroyed. The wars must be considered in the geo-political context of the time. The fact that there was a religious (Roman Catholic) imprimatur placed over the whole enterprise does not ultimately render it into a 'Christian war'. Since Jesus' kingdom is not of this world (John 18:36) and we are told to invest our futures in the next world in preference to this one (Luke 12:33), straight away we must conclude that *the fighting of aggressive expansionary wars is always in direct contradiction to the primary teachings of Jesus* — and to this extent is not only un-Christian, it is actively anti-Christian. Not for nothing is Jesus known as the *Prince of Peace* (Isaiah 9:6) and He commanded His disciples to 'turn the other cheek' when they are attacked for being His followers (Matthew 5:39). Many Christians conclude that fighting defensive wars is allowable for true Christians, but defining 'defensive' at a practical level and unravelling true motives has always been highly problematic. Some Christians have therefore developed a *totally* passive concept (conscientious objection) in relation to warfare. In this sense there can truly be no such thing as a 'Christian war', much as people may wish to conclude otherwise, whereas warfare among the other religions is specifically allowed and in places encouraged. God has made the need for peace between Himself and human beings and between His followers and the world at large abundantly clear (Romans 12:18 — **if it is possible, as much as depends on you, live peaceably with all men**, NKJV).[4] Where people choose warfare and cover it with *any* idea of God's approval, saying that this particular war is a Christian act or a Christian service, then ultimately they delude only themselves. In a very real sense they are taking the name of God in vain, in so doing, and are breaking the 3rd of the 10 commandments. **"Do not use my name for evil purposes, for I the LORD, your God, will punish anyone who misuses my name"** (Exodus 20:7, GNB). It is to be expected that God will always consider warfare to be an evil purpose, so it remains for the Godist to explain why so many of *the religions* actively flout this law.

Does Godism matter? As we continue in this book to explore God's revelation of Himself through the person of Jesus, we will continue to tease out inconsistencies in the Godist position versus God's self-revelation as found in the Holy Bible. We will hopefully conclude definitively whether this 'god' of all religions has any right to be called moral. But for the time being we will lay down this question as we take up others. Only this final comment needs to be made: we have noted that there is a good deal of self-justification behind the man in the street's desire that all religions should lead to 'god'. It really seems to the author that *all too many*

---

[4] Here the apostle Paul seems to recognise the possibility that there will be circumstances where un-peaceableness is forced upon Christians, which others have interpreted as the right to legitimate and proportionate self-defence. Within the context of a society, this might extend to warfare.

people want all religions to lead to God because this takes the heat off them and places it back upon God. It relieves them of the obligation to faithfully observe any religion. They can cherry pick the bits they like and ignore the bits they don't like. And when that inevitable day arrives when they have to face God (if 'he' or 'it' exists at all!) then they have their defence at hand — it was all much too confusing, so what chance did they really have of getting it right? This seems like cleverness — even deftness — but will God be so easily fooled? It seems that the answer is a resounding 'no' as God is not mocked (Galatians 6:7), as we have already noted. We should bear in mind then, a comment in the Old Testament book that we call Proverbs — actually Proverbs 21:30. We give it here in two different translations, although they each make exactly the same very profound point — *we cannot judge God.*

No wisdom, no understanding, no counsel can avail against the Lord (RSV)

Human wisdom, brilliance, insight – they are of no help if the LORD is against you (GNB)

We are never going to sit in judgement on God, and He cannot be tricked into missing our true motives. But God promises that He *will* judge us.

A Godist king for Britain?

It is hoped that non-UK readers will forgive a diversion into a singularly British question. Whilst in a real theological sense Godism may matter for little as noted in the preceding section, it is undeniable that the process of political correctness, which is morphing into *political correction* (and has alarming echoes of the re-education schemes so beloved of Communist aparachiks) is elevating the whole concept of a confluence of religions. We noted in Chapter 1 that there is a political imperative to this development, as governments throughout the West in particular see *religion management* as being a key plank in their cohesiveness policies for society at large. We noted, also, that the UK media — especially in the shape of the powerful BBC — are keen promoters of the idea of multiculturalism and therefore generally opposed to what they see as old fashioned and even damaging homogeneity within society. With these two undeniable developments within society it is not surprising that the assumed future King of the UK, (Prince Charles, *heir apparent* to Queen Elizabeth II at the time of writing this book), should take an interest in the subject of faiths. It is, at a high level, a part of his job description to be seen as a figurehead for all communities. Interestingly this idea of *all communities* already suggests that a form of societal Balkanisation is underway in the UK, but that is beyond the scope of this book. Prince Charles has for many years taken an active interest in comparative religion. It seems likely, taking into account past statements of the Prince and his very high profile and enthusiastic association with faith groups, that he would consider himself to be a Christian Godist, although he might well balk at the terminology.

In 1994 Prince Charles famously declared that as future King he wanted to be 'Defender of Faiths' rather than the *Defender of the Faith*, which is one of the official titles of the UK monarch. He went on to declare that he wanted to defend belief 'of the divine in existence, the pattern of the divine which is, I think, in all of us but which because we are human beings, can be expressed in so many different ways.' In practice this would not be as straightforward as the Prince seemed to have assumed and it appears that he was warned off this formulation by his advisers. Instead, and to mark his 60th birthday in 2008, the Prince modified his long held ambition by declaring that he wanted to be known as 'Defender of Faith'. This was so subtle a change that its importance may at first glance still be missed: as there were so many faiths, would the Prince be willing to defend them all? As was queried in 1994, would Charles for example defend Satanism — today an officially recognized religion? To circumvent this difficulty, Charles would simply see himself as defender of the concept of 'faith' itself, allowing him to defend peoples' rights to their own belief systems, and then to cherry pick those on which he would lavish royal patronage and recognition.

Charles' proposed change would mean the monarch, as Supreme Governor of the Church of England, would no longer be known as *Defender of the Faith* for the first time since the reign of Henry VIII — in other words for the first time in 500 years. Ironically, the Monarch has been known by this title ever since it was bestowed upon Henry VIII by the Pope in 1521 for Henry's early support for Roman Catholicism! Today there would be considerable obstacles to overcome before Prince Charles could fulfil his desire. It would, for example, require Parliament to agree to amend the 1953 Royal Titles Act which came into law after changes were made for the Queen's Coronation in the same year. Vernon Bogdanor, a constitutionalist and, at time of writing this book, Professor of Government at Oxford University, commented that in 1953 when Queen Elizabeth came to the throne, Britain was very much an Anglican society. Today the Prince of Wales would be expected to become king of a nation that is multi-faith, albeit that one predominates. Professor Bogdanor postulated the idea that after any future 'broadly Anglican' Coronation at Westminster Abbey, a second religious service might be held for other denominations and faiths, such as Muslims and Hindus, as a way of acknowledging their importance in the UK. This seemed to be a way to side-step potential constitutional difficulties whilst allowing the Prince to continue with his project.

On 14 November 2008 a major UK newspaper, *The Daily Telegraph* commented in its online edition about the massive implications of the Prince's proposal. Their commentator Andrew Pierce noted that, on the face of it, the loss of the grammatical *definite article* from the royal title carried by every English monarch since Henry VIII might seem a harmless gesture, but Pierce asserted that it was nothing of the sort. The proposed formula, he suggested, would cause considerable harm, not least because 'Defender of Faith' was just too vague a phrase to interpret clearly. Pierce continued that 'The Faith' in the original title referred directly to Christianity, originally Catholic, then Protestant; and in recent decades understood to mean Christianity in general. The Monarch's title, Pierce argued, was a specific recognition of his or her responsibility to preserve the unique and sacred status of Christianity in British society. In contrast, Pierce asked, what would 'Faith' without a definite article mean? Sociologists were still unable after 200 years to agree on a definition of religion, let alone one for faith! And where would we draw the boundaries of the 'Faith' that the future King wanted to defend? Would Scientology be considered a proper faith? Or Spiritism? How would the future King tiptoe through the theological and constitutional minefield exposed when unscrupulous, bizarre or extreme religions demanded Royal protection — as they surely would?

The implications, however, may go much further than most commentators have so far suggested. There are without doubt constitutional issues: the constitution of the United

Kingdom is the set of laws and principles under which the *UK* is governed, the UK having no single constitutional document comparable to those of many other nations. It is therefore often said that the country has an 'unwritten' or *de facto* constitution, but the bulk of the British constitution does in fact exist in written form in the shape of statutes, court judgments, and treaties, together with other unwritten sources, including *parliamentary constitutional conventions* and the *royal prerogatives*. The bedrock of the British constitution has traditionally been the doctrine of Parliamentary sovereignty, according to which the statutes passed by Parliament are the UK's supreme source of law. It follows that Parliament can change the constitution simply by passing new Acts of Parliament. The UK's membership of the *European Union* arguably complicated this principle and the UK today applies all EU law (and repeals any provisions of its own laws which conflict) that the Union passes in common with other member states.

UK Acts of Parliament in the early 21st Century remained among the most important sources of the constitution. According to the traditional view, Parliament retained the ability to legislate however it wished, and upon any subject it wished. For example, much of the iconic mediaeval statute known as *Magna Carta* was in fact repealed by Parliament in 1828,[5] despite previously being regarded as sacrosanct. It has traditionally been the case that the courts were barred from questioning any *Act of Parliament*, a principle that can be traced back to the mediaeval period. The sovereign remains the Supreme Governor of the established Church of England, with Archbishops and Bishops appointed by the monarch, on the advice of the Prime Minister. The Crown's

---

[5] In 1828 the Offences Against the Person Act was passed, which repealed clause 36 of Magna Carta.

role in the Church of England is mainly titular; the most senior clergyman, the *Archbishop of Canterbury*, remains the spiritual leader of the Church and (at the time of writing) of the worldwide *Anglican Communion*. The monarch is an ordinary member of the *Church of Scotland*, but he or she holds the power to appoint the *Lord High Commissioner* to that Church's *General Assembly*.

There seem to be two constitutional difficulties with Prince Charles' overarching desire to be known as *Defender of Faith*. The first difficulty is in relation to the 39 Articles of the Church of England, which state all the main distinctive beliefs of this Reformation church. Officially the Church of England accepts the full and final authority of Holy Scripture as the basis for all that it believes. Some of these beliefs were summarised in the historic creeds and at the time of the Reformation, the Church adopted those 39 Articles as giving a concise and systematic statement of the teaching of Scripture. The legal definition of the Doctrine of the Church of England can be found in the *Church of England (Worship and Doctrine) Measure 1974* which accords with what is also stated in *Canon A5*, which concerns the ordination of new ministers. These state clearly that the doctrine of the Church of England is particularly to be found in the 39 Articles, the Book of Common Prayer and the Ordinal. Indeed Ministers of the Church of England are still required to affirm their acceptance of the Church's doctrine but the wording of the declaration is now such that many feel able to say it without meaning what a simple reading might suggest.

The official text is that found in the 1662 Book of Common Prayer but is easily obtainable online. The 39 Articles cover the Doctrine of God and the human response to God's grace. They can be summarized as follows:

Article 1–5 (The substance of faith)

Articles 6–8 (The rule of faith)

Articles 9–18 (Personal religion)

Articles 9–14 (Doctrines connected with justification)

Articles 15–18 (Doctrines connected with sanctification)

Articles 19–39 (The Household of faith)

Articles 19–22 (The Church)

Articles 23 & 24 (The Ministry)

Articles 25–31(The Sacraments)

Articles 32–36 (Church Discipline)

Articles 37–39 (Church and State)

The centrality of the 39 Articles has been acknowledged since the time of King Charles I who stated that, '...the Articles of the Church of England ... do contain the true doctrine of the Church of England agreeable to God's Word ... no man hereafter shall either print, or preach, to draw the Article aside any way, but shall submit to it in the plain and full meaning thereof: and shall not put his own sense or comment to the meaning of the Article, but shall take it in the literal and grammatical sense.' Key among the 39 Articles that might be problematic for a future King who would defend all faiths *as essentially equal* are these:

I. Of Faith in the Holy Trinity

There is but one living and true God, everlasting, without body, parts, or passions; of infinite power, wisdom, and goodness; the Maker, and Preserver of all things both visible and invisible. And in unity of this Godhead there be three Persons, of one substance, power, and eternity; the Father, the Son, and the Holy Ghost.

II. Of the Word or Son of God, which was made very Man

The Son, which is the Word of the Father, begotten from

everlasting of the Father, the very and eternal God, and of one substance with the Father, took Man's nature in the womb of the blessed Virgin, of her substance: so that two whole and perfect Natures, that is to say, the Godhead and Manhood, were joined together in one Person, never to be divided, whereof is one Christ, very God, and very Man; who truly suffered, was crucified, dead and buried, to reconcile his Father to us, and to be a sacrifice, not only for original guilt, but also for all actual sins of men.

IV. Of the Resurrection of Christ

Christ did truly rise again from death, and took again his body, with flesh, bones, and all things appertaining to the perfection of Man's nature; wherewith he ascended into Heaven, and there sitteth, until he return to judge all Men at the last day.

XVIII. Of obtaining eternal Salvation only by the Name of Christ.

They also are to be had accursed that presume to say, That every man shall be saved by the Law or Sect which he professeth, so that he be diligent to frame his life according to that Law, and the light of Nature. For Holy Scripture doth set out unto us only the Name of Jesus Christ, whereby men must be saved.

How would an effectively Theist, if not actively Godist, King deal with these clear and unambiguous statements? The idea that the UK Government might amend the law to enable Prince Charles' ambition was viewed with no small alarm by many commentators, as it could entail the disestablishment of the Church of England by the back door. The Labour Party of Tony Blair in the 1990s and of Gordon Brown in the first decade of the 2000s was seen as being particularly keen to reduce the influence of the Church within the civic life of the land. Would the Prince present them with their opportunity?

To finally understand how this desire of the future King might affect the constitutional position we need to look at the promises made by his mother, Queen Elizabeth, in 1953, promises that, in effect, the future King would abrogate simply by not making them. Note that what follows is not the full text of the Coronation service (which again, is freely available online) but merely the parts that neither a Theist or indeed a fully Godist monarch could in honesty affirm without heavy amendment. The 1953 Coronation service was divided into distinct sub-sections, the headings of which we adopt below:

IV. The Oath

The Archbishop shall minister these questions; and the Queen, having a book in her hands, shall answer each question severally as follows:

Archbishop: Will you to the utmost of your power maintain the Laws of God and the true profession of the Gospel?

Will you to the utmost of your power maintain in the United Kingdom the Protestant Reformed Religion established by law?

Will you maintain and preserve inviolably the settlement of the Church of England, and the doctrine, worship, discipline, and government thereof, as by law established in England?

And will you preserve unto the Bishops and Clergy of England, and to the Churches there committed to their charge, all such rights and privileges, as by law do or shall appertain to them or any of them?

Queen: All this I promise to do.

V. The Presenting of the Holy Bible

When the Queen is again seated, the Archbishop shall go to her Chair; and the Moderator of the General Assembly of the Church of Scotland, receiving the Bible from the Dean of Westminster, shall bring it to the Queen and present it to her, the Archbishop saying these words:

Our gracious Queen:
to keep your Majesty ever mindful
of the law and the Gospel of God
as the Rule for the whole life and
government of Christian Princes,
we present you with this Book,
the most valuable thing that this world affords.
Here is Wisdom;
This is the royal Law;
These are the lively Oracles of God.

VI. The Beginning of the Communion Service
The Introit

O God, who providest for thy people by thy power,
and rulest over them in love:
Grant unto this thy servant ELIZABETH, our Queen,
the Spirit of wisdom and government,
that being devoted unto thee with her whole heart,
she may so wisely govern,
that in her time thy Church may be in safety,
and Christian devotion may continue in peace;
that so persevering in good works unto the end,
she may by thy mercy come to thine everlasting
kingdom;
through Jesus Christ, thy Son, our Lord,
who liveth and reigneth with thee

in the unity of the Holy Ghost,
one God for ever and ever. Amen.
And the Gospel ended shall be sung the Creed following,
the Queen with the people standing, as before.
I believe in one God,
the Father Almighty,
maker of heaven and earth,
And of all things visible and invisible;
And in one Lord Jesus Christ,
the only-begotten Son of God,
Begotten of his Father before all worlds,
God of God, Light of Light,
Very God of very God,
Begotten, not made,
Being of one substance with the Father,
By whom all things were made:
Who for us men, and for our salvation
came down from heaven,
and was incarnate by the Holy Ghost of the Virgin Mary,
And was made man;
And was crucified also for us under Pontius Pilate.
He suffered and was buried;
And the third day he rose again
according to the Scriptures,
And ascended into heaven,
And sitteth on the right hand of the Father.
And he shall come again with glory
to judge both the quick and the dead:
Whose kingdom shall have no end.
And I believe in the Holy Ghost,
The Lord and giver of life,
Who proceedeth from the Father and the Son,
Who with the Father and the Son together

is worshipped and glorified,
Who spake by the Prophets.
And I believe one Catholick and Apostolick Church.
I acknowledge one Baptism for the remission of sins.
And I look for the resurrection of the dead,
And the life of the world to come. Amen.

VII. The Anointing

The Creed being ended, the Queen kneeling at her faldstool, and the people kneeling in their places, the Archbishop shall begin the hymn, VENI, CREATOR SPIRITUS, and the choir shall sing it out.

Then shall the Dean of Westminster lay the Ampulla and Spoon upon the Altar; and the Queen kneeling down at the faldstool, the Archbishop shall say this Blessing over her:

Our Lord Jesus Christ, the Son of God,
who by his Father was anointed with the Oil of gladness
above his fellows,
by his holy Anointing pour down upon your Head and
Heart
the blessing of the Holy Ghost,
and prosper the work of your Hands:
that by the assistance of his heavenly grace
you may govern and preserve
the Peoples committed to your charge
in wealth, peace, and godliness;
and after a long and glorious course
of ruling a temporal kingdom
wisely, justly, and religiously,
you may at last be made partaker of an eternal kingdom,
through the same Jesus Christ our Lord. Amen.

Plainly the 1953 service was thoroughly Christian.

Although the wording has evolved and changed over the centuries, it is clear that the generic coronation service does not simply represent 450 years of Christian and Protestant observance — it represents in excess of 1,000 years of Christian tradition over the British lands. Prince Charles' attempt to end this reality by tinkering with the wording of the coronation service surely carried with it implications far beyond those he apparently had in mind. So why the constitutional difficulty? Have we not already observed that words can be changed? Why cannot at the end of the day, the King be the *defender of faith* as a concept, and indeed of multiple faiths? Surely Parliament could do the trick? And, at the time of writing, parts of it are itching to do so!

The true constitutional implication seems to be this: that England/the United Kingdom is a Protestant land by tradition. The monarch would defend that Protestant position if need be with his life (and it was genuinely that serious a matter for example, for the first Queen Elizabeth) because he or she understood that by so doing he was *personally preserving access to the Heavenly Father for his subjects through Jesus the Son without the intervention of Priests and all that this implied under Papacy*. This defence was bound up inseparably with and personified in the life of the King (or Queen). Without this singular role, which certainly cannot be personified by Parliament, there actually is no need for a monarch at all. Defender of *the* faith is *the* prime task of a British monarch. If that task is gone, there is surely no reason why Parliament cannot assume the role of defender of faiths or of faith. Indeed with its various religious hatred laws in the UK, it has begun to do so. Parliament at a practical level can be argued as defending peoples' health through the National Health Service, a task that need not be personified. It can be argued as defending the state through the military, something again that need not be personified. Parliament defends the laws of the land against the monarch — and fought a civil war to prove the point! If the monarch no longer defends *the* faith and if need be with his life, then the defence of people's rights to worship as they please can surely be guaranteed by Parliament. In deciding (arguably) to abandon the Protestant faith, Prince Charles may unwittingly have called into question the monarchy itself.

6

IS GOD GOOD?

Godism — another form of Gnosticism?

We ended the last chapter with the peculiarly British question as to whether the Prince of Wales, who at the time of writing this book was keen to become *Defender of Faith* rather than the *Defender of the Faith*, may unwittingly have called into question the continuation of the monarchy itself. We should perhaps close off this line of debate with these observations: clearly with the heavily politically-correct and multi-cultural leanings of much of the media-politico intelligensia in the UK in the early 2000s, it remained likely that the Prince would weaken (and be seen to weaken) if not actually abrogate the Crown's commitment to Christianity. This would be a departure of more than a thousand years of history, undertaken on the basis of just a few years of stunted debate engaged-in by a very narrow (post-modern in outlook, and generally anti-Christian in agenda) section of society. It remained likely at the time of writing this book that the Prince would get his way. The then Archbishop of Canterbury had surprised the nation in 2008 by seeming to call for parts of Islamic Sharia Law to be introduced into the UK, and political commentators believed that he and the Prince would take a similar line on multi-faithism in general. There would accordingly be no real *established church* opposition to the deletion of the definite article in that singularly important royal title of *Defender of the Faith*.

Many would argue, in any case, that the Monarch's job description can evolve and change over time and that, indeed, this is absolutely necessary if the monarchy itself is to survive. Would people march on the streets at the deletion of the definite article 'the' from the monarch's title in relation to faith and its defence? Plainly the answer would be 'no' so the ruling elite would surely achieve what they desired with no real 'capital investment' in terms of reduced popular support. Little if any real harm, they considered, would be done. If however it is considered, as some serious observers do, that the preservation of Protestant Christianity in this country has been a bedrock of its political and social development and that this (irrespective of whether you happen to be a Roman Catholic Christian or not) has been at the behest of Almighty God, then to refuse to defend *that same faith in the personified form of the monarch* means that the sole task that remains unique to the monarch no longer exists. All other aspects of the royal job description could be personified in other people and/or in other institutions. With no willingness to defend *the* faith at the personal risk of the life of the monarch, it was certainly arguable in the first decade of the 21st Century that there was no need for a British monarchy. If the defence of reformed Christianity (loosely Protestantism) for the UK had been part of God's plan for that nation for its preceding 450 years — and by this is meant, theologically, the right of access of the individual person to God the Father through the mediation of Jesus His Son without the aid of priests — if all of this had indeed been God's will and purpose — and if in the final analysis the future monarch was no longer willing to discharge this historically God-given duty, then would God ultimately see no further need for a British monarchy?

In the previous chapter we also noted that Godism generally is a mixture of religious philosophies and in particular of *Theism, Monism* and *Deism*. We added for good measure that peculiar philosophy with the improbable title *Holistic Gnoseology* which holds rather vaguely that only a global approach to reality by means of a global knowledge is able to reach the truth of the Eternal. Holistic Gnoseology then is considered to be a general philosophy to achieve a supposedly deeper and more comprehensive reality for the individual. The word 'gnosis' is an English translation of the classical Greek word meaning knowledge. Fully developed Gnosticism is a philosophical-religious movement that became prominent in the Greek/Roman world of the second century AD. While Gnosticism drew from many traditional religions its effect was most clearly felt in the very early Christian church, and led that church to form what we now call the agreed and authorised *canon* of Scripture, the *creed*, and the formalizing of *episcopal organisation*. Evidence for the Gnostic threat to the early church is found mainly in the writings of the early Church Fathers who opposed Gnostic teachings — especially Irenaeus, c. 185, Hippolytus, c. 230 and Epiphanius, c. 375. Their writings indicate a diversity in the Gnostic theology, as well as in their ethics and ritual, which makes strict classification quite impossible. Gnosticism, like so many other *isms*, is a very mixed-up thing! Although Gnosticism seems to reach back before the time of Jesus, the first Gnostic of whom we can speak with certainty was one Simon Magus, a first century Jewish teacher of unorthodox views who introduced the basic idea that evil resulted from a break within the Godhead. Simon Magus' beliefs remained basically Jewish and monotheistic. The dualistic phase was reached following the expansion of Gnosticism into the Greek/Roman world of the early church, particularly borrowing from Platonic philosophy the idea that a 'lower god' or demiurge, had created the world. As always, readers who want to look further into this will find material widely available, especially on the internet. Care should always be taken with internet resources, however, because they are not rigorously quality-controlled in a scholarly sense, no matter what they may say to the contrary!

In the Gnostic view, the unconscious self of man — his soul, if you prefer — is consubstantial with the godhead, but because of a tragic fall (ideas borrowed indirectly from the biblical account of Adam and Eve) his soul is thrown into a world that is completely alien to its real being. Through revelation from above, man becomes conscious of his origin and of his transcendent destiny. Gnosticism is different from philosophical enlightenment, because it cannot be acquired by the forces of reason, and different from Christian revelation, because Gnosticism unlike Christianity, is *not* rooted in history — it is rather a sort of sophisticated *religious intuition*. Using our definition of Godism from the previous chapter, we can easily see that there are aspects of Gnosticism within broad Godist thought. As most Godists believe that the various religious scriptures have been contaminated by humans, like Gnostics they rely instead on their own *attained knowledge* which (a) transcends the higher religions as and when those religions clash with the philosophy of Godism and (b) enables them to 'see' things that are hidden from singular adherents of those religions. A Godist therefore looks with some disdain upon the singular adherents of *the religions* (although many would deny it most emphatically!) as being a religious class of also rans' in *mankind's great religious quest*. Godists concede that these singular religious types may indeed be 'saved' by their slavish acceptance of their own religion (which 'god' will find acceptable) but the Godist himself has seen beyond what has been revealed and has achieved a higher esoteric knowledge of 'god' wherein these various religions can be harmonized in spite of their glaring differences. The most direct and popular articulation of this quest for religious harmonisation in the early years of the 21st century was perhaps the so-called 'Golden Rule' which we encountered in Chapter 1.

We need to look at Gnosticism as a Christian heresy: it appears that in the first and second centuries AD a number of Gnostics remained as members of local churches and some even served in high offices within those churches. Indeed there is speculation that Valentinus[1] may have been considered as a possible Bishop at Rome. Marcion,[2] perhaps the greatest heretic of the early church period, although probably not fully Gnostic, did certainly assist in the development of Gnostic ideas. He reinterpreted the apostle Paul in such a way that the Old Testament God became the 'god of evil' and Christ became the messenger of the good 'god of grace'. Marcion developed his own

---

[1] 2nd century AD Egyptian religious philosopher and founder of the Roman and Alexandrian schools of Gnosticism. Baptised as a Christian, during the time of Pope St Hyginus he taught a synthesis of Christian and oriental Gnosticism. Aspiring to become a Christian bishop, he left the faith after being passed over for a bishopric in Rome. Even in later years, Valentunus' teaching continued to argue for the need for Christ's death and resurrection as effecting Christian deliverance, alongside other esoteric teachings.

[2] 2nd century theologian who was excommunicated by the church at Rome as a heretic. His teachings were influential during the 2nd century and a few centuries after, rivalling that of the Church of Rome. As he offered an alternative theology to the Canonical, Proto-orthodox, Trinitarian and Christological views of the Roman Church, the early Church Fathers denounced him. Their views continue to dominate authentic Christianity today. One of the greatest heretics in church history, Marcion is condemned by all branches of the Christian Church.

censored canon of New Testament Scripture and in so doing, compelled Christians to counter by clarifying their own canon. Interestingly in the author's personal experience, this idea of a 'god' who has both good and evil facets is propounded by at least some who are involved in modern Christian churches, so it appears that in the shape of Godism generally we *do* see views being expressed that it is impossible to describe as being anything other than a Christian heresy. Classical Gnostic teachings are so involved and so bizarre that we will waste no further time on them in this book,[3] except to observe that Godism, in its insistence on the polluted nature of the various scriptures of the 'higher religions' and with the inability of their 'god' to have secured for 'himself' or 'itself' fully dependable scriptures, do show clear Gnostic leanings. This is combined, as we have already noted, with the Godists' own esoteric ability to 'see' the truth that unites all the so-called higher religions. It seems then that Godists consider themselves to have a *gnosis*, a knowledge, which is simply not attained by those people with less sophisticated theological understanding. The word 'arrogant' springs to mind in this regard! There really is a breathtaking arrogance in those Godists who hold so unswervingly to this idea that they 'see' things in *the religions* and in the sacred writings of those religions that are hidden from others, but without the slightest blush will admit they cannot read those scriptures in their original native language! Finally we observe that Godists often hold views about *the religions* which are generally not shared or recognised by the adherents of those same religions. The adherents of *the religions*, it might be added, ought to

---

[3] There are some useful books and some useful material on the internet freely available. As always with the internet, however, be sceptical of scholarly quality control!

be presumed to be far better versed in their own religious theology than the average Godist! Later in this book, as we begin to look again at the nature of the unswervingly good God that the Holy Bible reveals, and at Jesus Christ His Son, we will begin to see the clear dividing lines between orthodox Christian belief as revealed from the pages of Scripture and the heterodox beliefs of the various ideas that comprise 21st century Godism.

What exactly is 'good'?

It is at this point in our study that we challenge the Godists' first great weakness when viewed from an orthodox Christian position. They do not believe in a God who is unswervingly or totally good. In our straightforward day to day understanding of what should be considered to be good, we can readily see based upon our own faulty and worldly morality that a 'god' who 'revealed' himself in umpteen different guises (religions), and in guises that are diametrically opposed to each other, and in the knowledge that by so doing he would cause spiritual and temporal conflict between the adherents of those 'faith systems' — such a 'god' would have no claim to be good. We need to consider then, what does the Bible say about God's goodness, and what does experience teach us?

The Holy Bible simply oozes the goodness of God. Anyone with access to a quality Bible Concordance[4] and who looks up the word 'good' will find hundreds of references. Leaping back to the very beginning of the Bible in Genesis chapter 1, we see that as God creates the world He declares it to be good. Some may object that in creation we find too much that is bad (earthquakes,

[4] A sort of Bible dictionary showing where in the Bible words and phrases may be found.

tsunamis, disease, failed harvests) and that it is God's 'fault' for having made this sort of a world. But they perhaps too easily forget what appears to be a historical reality alongside a spiritual reality, that, at some point in our time-space world, mankind decided to rebel against God and with that rebellion brought sin and evil into this world in which we must continue to live. This rebellion has huge implications for the happiness and security of the planet as a whole. Mankind, having been unfaithful in actively disobeying God (in order, as they hoped, to become like God), brought into this world a deadly disease that runs throughout all of mankind — the Bible calls it sin. What was created good was rendered 'fallen' from that state of goodness. From now on, men and women would continually try to be 'like God', but without His goodness and holiness, and in the attempt would immerse themselves ever more deeply into the mire of sin and corruption.[5] But in spite of this God's goodness continues to shine through into this, His world.

What is meant by the phrase 'the goodness of God'? At its most basic theologians tend to focus on the bounty of God. When we say that a person is good, we think of his dependability and moral uprightness, or else of his charitable and liberal disposition in the management of his goods and his time. Goodness in humans is generally thought of as the way they 'do good' to other humans. The goodness of God can be described as His permanent and unwavering inclination to deal well and bountifully with His creatures. In considering His creatures, God delights in them and is beneficial to them. God is the highest goodness, because He

---

[5] For someone to want to be more like Christ is not in itself a sin — see Matthew 5:48 and Ephesians 5:1. Becoming more like Christ is one consequence of becoming a disciple of Jesus (note His obedience to His Father; and see Philippians 2:5–11 and 2 Peter 1:2–11; also John 17:20–21. The Satanic deception is to make humans think that God is not telling us the truth. (See Genesis 3:1–7.)

does not act for His own benefit, but acts for His creatures' welfare, and to demonstrate His own goodness.

The original Saxon meaning of our English word 'God' is *'The Good'*. God is not only the greatest of all beings, but the best. Christians assert that all the goodness found in any creature has been imparted from the Creator, but God's goodness is un-derived, because it is the essence of His eternal nature. As God is infinite in power and has been from all eternity, even before there was any display of that power, so He was eternally good before there was any communication of His bounty, or indeed any creature to whom it might be imparted or exercised. So, the first manifestation of this Divine perfection was in giving existence to all things. **You are good, and what you do is good; teach me your decrees** we read in Psalm 119:68. God has in Himself an infinite and inexhaustible supply of all blessedness and it is sufficient to fill all things. Of course, sadly, not all things want to be filled with His goodness.

The goodness of God underpins all His attributes, some of which we explored in Chapter 2. All the activities of God are nothing more and nothing less than the radiance of His goodness: **And the LORD said, "I will cause all my goodness to pass in front of you, and I will proclaim my name, the LORD, in your presence. I will have mercy on whom I will have mercy, and I will have compassion on whom I will have compassion"** (Exodus 33:19). God's goodness is His crowning glory and is delightfully visible to His creatures: **And he passed in front of Moses, proclaiming, "The LORD, the LORD, the compassionate and gracious God, slow to anger, abounding in love and faithfulness"** (Exodus 34:6). There are many, many millions of people in the world today who would be able to echo that truth, having found God to be precisely that — loving and faithful.

God is the prime and chief goodness. In God there is nothing but goodness; and our own goodness, such as it is, would be non-existent without Him: **I said to the LORD, "You are my Lord; apart from you I have no good thing."** (Psalm 16:2). For the Christian believer God is the *summum bonum*. God is good by His own essence — good of Himself, eternally good and abundantly good. God is necessarily good, but He is also freely good. The necessity of the goodness of His nature does not restrict the freedom of His actions. This goodness is communicative with those He has created — in other words we can encounter it and understand it. What God gives out of goodness, He gives with joy and gladness. He did not only Will that we should be, but rejoiced that He brought us into being. He rejoiced in His works. **May the glory of the LORD endure forever; may the LORD rejoice in his works**. (Psalm 104:31).

The goodness of God is a real and genuine characteristic. He has always been and will always be infinitely good. In His goodness He is prompted to deal bountifully and in kindness with all His creatures. God's attribute of complete holiness emphasises His transcendence and condescendence toward His creation. **Surely God is good to Israel, to those who are pure in heart** (Psalm 73:1). We noted earlier in this book that God's progressive self disclosure as revealed through the pages of the Old Testament shows Him in ever clearer detail and increasingly in the pages of the Old Testament we see that self-disclosure leading, in turn, to love and worship on the part of His servants. At this point readers may want to pause to read in their entirety all of Psalms 103, 104 and 107, where we see and experience some of this outflow of love returned from God's people to their God Who is fundamentally good.

From the many references to the goodness of God we can draw certain clear deductions.[6]

God is originally good

God is good of Himself and has been always. Creatures may be good, but any goodness is derived and granted to them by God, without whom there can be no goodness, since He is the source of all goodness.

God depends on no one else for His goodness; he has goodness in and of Himself. He depends on no one, but all things depend of Him. He is so good, that He gives all and receives nothing in return; He only is good, because nothing is good but by Him: nothing has goodness except from Him.

God is infinitely good

God alone is infinitely good. His goodness is boundless and knows no limits; His goodness must necessarily be as infinite as His essence. All possible creatures are, and the entirety of creation is, incapable of exhausting the wealth and the treasures that the divine bounty is filled with. Since God is immeasureable, all His attributes or characteristics must also be without measure.

God is perfectly good

As in Him we find the whole nature of entity, so in Him is the whole nature of excellency. As nothing has an absolute perfection except God, so nothing has an absolutely perfect goodness except God.

The goodness of God is logically the measure and rule

---

[6] The author is indebted to website www.tecmalta.org/tft140.htm ('Truth for Today') for permission to borrow the structure and some of the arguments set out in this section.

of goodness in everything else; hence it must necessarily be perfect, as all the other divine attributes are perfect.

God is immutably good

Glorified saints are now immutably good by divine power and purpose; elect angels are immutably good by God's original decree to keep them good; other things may be perpetually good by supernatural power, but not immutably good in their own nature. Only God is immutably good, from eternity to eternity, for there can be no change in God. **Every good and perfect gift is from above, coming down from the Father of the heavenly lights, who does not change like shifting shadows**. (James 1:17)

Goodness is not the same as holiness

Again, God's goodness must be distinguished from His holiness, which is the rectitude of His nature, whereby He is pure, and without spot in Himself.

The goodness of God is the outward manifestation of His will, by which He shows Himself beneficial to His creatures.

The holiness of God is manifest to His rational creatures, and nothing else; but the goodness of God covers all the works of His hands. **The LORD is good to all; he has compassion on all he has made**. (Psalm 145:9)

God's goodness is a communicable attribute

Pure and perfect goodness is the royal prerogative of God; goodness is a choice perfection of the divine nature. This is the true and genuine character of God; He is goodness, good in Himself, good in His essence, good in the highest degree, possessing whatsoever is comely, excellent, desirable; the highest good, because He is the source of good. All gifts, all variety of goodness, are contained in Him as one common good. In reaching out to His creatures, and manifesting His goodness to them, this is certainly a communicable attribute. For His goodness is not only seen but is extended to others. A Christian may be a good person, but his goodness is the work of God in him and through him. Whatever goodness a Christian may have and exercise, he is ultimately a channel for the Divine goodness to reach out to others.

God's goodness is not lessened by His punishment of sin

When offenders are punished, we do not conclude that the Judge is devoid of goodness, but rather that the Judge is righteous. God's vindictive justice is as naturally His as is His goodness; both are necessarily His, and one does not exclude the other.

God is not bad because He is just; nor unrighteous, because He is good. God being infinitely good, cannot possibly intend or act anything but what is good: **You are good, and what you do is good** (Psalm 119: 68). Whatever God does is good, whether it may be pleasant or painful to His creatures. To punish evil is right, and therefore good.[7] We need to bear in mind the following points:

1. The justice of God is a part of the goodness of His nature. (See Exodus 33:19.)

2. Evidence of the goodness of God is the fact that He has made laws, and indeed has added to them warnings about what is involved in transgression. The design of laws, and the purpose of upholding the honour of those laws by the punishment of offenders, is to promote goodness and

---

[7] In Romans 1:24, 26 and 28 we learn that God will 'give us over' (NIV) to our sins. In this we understand that where a persistent and determined rebel/sinner decides he is going to attempt to be 'like God' in determining right from wrong, God will reluctantly allow them to have full rein for a period and endure the full consequences of that sin. But a time of judgement will come.

restrain evil. That is actually a normative legal position which would be recognized in secular jurisprudence as well as in theology.

3. It follows, then, that failure to punish evil would be evidence of a lacking in goodness. We need to remind ourselves, though, that punishment as an end in itself is negative. On the positive side, God in His mercy seeks the salvation of all.

4. Punishment is not the primary intention of God. When He created, His intention was fundamentally to manifest His goodness. He actually calls the act of his wrath His strange work, His alien task (see Isaiah 28:21). Finally, He finds no pleasure whatsoever in the death of a sinner (see Ezekiel 33:11).

God's goodness is manifested in various ways

God's supreme goodness is displayed in:

a. The creation

Just as His wisdom was the cause of making everything in order and harmony, His goodness was the cause of the very act of creation. He pronounced it 'very good,' that is, such as became His goodness to bring forth into being. So:

1. *Creation proceeds from goodness*; From the biblical perspective, we can affirm that God extracted vast numbers of things out of the depths of nothing. We can say this biblically in spite of and theories about creation or about evolution. Because God is good, things have a physical being. It has rightly been observed that *by God's goodness, the whole was brought out of the dark womb of nothingness*.

2. *Creation was the first act of goodness external to Himself*; the Persons of the Holy Trinity are good to each other (*ad intra*). The creation is the proof of God's goodness *ad extra*.

3. Especially in the case of man, *God's goodness is made manifest*. He empowered humankind with choices over and above any other creature; humankind was made a little lower than the angels, and crowned with glory and honour above any other creatures (Psalm 8:5).

4. *God provides for man*, as His supreme Benefactor. **O Lord, how excellent is thy Name in all the earth** (Psalm 8:1, 4).

5. When man sinned, God, in His goodness and for man's sake cursed the creation with the inevitable consequences of that rebellion. Creation still today *groans* because of Man's sin. But creation will finally be delivered from bondage (see Romans 8:20–22).

b. Man's redemption

The core of the gospel can be justly said to be a mirror of divine goodness, a special kind of goodness: 'Goodwill towards men' (Luke 2:14). Although if we read Luke 2:14 more accurately we need to add, in the words of the *Revised Standard Version* of the Bible, that God's peace is lavished upon humans with whom He is pleased. God's good will *does* extend to all men in the sense that He desires their salvation and makes it possible. But His highest goodwill is lavished upon His disciples.

It might be said, then, that God's goodness was the inspiration for His plan of redemption. It must have been an unimaginable and a miraculous goodness that impelled the Father to expose the life of His beloved Son to the difficulties and uncertainties of this world, and ultimately to death upon an evil cross of crucifixion, for the redemption of wicked rebels. God's great objective, perhaps, was to give a precise and unmistakable demonstration of the liberality of His nature (see John 3:16–17).

Redemption comes out of pure goodness. God was under

no obligation to pity our misery or repair our ruin — but He has done both. This is the *good news* of a God abounding in His own blessedness (2 Timothy 1:8–11). Hence we may estimate the extent of God's goodness in the great act of salvation to be much greater even than that of creation. God's goodness is amply demonstrated when we consider Whom He 'gave':

1. His Son is a greater gift than creation itself (Hebrews 1:2–3).

2. His Son is the only-begotten, the unique Son of God, not an angel.

3. His Son was given the task to rescue us from eternal damnation (Mark 8:36–38); He was made poor that we might become rich in Him (2 Corinthians 8:9).

4. Jesus is the epitome of goodness. The Lord Jesus through His love became what we humans are — mere flesh and blood, so that He might then bring us to be, ultimately, what He is — holy and beloved of God. An amazing thought! As someone once said: the Son of God became the Son of Man, so that the sons of men might become Sons of God.

c. Providence

Psalm 107 celebrates the goodness of God in the continued supply of His providence throughout all the ages. It credits to God's goodness all the advantages men meet with as they seek to serve Him. God helps them in their actions, presides over their plans, reviews and understands their different circumstances, and perpetually cares for them. The emphasis in this Psalm is expressed in the first and last verses (v. 1: **give thanks to the Lord, for he is good; his love endures forever**; v. 43: **whoever is wise, let him heed these things and consider the great love of the Lord.**)

1. This goodness is obvious in the care God exercises over all creatures. There is a special goodness displayed to His

people; but this does not take away His general goodness to the world. The earth is still 'full of His riches' (Psalm 104:24).

2. His goodness is seen in the preservation of all things. **O LORD, you preserve both man and beast** (Psalm 36:6; see also 65:9,10; 107:35,36). Every day He 'prepares a table' for us (Psalm 23:5), and proves to be the 'stronghold of our life' (Psalm 27:1).

3. In His goodness He employs His angels on our behalf, to help and assist us, in ways most often unknown to us (Hebrews 1:14).

4. The goodness of God is seen in taking care of the meanest rational creatures — as servants and criminals. Widows, orphans and foreigners are under His care.

5. His goodness is evident in the preservation of human society. Because of His power He is able to do it, but because of His goodness He is willing to do it. This idea is often summed up in the idea of *common grace*.[8]

Much of what we have explored so far has been found in the pages of the Old Testament. As noted previously the author finds it helpful to consider the Old Testament as *the history of the promise*, and the New Testament as *the promise fulfilled*: the Old Testament points towards the promise of the Messiah, and the New Testament shows the nature of that same Messiah who shares with the Father the absolute claim to be good. Jesus challenged the rich young ruler in Matthew 19:16–17 (repeated in Mark 10:17–31 and in Luke 18:18–30) in this way: **"Why do you ask me concerning what is good? There is only one who is good ...."** (GNB). Jesus challenged the young ruler,

---

[8] Readers who want to get a good biblical perspective on this subject may want to read N. R. Needham's short (30 page) booklet *Common Grace* published 2008 by the UK Christian Institute (ISBN 978-1-901086-38-6).

but He did not rebuke him for assigning that title to Jesus Himself. The New Testament also reminds us that **God is light, and in Him is *no* darkness at all** (1 John 1:5). As we will explore in greater detail the good news of the New Testament elsewhere in this book, we will conclude our thoughts on the goodness of God with these general observations: there is an absolute perfection in God's nature and being. There is nothing wanting to it or defective in it, and nothing can be added to it to make it better. All that emanates from God — His laws, His creation, and His providences — cannot be otherwise than good. As is made clear in Genesis chapter 1 in several places, as God surveyed all that He had made He saw that it was — good.

Measured in the way the Bible uses the word 'good' it can easily be seen that we tend to misuse and devalue the word good in our everyday language. Some Bible teachers assert that they try to avoid using the word 'good' at all in common parlance, and instead reserve it only with reference to Almighty God. Whilst on the face of it this may seem slightly eccentric, it is actually biblically sound. If we all were to adopt that approach to this word, then we would probably enlarge immeasurably our understanding of the goodness of God.

Could a good God 'reveal' Himself in different guises?

We really do now have to throw down the gauntlet to the Godists on this question. The goodness of God is amply demonstrated in the pages of the Holy Bible. It is amply demonstrated in the lives of individuals who have put their trust in Him. It is amply demonstrated in the life and teachings of Jesus, His Son. We might first pose the question, why should such a God feel the need to invent other and conflicting 'messages' about Himself? What, precisely, is the deficiency in His biblical revelation and in His revelation through Jesus that needs to be remedied by other revelations? Just how can it be good to allow the confusion of multiple religions? How can it be good to demonstrate deity in *many* religions that demand from their followers salvation by works, and just *one* that allows salvation by grace? In many religions that reach up, and just one that reaches down?

How could a good God reveal Himself in commands and concepts that are diametrically opposed? How could He allow such massive confusion to reign? How could He allow the inevitable conflict of ideas and aspirations and understandings and still merit the title 'good'? Some examples of what we mean are set out on the next three pages, but please consider this cautionary note:

IMPORTANT NOTE : NO REAL COMPARABILITY!

Many terms have meanings that shift dramatically in the context of each religion, as each has its own belief structure. Not only does the word 'god' or 'God' have very different meanings, so do words like 'heaven', and so on. Therefore, at best, this can only be a rough illustration of some areas where clear differences in understanding and conflicts in practical outworking on fundamental issues are very obvious. There are many other differences, and nothing is explored in depth in these brief notes! Beware: even the expression 'believe in' has different meanings, as the Christian believer's relation to God the Father — through faith in Christ Jesus (and being found 'in' Him) — is unique; it differs from the modes of 'believing' found in any of *'the religions'* as it signifies a personal relationship with the risen, *living*, ascended, glorified Lord Jesus, the only way to the Father. Believing in (or 'on') a living person is not just believing that something happens to be true (though it certainly does entail belief that certain claims are historically true!) It is not possible to quote documentary sources for beliefs of *the religions* as they are so diverse. There are, of course, many other religions besides those mentioned, so these are just a few examples of how they all differ radically from true, biblical Christian faith.

The Bible teaches . . .

GOD REACHES OUT TO PEOPLE

The Word became flesh and made his dwelling among us (John 1:1–18). For God so loved the world that he gave his only son (John 3:16–21). The wrath of God is being revealed from heaven against all the godlessness and wickedness of men (Romans 1:18–2:6).

But 'the religions' teach . . .

- Buddhists do not believe in God.
- Hindus believe in many 'gods' (circa 7,000 with about 20 important ones). Some maintain that 'god' is one but revealed in thousands of guises.
- Muslims believe in 'Allah'. They ascribe to 'Allah' many names but do not see 'Allah' as reaching down to rescue mankind.

The Bible teaches . . .

WE MUST FACE DEATH ONCE, THEN JUDGEMENT

Man is destined to die once, and after that to face judgement (Hebrews 9:27).

But 'the religions' teach . . .

- Buddhists believe in reincarnation — their concepts of 'heaven' and 'hell' (very different meanings) are considered allegorical.
- Hindus believe in reincarnation.
- Muslims believe in a 'paradise', also called 'The Garden', a place of pleasure, with lofty mansions, delicious food and drink, and virgin companions. There are thought to be seven 'heavens'.

The Bible teaches . . .

JESUS' SACRIFICE ON THE CROSS IS ALL SUFFICIENT

In him we have redemption through his blood, the forgiveness of sins, in accordance with the riches of God's grace (Ephesians 1:3–14). Christ died for sins once and for all, the righteous for the unrighteous, to bring you to God (1 Peter 3:18–22).

But 'the religions' teach . . .

- Buddhist beliefs about Jesus defy quick summary. Some believe he moved to India and became a Buddhist.
- Hindu beliefs about Jesus defy quick summary. Some believe he is one and the same as 'Krishna', ignoring the fact that Jesus was born a Jew in a particular place, was crucified, dead and buried; and that he was raised from the dead and is alive now, reigning in glory.
- Muslims – do not believe that Jesus was crucified. A recent Islamic booklet in UK is titled *Crucifixion or Cruci-Fiction?*

IS GOD GOOD?

The Bible teaches ...
GOD IS THREE PERSONS IN ONE GOD
See Deuteronomy 6:4; Galatians 3:20 (see also verse 16);
1 Timothy 2:5; James 2:19.
But 'the religions' teach ...
- Buddhists do not believe in God.
- Hindus believe in many 'gods' (circa 7,000 with about 20 important ones). Some maintain that God is one but revealed in thousands of guises.
- Muslim beliefs vehemently condemn the Christian understanding of Holy Trinity – God in three Persons. Muslims think this signifies three gods.

The Bible teaches ...
REDEMPTION
The Son of Man did not come to be served, but to serve, and to give his life as a ransom for many (Matthew 20:28; Mark 10:45).
But 'the religions' teach ...
- Buddhists – The concept as the Bible expounds is not recognised. Self effort is stressed.
- Hindus – The concept as the Bible expounds is not recognised. Self effort is stressed.
- Muslims – Think 'paradise' awaits those who have followed the Muslim way of life; hell for non-believers. Essentially self effort.

The Bible teaches ...
THE NEED TO BE BORN AGAIN
I tell you the truth, no one can see the kingdom of God unless he is born again. (See John 3:1–21)
But 'the religions' teach ...
- Buddhists – do not believe in God – concept of new birth leading to regeneration is not recognised.
- Hindus – believe in many deities – concept of new birth leading to regeneration is not recognized.
- Muslims – this concept is not recognized.

The Bible teaches . . .
THE RESURRECTION OF THE DEAD
The Lord Himself will come down from heaven, with a loud command . . . and the dead in Christ will rise first (1 Thessalonians 4:16–17). (See also 1 Corinthians 15:35–58.)
But 'the religions' teach . . .

- Buddhists – reincarnation.
- Hindus – reincarnation leaving to 'nirvana'. The position of women is unclear.
- Muslims believe that Muslims will be 'resurrected' but the concept is quite different from that of Christianity.

The 'god' of the Godists has a lot of explaining to do if 'he' or 'it' has made key revelations as contained in the comparison above in so many different and opposing ways. It can be argued that the message of Christianity is fiercely logical, is internally consistent, and is self-authenticating in the lives of true Believers.[9] It must of course be readily acknowledged that true Christian Believers may not always see eye to eye on every theological issue within Christianity. In point of fact the apostle Paul does seem to have made provision for this by acknowledging that the church is analagous to a body, with many parts, but still living in harmony with itself: **Just as each of us has one body with many members, and these members do not all have the same function, so in Christ we who are many form one body, and each member belongs to all the others. We have different gifts, according to the grace given us. If a man's gift is prophesying, let him use it in proportion to his faith. If it is serving, let him serve; if it is teaching, let him teach; if it is encouraging, let him encourage;**

---

[9] Some Christian denominations resist the pull of logic and prefer to emphasise the mystical traditions of Christianity. Providing that these traditions do not run counter to clear biblical teaching, there seems to be no harm in exploring these mystical dimensions of God's revelation.

**if it is contributing to the needs of others, let him give
generously; if it is leadership, let him govern diligently;
if it is showing mercy, let him do it cheerfully.** (Romans
12:4–8).

Whilst the above seems to talk of individual church
communities, the lesson of diversity can surely be applied
to the wider church and by extension to the so-called
denominations. Western Christians sometimes consider it to
be a strength, rather than a weakness, that God has allowed
and empowered a broad church — providing that this broad
church treads a narrow doctrinal path. Looking again at
the comparisons set out above, it is a fair comment that the
biblical truths set out would be gladly acknowledged by
the vast majority of practicing Christians, no matter their
denominational affiliations. The glaring inconsistencies
demonstrated by comparing biblical Christianity with the
beliefs of *the religions*, even allowing that we are only able
in such a short discourse to highlight a summary of these
classic religious beliefs, means that either the Godists' 'god'
is inconsistent and therefore not to be trusted, or that *the
religions* are in fact 'external noise' that clutter the clear
and simple message of the gospel. A 'god' who, it must be
argued, callously and carelessly fails to harmonise even the
basic tenets of faith and of peace among the majority of
the people who inhabit this planet, cannot warrant the title
'good'. It is for Godists to demonstrate otherwise.

7

IS GOD HOLY?

The holiness of God as revealed in the Bible

It has been mentioned several times in this book that the author finds it helpful to consider the Old Testament as *the history of the promise* and the New Testament as *the promise fulfilled,* in the sense that the Old ultimately can be seen as God's dealings with the human race through His chosen and rebellious people (the Hebrews) under the old covenant, whilst the New deals with God's dealings with the human race through His new covenant made with all peoples, everywhere, who are in practice just as rebellious as the chosen people. Readers may again want to hold this thought of promise and fulfilment in mind as we look back once more into that Older Testament[1]. We explored in chapter 2 some of the key *inherent attributes* of God and we noted that, amongst these, the attribute of holiness is a communicable attribute – in other words one that He can and will share with His children.

The word 'Holiness' and the adjective 'Holy' are found more than 900 times in the Bible. Precise definition of the

---

[1] The Word 'Testament' really means, and carries the idea, of a witness giving testimony. Hence the two halves of the Bible could equally be called the Old Witness and the New Witness.

word is not altogether straightforward and there remains some divergence of view among theologians as to its exact meaning. The etymology of the Hebrew word *qadosh* is uncertain. It may come from a Hebrew root 'to shine', or from a Semitic/Arabic root 'to cut or separate'. Both interpretations do seem to illustrate in a meaningful way what we understand of holiness at the most basic level. What is truly beautiful about God – His utter holiness, does seem to shine out like brilliant light into this all too often wicked and dark world. When found in the Old Testament the word 'holy' focuses on that idea of separation. We can say that at its most basic, holiness is (negatively) a cutting off or separation from that which is unclean and (positively) a consecration to that which is pure. In the Old Testament the word holiness signifies God's transcendence over all that He has created, as well as the moral perfection of His character. God is holy in that He is totally different from all that He has created and yet still exercises power and sovereignty over it. The following verses help to illustrate the Old Testament view of the holiness of God:

God reigns over the nations; God sits on his holy throne (Psalm 47:8 NKJV).

I will make My holy name known in the midst of My people Israel, and I will not let them profane My holy name anymore. Then the nations shall know that I am the LORD, the Holy One in Israel. (Ezekiel 39:7 NKJV)

> **For thus says the High and Lofty One**
> **Who inhabits eternity, whose name is Holy:**
> **"I dwell in the high and holy place,**

With him who has a contrite and humble spirit,
To revive the spirit of the humble,
And to revive the heart of the contrite ones.

(Isaiah 57:15, NKJV).

I am the LORD, your Holy One,
The Creator of Israel, your King.

(Isaiah 43:15, NKJV)

For our shield belongs to the LORD,
And our king to the Holy One of Israel.

(Psalm 89:18, NKJV)

Also the sons of those who afflicted you
Shall come bowing to you,
And all those who despised you shall fall prostrate at
the soles of your feet;
And they shall call you The City of the LORD,
Zion of the Holy One of Israel.

(Isaiah 60:14 NKJV)

From the suffering, though faithful and morally upright biblical character Job, we encounter the following recognition of God's beautiful holiness as Job affirms that, in spite of all his underserved and inexplicable suffering: **. . . no matter how great my pain, I know that God is holy; I have never opposed what he commands.** (Job 6:10, GNB)

So in the Old Testament God's holiness, as a concept, helps us to understand that He is completely separated from all that is evil and defiled. God cannot do evil and His character really is the standard for moral perfection.

It is again from the book of Job that we hear this clarion truth: . . . **listen to me, you men of understanding: Far be it from God to do wickedness, and from the Almighty to commit iniquity**. (Job 34:10, NKJV)

The NIV translation of Psalm 34:10 renders wickedness as 'evil' and iniquity as 'wrong' – but the essence of the verse in both translations is much the same. Far from being unjust, God will be praised for His standards of morality and justice: **But the LORD of hosts shall be exalted in judgment, and God who is holy shall be hallowed in righteousness**. (Isaiah 5:16).

God's holiness – His purity of character and His transcendent majesty are wonderfully balanced in Psalm 99. To modern readers the language may seem extravagant, but we need to understand that this is the outpouring of a heart melted into the love of a totally good, a totally dependable and a totally holy God, Who has proved His faithfulness to previous generations:

> **The LORD reigns;**
> **Let the peoples tremble!**
> **He dwells between the cherubim;**
> **Let the earth be moved!**
> **The LORD *is* great in Zion,**
> **And He *is* high above all the peoples.**
> **Let them praise Your great and awesome name—**
> **He is holy.**
> **The King's strength also loves justice;**
> **You have established equity;**
> **You have executed justice and righteousness in Jacob.**
> **Exalt the LORD our God,**
> **And worship at His footstool—**
> **He is holy.**
> **Moses and Aaron were among His priests,**

**And Samuel was among those who called upon His
name;
They called upon the LORD, and He answered them
He spoke to them in the cloudy pillar;
They kept His testimonies and the ordinance He gave
them.**

**You answered them, O LORD our God;
You were to them God-Who-Forgives,
Though You took vengeance on their deeds.
Exalt the LORD our God,
And worship at His holy hill;
For the LORD our God is holy.**

(Psalm 99 NKJV)

The Old Testament also demonstrates to us the inner,
moral and spiritual dimensions of God's holiness. Human
beings, men and women, have been created in the image of
God (Genesis 1: 26) and are called to cultivate the holiness
of God's character in their own lives. **"Be holy because
I, the LORD your God, am holy"** (Leviticus 19:2). God
wants and expects us to be holy, for only in that way can
we ultimately have communion with Him. Recognising that
we are by our own rebellious nature unholy, God has made
it His business to provide a pathway for us to become like
Himself. Psalm 15 looks at the ethical implications of God's
demand that we should be holy. So the psalmist asks:

**LORD, who may abide in Your tabernacle?
Who may dwell in Your holy hill?
He who walks uprightly,
And works righteousness,
And speaks the truth in his heart;
He who does not backbite with his tongue,
Nor does evil to his neighbor,**

Nor does he take up a reproach against his friend;
In whose eyes a vile person is despised,
But he honors those who fear the LORD;
He who swears to his own hurt and does not change;
He who does not put out his money at usury,
Nor does he take a bribe against the innocent.
He who does these things shall never be moved.

(Psalm 15, NKJV)

When we decide to follow God, our lives will display real evidence of that decision. In much the same way, the prophet Isaiah characterizes God's ransomed community as **the Holy People, the Redeemed of the LORD** (Isaiah 62:12). Through the Lord Jesus a new covenant is established with a new *redeemed people* — those who have put their faith in God through Jesus. So in the New Testament in the letter to the Hebrews we read: **He is the Mediator of the new covenant, by means of death, for the redemption of the transgressions under the first covenant, that those who are called may receive the promise of the eternal inheritance.** (Hebrews 9:15, NKJV).

We will leave for the time being this concept of the Lord Jesus as mediator of a new covenant because we are entering into some deep theological areas that will be explored more fully in chapter 10. For now it is sufficient simply to note that a holy God would be expected to have a holy Son. Everything that we encounter in the Old Testament points, ultimately, towards the world's need for a Saviour (or a Messiah), and He is precisely the person God sends to the world according to the New Testament.

Holiness is regarded by many as a moral attribute of God as it shows us *positively* His purity and *negatively*, His complete freedom from sin. Holiness, then, is a general term for the moral excellence of God as well as His freedom from all moral limitations in His moral perfection. As the prophet Habakkuk reveals: **You are of purer eyes than to behold evil, and cannot look on wickedness** (Habakkuk 1:13, NKJV). This is a clear declaration expressing the moral sensitiveness of God, Who shrinks from all evil and sin. He shrinks from it not because He is afraid of it, but because He is holy and sin is deeply offensive to Him. Hopefully by now we are getting a sense of what the holiness of God is, but what we have explored so far is rather more negative than positive.

We gain a fresh insight into God's holiness as we consider that holiness is the summation of all those characteristics that theologians generally call the attributes of God, some of which we looked at in chapter 2. Holiness can be thought of as the *whole* of which other attributes are a *part*. Holiness might then be thought of as the Divine nature in which all His attributes subsist, or as 'the attribute of attributes'. Some have suggested that holiness is a *transcendant attribute* that runs through all the other attributes and casts glory upon each of them. Jonathan Edwards,[2] with his classic Christian insight, wrote: 'The holiness of His nature is the cause and reason of holy determination ... the foundation of all His will, purpose and decrees'. He said it was 'the beauty of God's moral attributes', and that 'no other attribute is truly lovely without this, and no otherwise than it derives its loveliness from this.'[3]

Another great theologian, Professor R.A. Finlayson,

---

[2] Jonathan Edwards (October 5, 1703 – March 22, 1758) – Eighteenth century colonial American preacher and one of the greatest and most profound American evangelical theologians. His sermons and writings stimulated a period of renewed interest in Christianity in America.

[3] *Works*, vol. II, p. 143.

made the similar point[4] — that Holiness is more than a mere attribute of God — rather it is in a very real sense the sum of all His attributes, the outshining of all that God is. Finlayson used the simile that just as the sun's rays containing all the colours of the spectrum come together and blend into light, so all the attributes of God come together in His self-manifestation and blend into holiness. To conceive of God's being and character as merely a synthesis of abstract perfections would be, said Finlayson, to deprive God of all reality. In the God of the Bible these perfections live: they function, they operate, they burn — in holiness! Our God is a consuming fire! If we consider holiness, then, as the overall expression of the Divine perfection, we will begin to grasp why God's holiness and His glory are so frequently associated in Scripture, as the One who is 'glorious in holiness, fearful in praises', and as the One who 'swears' by His holiness, as though it were the fullest expression of Himself. It is not surprising, therefore, that holiness is expressly linked in Scripture to each Person in the Trinity, not only to the Father, but also to the Son and the Spirit, as the highest expression of divinity, and claiming for them the excellence of the Divine nature.

Because God is holy He cannot be indifferent to sin. He cannot ignore it, for example by the mere exercise of His clemency. God will never wink at our sin and 'make everything all right in the end'. It must be added, because God is holy He cannot be appeased by the sinner's own effort to 'make-up' for his wrongdoing. In all other religions, notes Finlayson, salvation is sought by self-effort, because God is not conceived to be absolutely holy.

---

[4] In a June 1955 lecture to Westminster Chapel in London on the holiness of God. Interested readers will find this full lecture available on the internet.

'There are but two religions in the world: salvation by grace and salvation by works. Salvation by works is based on too low a view of the holiness of God. There is so much aesthetic religion which is nothing else than bringing man's artistically conceived religion to God in an attempt to know and please Him. True religion consists in the sinner coming into the presence of God that he may get Divine religion. The one makes religion his god, the other makes God his religion.'[5] The author suggests that readers may want to re-read Finlayson's comment immediately above several times as it is really quite profound and speaks directly into the Godist philosophy with its overarching desire to create a synthesis of religions.

The holiness of God revealed through Christ

As we intend to return to this subject later in chapter 10 we simply need to note here that in Christ's redemptive work we see an amazing manifestation of God's holiness. We see a vindication of God's right to give (or more correctly, using two theological technical terms, to *impute* and to *impart*) holiness to human beings who are, both in state and condition, unholy. He is holy, yet he gives holiness to those who are unholy. In the atoning work of Jesus Christ we have an act of God which removes all that hinders our participation in His holiness. The Bible summarises the overall problem in these words: **For He made Him who knew no sin to be sin for us, that we might become the righteousness of God in Him.** (2 Corinthians 5:21, NKJV). In the Lord Jesus we find holiness manifested and holiness vindicated: the Cross in practice reconciles

---

[5] Professor R.A. Finlayson — The Campbell Morgan Memorial Bible Lectureship — 22nd June 1955, Westminster Chapel, Buckingham Gate, London

holiness and love. It was common during the twentieth century to regard love as the overriding feature of the Divine character, and indeed in much of contemporary Christianity Divine holiness is unhealthily subordinated to Divine love, with the dangerous side effect of distorting both holiness and love. So today in much of Christianity Divine holiness is compromised and Divine love has been transmuted into something that is too often little more than sheer sentimentality.

Without the Cross, love and holiness are often considered to be rival attributes, in some way negating or cancelling each other, either holiness overruling love, or love obscuring holiness. But in the Cross of Christ Divine love and Divine holiness combine perfectly to create a unique relationship with mankind. The necessity of the atoning sacrifice (of Jesus taking our place on the cross) arises from God's holy character — the principle simultaneously of His love and righteousness. The difficulty of how to reconcile the reality of God's holiness with Divine justice in relation to sin, receives its answer in the Cross of Christ. There holiness is not only vindicated but made available to humans. The problem of how God could hate and condemn the sin and yet love and save that same sinner has found its solution in the death of Jesus Christ His Son.

Can the Godists' 'god' claim holiness?

The author once engaged in a debate with an older (and wiser!) Christian about the interpretation of Genesis chapter 1. Without a clear recollection of the debate and precisely what was said, the author recalls well that the wiser Christian gently rebuked him with the comment, which he made with a slight and patient smile. Extending his Bible in his hands he said: "So you think that God has given us a pack of lies to believe, do you?" He had made a telling point: it is difficult and dangerous to 'write off' anything in the Holy Bible or to say that what is written needs to be reinterpreted in the light of modern circumstances. Reverting to the Godists' core beliefs, we need to measure these against the standard of holiness we have begun to explore in this chapter and to challenge whether their understanding of 'god' can match the requirement of moral perfection that is encompassed in holiness. We remind ourselves at this point, that Godists variously believe that:

- God has revealed Himself in many different ways, especially in the so-called 'higher religions';
- God has revealed Himself in ways that are (or may very easily be considered to be) contradictory;
- The various scriptures of the various religions have been tampered with and/or misinterpreted by humans (implication: God has not troubled Himself to procure for us dependable holy writings, nor has He procured for us trustworthy religious teachers, howsoever known);
- There are many paths to God and no one religion holds all the answers.

Godism, we discovered, shares and borrows beliefs selectively from other philosophies: a Godist would share with a Deist the view that God can be discovered through reason, although the Godist would add that this is not the sole means of an authentic encounter with the Eternal. In chapter 5 we discovered that Monism is the philosophical idea that there is unity in any given field of inquiry, even where this is not to be expected. Some Monist philosophers hold that there is one god, with many manifestations in different religions. *Deism* is both a religious and philosophical belief that a supreme 'god' exists which created the physical universe and that religious truths can be arrived at by the application of reason and observation of the natural world. ***Theism***, a philosophical position not to be identified with any particular religion, believes in the existence of God/gods and that this God or 'gods' reveals Himself to His creatures. Godists do not believe in the total veracity of any of the 'scriptures', all of which they believe have been corrupted by humans, so Godists have 'seen' a greater truth than that acknowledged by singular adherents of *the religions*.

We noted in chapter 5 that Godism shares or borrows beliefs of all the major religious philosophies. It is God-centric, to the extent that it believes in a deity or deities which have an 'emotional' interest in the mortal. Some Godists are indeed adherents of particular religions but they are all *religion–negative* to the extent that where a religion's teachings get in the way of the overall thrust of Godism then the Godist is happy to bypass or trample the religion, which is not allowed to stand in the way of the overall belief. Godism seeks to draw out and amplify a theme that is seen to run through all the (higher) religions — that of compassion. A Godist generally believes that God has established religions to help humans to encounter 'him' or 'it'. All religions contain good and all contain bad: it is up to the individual to discern what is good and to 'follow' that. Godists hold their 'god' culpable and answerable for the sins and woes of this world, even if 'he' or 'it' in turn has the power and the authority also to hold us responsible. Godist belief is therefore a sort of mutual moral accountability but where 'god' will have the final say. Godists hold the slightly arrogant view that they can 'see' more perceptively than those of no faith (agnostics or atheists) as well as more clearly than those of *the religions*, who are limited to perceiving the 'truths' only within their own dogma.

Having looked briefly at the holiness of God as revealed from the pages of the Bible and reminded ourselves of the basic beliefs of Godism, we must once again challenge whether this Godist 'god' has any right to be considered holy — certainly by the standards of the Holy Bible. A few key observations should make this point for us: **I will make My holy name known in the midst of My people Israel, and I will not let them profane My holy name anymore. Then the nations shall know that I am the LORD, the Holy One in Israel.** (Ezekiel 39:7, NKJV)

God's name is holy, yet Godists say 'god' has allowed his name to be used in a multiplicity of conflicting ways. They think some humans are allowed to know god as a single divine person and others are allowed to see god in a multiplicity of guises; that for some there will be a single death and judgement to be faced, yet for others there will be a constant reincarnation until (perhaps) they reach an exalted state by their own good efforts. For Christians there is an understanding that by their own efforts they can never be found right with God and must accept the sacrifice of Jesus on the cross. But for Muslims the cross is a fiction ('the cruci-fiction') and Jesus cheated the executioner. Can a 'god' who supposedly reveals 'himself' or 'itself' in such diverse ways be called morally pure, especially when it leads to a lifetime of confusion between 'his' religions?

Therefore listen to me, you men of understanding: far be it from God to do wickedness, and from the Almighty to commit iniquity. (Job 34:10, NKJV)

Far be it from God to do wrong, stated Job, emphatically. Yet the Godist accuses god of telling the Christians that there is one path to God (Matthew 7:13 — **small is the gate and narrow the road that leads to life**), yet to Hindus that there are thousands! Is this good or evil? God presents His Son as a prince of peace, yet the godists tell us sent Muhammad who led the Battles of Badr, Uhud, Dumatul, Banu, Ahzab, Khibar, Mutah, Hunain, Taif, and Tabuk. Are these two revelations compatible? If not, but if both come from 'god', then surely 'god' cannot be holy? To the Christians, the death of the Lord Jesus on the cross of crucifixion is the locus of history: **And Jesus cried out again with a loud voice, and yielded up His spirit.** (Matthew 27:50, NKJV). But to Muslims this is a lie: 'They uttered against Mary a grave false charge; they said (in boast), we killed Christ Jesus, the son of Mary, the messenger of Allah; but they killed him not, nor crucified him, but so it was made to appear to them' (Q4: 156-158). If 'god' has revealed these two diametrically opposed statements, then 'god' is not committed to truth. If 'god' is not committed to truth, then 'god' is not holy. It really is for the Godists to justify their position. As the author's wise Christian mentor challenged so many years ago, the author repeats the simple question to people who consider themselves to be Christians who also hold Godist beliefs: 'So you think that God has given us a pack of lies to believe, do you?'

But the LORD of hosts shall be exalted in judgment, and God who is holy shall be hallowed in righteousness. (Isaiah 5:16, NKJV.) Righteousness and justice flows like a mighty river from the God of the Bible. Readers may want to access a good Bible encyclopedia and follow the concept of righteousness in detail. In this chapter we simply pose the question again to the Godist: how can a 'god' be considered to be righteous when 'he' or 'it', tells Jews through the old covenant (fulfilled in the new covenant) and repeats in the New Testament, that they must not worship idols (e.g. Isaiah 44; Jeremiah 10:2–5; Psalm 115:2–8; Zechariah 10:2; Isaiah 45:16 and 20; Isaiah 46; Psalm 40:4;

Acts 17:29–30, as just a few references) and yet that same 'god' allows other religions, Hinduism and Buddhism in particular, to worship idols? Apart from being inconsistent, could this be considered a remotely 'righteous' action on the part of God? How does such a confused revelation from this 'god' square with the attributes of Truthfulness, Wisdom , Holiness, and Love that we began to explore in chapter 2? We are bound to repeat, in the context of holiness which we have begun to explore in this chapter, can the Godists' 'god' be called holy? **"You shall be holy, for I the LORD your God am holy"** (Leviticus 19:2, NKJV). When God made this command, had He forgotten that in the past and in the future He would also reveal Himself in ways that He had already pronounced as unholy?

The Holy Spirit

Many good books have been written about the Holy Spirit, so what follows here need only be a brief summary. But in the context of a Holy God we must consider the Holy Spirit and the normative Christian view of that Spirit. He is the third person of the Trinity: the Hebrew word *ruah* and the Greek word *pneuma* are the words used from earliest times to explain and describe the experience of Godly power working in, upon and around humans, and understood by those humans as the power of God. The Bible reveals to us the Spirit as truly God, a personal being and not merely a power for good. Everything said of God can be said of the Holy Spirit and we should speak of Him with reverence, and indeed approach the whole subject with the utmost reverence. Since the Holy One does what is holy, we are to beware of any idea that He might command us to do something that is unholy. Things that are said of a person are said of the Spirit in the Bible, as well as things that could

only be said of a divine being, as this quick Bible search
may help us to see:

Matthew 28:19

2 Corinthians 13:14

Luke 1:35

Psalm 139:7 – 10

Matthew 12:31

John 14:26; 15:26; 16:13 – 14

Acts 5:3

Romans 8:26 – 27

Galatians 4:6

Ephesians 4:30

Hebrews 9:14

1 John 4:1 – 3

In the Old Testament the Holy Spirit came upon particular
men and women for special tasks, but a future outpouring
was promised — another case, if you like, of the promise
(Old Testament) and the fulfilment (New Testament). In the
Old Testament the Spirit was not given to God's people in
general, as He has been since Pentecost (Acts chapter 2).
He is the spiritual presence of Christ with His people:

Matthew 1:18; 3:11; 10:20

Luke 1:15; 2:25 – 27; 3:16, 22; 4:1

Luke 11:13

John 3:5, 6, 8

John 7:39; 14:17; 16:7 – 8; 20:22

John 14:16 – 18, 26; 15:26

At Pentecost a new day dawned. The Holy Spirit became
a free gift of grace available to all who believe:

Acts 1:4, 8; 2:1 – 7

Acts 2:18, 38; 4:8, 31; 7:55; 8:18 – 22

Acts 10:44 – 45; 13:2, 4; 19:2

The Bible distinguishes between *having* the Spirit and being *filled* with that Spirit. The ultimate command for Christians remains: be filled with the Spirit (Ephesians 5:18). In the life of a Christian believer, in greater or lesser measure, we will expect to see the fruit of the Spirit in evidence. Like fruits on a tree this will 'grow' naturally and will be the natural outcome of a life spent as a disciple of Jesus. That fruit, set out in Galatians 5:22–26 is: love, joy, peace, patience, kindness, goodness, faithfulness, humility (or gentleness) and self control. Where these things are absent in the life of a believer, or where there is a preponderance of unholy fruit (probably the opposite of each of those mentioned above) then we may have to doubt the reality of any profession of faith in Jesus. So, for all those Godists who try to claim that 'Christians' get involved in brutal religious wars (something we explored in chapter 5) then we have to point out that, not only is such temporal warfare condemned by Christ, but those who prosecute such warfare are unlikely to be evidencing all that fruit in their lives. No matter what an IRA[6] terrorist may say or think, he cannot be cited as a disciple of Jesus and filled with the Holy Spirit! But the Bible goes further: not only are there natural fruits that will be evidenced in the lives of all true followers of Jesus, there are also special gifts, given to His disciples in order to carry out whatever ministry Jesus has planned for them. These gifts are listed in 1 Corinthians 12:4–11 and 28. They are: the message of wisdom; the message of knowledge, faith, gifts of healing, miraculous powers, prophecy, distinguishing between spirits, different kinds of tongues, interpretation of tongues —and, finally, the gift of administration.

---

[6] Irish Republican Army

The challenge goes back to the Godist who insists that 'god' is revealed in different ways through different 'faith systems': can a God who promises to lavish all this good fruit and good gifts to one set of followers, and provide to Christians fruit and gifts that are *prima facie* so much better and so much more sublime than the gifts and fruits evidenced in *the religions*,[7] be considered to deal with followers on a fair and equitable basis? Godists need to tell us what are the counterpoint/compensatory 'gifts' and 'fruit' evidenced in their other religions. Surely we would expect to find at least as many? If 'god' gives special gifts only to a favoured set of believers, then surely this is unfair to the followers of his (its) other religions? If the Godists' 'god' is unfair, as we have just explored, then surely at the end of the day 'he' or 'it' must fail the test of holiness? It seems to be an open and shut case: the Godists' 'god' is unholy.

---

[7] See chapter 11

8

IS 'GOD' A SPLIT IDENTITY?

Is Godism a new form of Arianism?

'There is nothing new under the sun' has become a well known proverb.[1] As we look into economics, politics, history, and in the seemingly endless series of comedy and drama 'repeats' served up to the consuming public by the broadcast media, we do see a pattern of repetition through many aspects of human endeavour. History does seem to repeat itself. Another, slightly hackneyed, proverb is that 'the lesson of history is that we never learn the lessons of history' and so we carry on making the same old mistakes that were made by our grandfathers. In chapter 6 we considered whether Godism is in fact another form of Gnosticism and concluded that Godism does indeed share features of that early heresy. We pause now to consider whether Godism also borrows from the second major heresy encountered by the Christian church – Arianism. At the risk of being repetitive, let us remind ourselves once again of what Godists generally believe, but noting there is divergence of belief: a Godist is someone who believes that there are many paths to 'god' and that no one religion

---

[1]   Ecclesiastes 1:9 – Ecclesiastes is the Old Testament 'philosophical' book that demonstrates the meaninglessness of a world view that does not press beyond the limits of human experience to include God.

holds all the answers'; 'god', whoever 'he' or 'it' is, wants us all to live in harmony: our individual beliefs matter far less than the way that we conduct our lives. Concepts such as sin and salvation if accepted at all, need to be reinterpreted and constantly updated to fit with the complex and diverse world in which we live. Only serious misdemeanors, offences against our fellows when we should observe a 'Golden Rule' of compassion, will achieve God's displeasure.

Godism borrows from Theism, Deism, Monism and Gnosticism, as well as from the so-called 'higher religions'. It is God-centric, to the extent that it believes in a deity or deities which have an emotional interest in the mortal. Some Godists are adherents of particular religions but all are *religion–negative* to the extent that where religion gets in the way of the overall thrust of Godism (and it frequently does!) then the Godist is happy to bypass or trample the religion, which is not allowed to stand in the way of the overall belief.

It does not matter ultimately what you believe about God providing (a) you are sincere and (b) you do not hold your belief with excessive conviction. Something called 'compassion' is the highest virtue and is demonstrated by charitable acts. Godism is (generally) intolerant of exclusionary beliefs held with conviction by the adherents of *the religions*. To that extent Godism is as intolerant as any religion, but Godists purport to be otherwise.

Godists believe they have a heightened perception or truth as compared to the slavish adherents of *the religions* — this is *attained knowledge* rather than revelation.

All the scriptures of the higher religions are tainted, to the extent that either mankind has superimposed his beliefs and agendas onto what 'god' has revealed and/or there have been serious mistranslations of ancient documents.[2] God can be held accountable for the effects of sin in this world

As Godism is a malleable thing, a sort of do it yourself (DIY) religion made up of bits and pieces of the 'higher religions' leading towards an identikit 'god', it is difficult to devise a final definitive statement of what it is. Rather we need to be alert for its inherent characteristics as we encounter it both in religious discourse and in the secular mindset. We can, however, posit this as a sort of pseudo-formula to describe Godism:

Godism is $G + R[N] + RI + AK - TS$ *where*

G = 'god'

$R[n]$ = the 'higher religions' multiplied by $[n]$ being the number of such religions as the Godist is willing to call an authentic religion of 'god'

RI = religious intuition

AK = attained knowledge

TS = tainted scriptures

The Godist belief takes priority. Where the so-called religious 'scriptures' are difficult, or contain embarrassments, or clash with other scriptures, then the Godist simply discounts them. Hence the 'minus TS' in the pseudo-formula above. We can see then that Godism is a veritable Googled belief system with a Googled 'god' — cutting, pasting and amending as seems appropriate. Although it borrows from ancient philosophies, it is postmodern in its willingness to shift ground easily and to ignore inconvenient truths. In conversation with some rather determined Godists, the author mentioned the historical and resurgent plight of

---

[2] Godists might add, aligning themselves with the Dan Brown (The DaVinci Code etc) school of 'theology', various ancient documents may have been suppressed and replaced with other writings.

the Dhimmi[3] peoples as experienced in Muslim majority countries and the plight of the estimated 25,000 shrine prostitutes in Hindu India. Both these inconvenient truths were simply ignored as though they did not exist. How, we may wonder, can such troubling issues be so easily swept under the carpet? The answer seems to be because they challenge (and seemingly cannot be answered) the basic belief that 'god' invented **all** *the religions*, with their beliefs and practices, which are seen as fundamentally 'good' and harmonious. Accordingly, any unanswerable challenge to that 'fundamentalist Godist' view must be ignored and bypassed.

Godism, when viewed from a biblical and traditional Christian perspective, is seen to 'borrow' from specifically Christian heresies. A heresy (from a Christian perspective — noting that *the religions* also have definitions of heresy from their perspectives) is a belief or practice contrary to the orthodox doctrine of the Church.[4] We might go a little further, noting that because there are different Christian denominations that hold sharply differing views, a Christian heresy can be defined as a teaching that is in clear contravention of the specific teachings of the Lord Jesus, or a teaching that is in clear contravention of what the Bible teaches and is widely understood to teach, and/or is a teaching or practice that runs counter to a straightforward understanding of the Apostles' Creed (see below).

---

[3] Historically non-Muslim peoples supposedly 'protected' by Islam. In practice under Shariah their lives became very much those of second class citizens with very few legal protections and the requirement to pay an additional tax called Jizya. The best known history of the Dhimmi peoples is that by Bat Ye'or 'Islam and Dhimmitude' ISBN 0-8386-3942-9 (cloth) 0-8386-3943-7 (pbk), a 500 page history from the earliest days of Islam to the 1980s.

[4] It should be noted that we are not referring to the Eastern Orthodox tradition. By 'orthodox' we mean beliefs that are essentially in agreement with the clear teachings of the Bible and align to broadly mainstream Christian views.

Arius (born circa 250 AD; died 336 AD in Constantinople) was an initially Christian priest in Alexandria (Egypt) whose teachings created a theological system known as Arianism. This affirmed the Christ was not truly divine but a created being. Arius focused on the idea of the uniqueness of God, who alone is immutable (unchangeable) and self-existent. The Son, Arius claimed, is not self-existent and therefore cannot be God. Arius reasoned that the godhead, being unique, cannot be shared or *communicated*, so the Son cannot be God. The godhead is immutable, but the Son who grew and changed must be considered as *mutable* — and therefore cannot be God. Arius further reasoned that the Son must be a creature *created out of nothing* and must therefore have had a beginning, unlike God. The Son is therefore finite and of a different order of existence to the godhead.

Opponents were quick to see where Arius' teachings were heading: they reduce the Son to a demigod (or demiurge — part of the Gnostic philosophy); reintroduce polytheism, since worship of the Son was not abandoned by Arianism; and undermined the fundamental concept of redemption because only He who is truly God can be deemed to reconcile man to the godhead. The controversy seemed to have been brought to an end by the first ecumenical council held in Nicaea (May, AD 325) which condemned Arius and his teachings as heretical after he refused to sign the formula of faith stating that Christ was of the same divine nature as God. Influential support from church leaders in Asia Minor and from Constantina (Emperor Constantine I's daughter) succeeded in effecting Arius' return from exile and his readmission to the church after he agreed to a compromise formula. Shortly before he was to be formally reconciled, however, he collapsed and died whilst walking through the streets of Constantinople. The controversy did not die with him and readers may want to consult a good encyclopedia or history of the early Church to follow the rather sad story. Essentially the heresy collapsed in 381 when the second ecumenical Council was held in Constantinople, when Arianism was once again proscribed.

Although this ended the battle within the Roman empire, Arianism continued amongst some Germanic tribes until the end of the seventh century. Truly there is nothing new under the sun! Today it is noteworthy that some Unitarians are virtually Arian in that they are unwilling either to reduce Christ to a mere human being or to attribute to Him a divine nature identical to that of the Father. The Christology of the Russelites (better known as the Jehovah's Witnesses) is also a form of Arianism. Although sociologists tend to lump together the Russelites and Unitarians as 'Christian' organisations, most of the orthodox church treat their belief systems as heretical and do not consider them to be part of the church. Godism, where held and accepted by church-goers as a philosophy, may not be Arian, as 'Christian Godists' would say that they affirm the Apostle's Creed: they affirm it, but in effect they add to it! So what precisely is the Apostles' Creed, and why do we conclude that 'Christian Godists' manage to affirm it? It is set out below:

I believe in God the Father Almighty, Maker of heaven and earth: And in Jesus Christ his only Son our Lord, Who was conceived by the Holy Ghost, Born of the Virgin Mary, Suffered under Pontius Pilate, Was crucified, dead, and buried, He descended into hell; The third day he rose again from the dead, He ascended into heaven, And sitteth on the right hand of God the Father Almighty; From thence he shall come to judge the quick and the dead.

I believe in the Holy Ghost, the holy Catholick Church; the Communion of Saints; The Forgiveness of sins; The Resurrection of the body, And the life everlasting. Amen.

A 'Christian Godist' would have no difficulty in 'confessing' all the words given above. They would simply rationalise their overall belief that Christianity is only one god-approved faith system and that 'god' loves and affirms them all. This means that all religions can affirm their creeds but Jesus, these particular 'Christian Godists' say, will 'save' all humans via their own religions. Some would add that Jesus remains the true way to God the Father and that religionists will be delighted and surprised when Jesus admits them to heaven! However the challenge reverts to the Godist: as we suggested in the Foreword to this book, if a Labour MP[5] were to consistently sit and vote with the Conservative party there would come a point where the question had to be addressed: is this person truly a *Labourite*? The same challenge is offered to those of Godist persuasion where they are found in Church contexts. As their beliefs borrow so heavily from other religions, and from at least one clear heresy (Gnosticism), at what point do their heterodox views cease to be Christian?

Godism is not Arianism, directly. But since the Arianist view is close to the Muslim view of Christ, and since Godism borrows so heavily from or is enthusiastic about the teachings of *the religions*, there must logically come a point at which a church-based Godist, or a 'Christian Godist',[6] ceases to be in any real sense a Christian, no matter what they think or say.

Differences Between the religions

We promised in Chapter 1 that this book would not be a comparison of religions. However we will spend a few

---

[5] Member of Parliament in the UK

[6] We use this term advisedly. A Godist cannot be a true Christian in the normative sense when we take into account the exclusive claims of Christianity.

moments once again to examine some glaring differences between the world's major *faith systems* as a precursor to querying the Godist idea about the identity of God. The main faith systems in this world, or the 'higher religions' as they are increasingly dubbed, believe markedly different things. Readers may want to look again at the comparisons in chapter 5 where key religious beliefs are listed and summarized. We do at this point need to ask the logical question of all categories of Godist, whether church-based, or of *the religions* or of no-particular religion: does your 'god' have a split personality in that 'he' or 'it' can present himself/itself in such opposing ways? In chapters 6 and 7 we have posited that any 'god' who reveals himself like this could not be truly good, nor truly holy. As Godists generally believe that 'god' is ultimately responsible for sin in this world and is to some extent culpable for its effects, we conclude inevitably that along with 'his' or 'its' lack of goodness and holiness there must be something capricious in this deity. We begin to see that the Godist view of 'god' is in fact rather dismissive and irreverent. Readers may want to look at Appendix 1 to see some of the implications of basic Godist beliefs in a simple *mind-map* format. To argue that there are multiple paths to God quickly suggests, as has been argued earlier in this book, that God could not be good in the sense that we understand that term. Godists believe that their 'god' does not (really) mind about confusion between *the religions* with all the terrible implications that flow. It seems in the *mind-map* diagram at Appendix 1 that whichever path you take, ultimately it ends in a dismissive attitude to the Almighty.

We might again ask ourselves why anyone should want to create a 'god' at variance with the beliefs of all of the key religions in this world, then believe in and claim to follow such a 'god'. In the politically correct West there is a supposed desire not to offend and to 'respect' everyone's beliefs. But this philosophy is not applied even-handedly — there is an increasing willingness to disrespect traditional Christian beliefs, so we may conclude that Western society as a whole is not shy about offending at least some of its members! There really must be a deeper reason why people seem today to be so anxious to have a 'god' whom it is difficult to discern, being comprised of different facets of different religions and belief systems – an identikit 'god'. So just what is that deeper reason? The most likely explanation is that such a 'god' is undemanding. Whilst writing this book the author was told about an interesting debate between a Christian and an acquaintance we will call Jack, who was an adherent of a traditional Christian denomination, but claimed to believe that all religions lead to God. A slightly tongue in cheek challenge was issued to 'Jack' to make up his mind about where he stood, as sitting on the religious fence for your whole life would be a distinctly uncomfortable spiritual experience for anyone! Jack's 'god' proved to be an easily controllable one. 'It' did not make any real demands upon Jack, who continued to lead a mildly hedonistic, Christ averse but 'god' tolerating lifestyle. This was a man who would not under any circumstances claim re-birth! Indeed he was suspicious of anyone who believed in such a notion, and yet he was an occasional church attender! His God was 'in a box' which is just where Jack wanted to keep the Deity. Jack could 'open the box' and access the Deity if things got tough, and keep the box lid tightly shut at all other times.

The challenge issued to Jack went something like that depicted on the next two pages . . . .

'GOD IN A BOX'

Is Jack listening to God? Or is Jack simply justifying his position?

Jack's accusation:

God is incompetent

You cannot get a reliable translation of the Bible — or any other religious book, and you cannot get trustworthy shepherds to look after your flock.

Everything is relative
(there are no absolutes)

Nothing is definite = very convenient!

Since nothing is dependable, Jack cannot be held to account, therefore Jack can do ('what the hell') he wants, providing it is within Jack's personal credo.

= privatised religion
Jack's religion doesn't challenge, doesn't require change, doesn't require re-birth — and it allows Jack to do pretty much what he wants.

God under Jack's thumb

Don't you dare try and get out, or I'll accuse you of misleading people, of allowing lots of (perfectly plausible!) religions to emerge and of damning people out of hand.
Don't you dare try and get out, or I'll crucify you!

Since every translation of every religious scripture has been corrupted, and therefore nothing can be trusted, Jack is free to make up his own credo.

It's a case of 'Heads, Jack wins, tails God loses!'. It is all very, very convenient!

Jack put his faith in the Dan Brown school of 'theology'; religion is a big conspiracy, a few people pull all the strings and religion is the opiate of the people.

Poor, stupid people. Shrewd old Jack!

But Jack is not totally certain, so he continues to curry favour with God ('just in case'). So he attends 'church' occasionally. Jack is hedging his bets!

The financial industry hedge funds hit the buffers in the financial crisis of 2008-9! Religious hedging may not be a good strategy either!

At heaven's 'pearly gates' Jack's defence is going to be: 'I went to church; if it wasn't any good then that's your fault, not mine.

Score: Jack 1 — God 0

'I'm sorry I couldn't trust your Bible; everyone was saying it was wrong so how was I to know? So that's your fault again.'

Score: Jack 2 — God 0

I picked the strongest 'Christian brand'. If it was no good, how was I to know? I'd already dismissed your Bible as unreliable — and I never fancied other churches!

Score: Jack 3 — God 0

All the religions looked OK to me — or at least all as bad as each other. If they weren't real then you should have done something about it. So it's your fault.

Score: Jack 4 — God 0

I lived my life as best I could. I sang the Frank Sinatra hymn 'I did it my way'!

BUT Jack still has the empty cross to contend with. Jack still has the empty tomb to contend with.
See Revelation 1:16.
The risen Lord Jesus when we next meet Him will be Jesus the judge, not 'gentle Jesus, meek and mild'.

The big question is: will Jack's defence stand up in the court of heaven? Does Jack believe in God or not? Is Jack simply hiding?

Jack must finally decide — and then declare just what sort of God he believes in.

Whilst this character 'Jack' may be an unusually cynical church attender, his beliefs may not actually be so far from the beliefs of the 'average' man-in-the-street who, having thought for a few moments will declare that 'all the religions follow the same "god" and what you have got to do is lead the best life you can, being compassionate where you can. The Almighty will be satisfied with that!' It is precisely this sort of a 'god' that makes no (serious) demands and leaves us to get on with our lives more or less as we want to. Troublesome moral restrictions will be overlooked by this sort of 'god' and if we have got any of our 'theology' wrong, then this 'god' will see us all right in the end!

But is 'god' a split-identity as many seem to (want to) believe? Is such a 'god' a comfort-blanket rather than a consuming fire? [7] Such a 'god' may seem to be consoling for a while, but we ought to echo the Old Testament character Job who demanded from his so-called comforters **"How then can you comfort me with empty words, since falsehood remains in your answers?"** (Job 21:34, NKJV) Where churchmen, especially church leaders, teach about a 'god of *the religions*' are they in reality consoling us with nonsense (in the words of the NIV) or empty words (in the NKJV translation)? We have noted elsewhere that Godists rely ultimately on a sort of *religious intuition*. Godists think they can 'see' things that are hidden from the singular adherents of the various religions. Godists have a special knowledge or *gnosis* of these things; they are perhaps, wise in their own eyes. But the apostle Paul in his first letter to the Corinthians poured scorn on what the world considers to be wisdom. We do well to listen to him: **Where is the wise man? Where is the scholar? Where is the philosopher of**

---

[7] See Hebrews 12:29.

this age? Has not God made foolish the wisdom of the world? For since in the wisdom of God the world through its wisdom did not know him, God was pleased through the foolishness of what was preached to save those who believe. Jews demand miraculous signs and Greeks look for wisdom, but we preach Christ crucified: a stumbling block to Jews and foolishness to Gentiles, but to those whom God has called, both Jews and Greeks, Christ the power of God and the wisdom of God. For the foolishness of God is wiser than man's wisdom, and the weakness of God is stronger than man's strength. (1 Corinthians 1:20–25, NIV)

The consistency and cohesion of God's personality

A convenient god or even a *convenience* god, that is a 'god' who reveals Himself to different audiences in totally different ways ('and to hell with the consequences'!) might fairly be accused of having a split personality. We have already reviewed whether such a 'god' could be called good and holy by the yardstick of the Holy Bible, and concluded that the answer to both questions is a resounding 'no'. If people really want to invent and believe in a 'god' that behaves in such a manner then, at the end of the day, that must be their own affair. We should take a few moments however, in concluding this chapter, to ask whether God as revealed in the Holy Bible can be accused of having a split identity – in other words *is* there any justification from the pages of the Bible in saying that God actually behaves as the Godists accuse Him of behaving?

We noted earlier in this book that some critics of Christianity accuse the Old Testament revelation of God as representing the 'harsh' face of God, and the New Testament of representing the 'nice' God that we all want to follow today. But as we looked in earlier chapters at God's holiness and at His goodness we began to see even in some of the superficially 'harsh' commands of God, the fundamental compassion and goodness of God, and His overriding concern for the weak and the defenceless, as well as His opposition to the overweening power of the world's rich and powerful who all too often abuse their positions of influence and who oppress the weak. The author prefers increasingly to consider the Old Testament as *the promise* (of the Messiah) and the New Testament as *the promise fulfilled* (in the person and work of the Lord Jesus). As we consider the increasingly insistent promise of a Saviour to come, and at the reality of that Saviour when finally He arrived and had His earthly ministry among us, we see a real consistency at work. At its most basic, God always had in mind to provide a Saviour to all who would receive Him, not just to the chosen Hebrew people.[8] But God decided that He would represent Himself first in His chosen people, then in the Law, and finally in His Son, the fulfilment of that Law. God's manifesto, we might say, was set out definitively in the Ten Commandments (see chapter 3). God established an agreement — or a covenant — with the Jewish people[9] but promised from earliest of times that one day that covenant would be expanded to cover all peoples. In this regard, readers are directed to Isaiah chapter 56 and its first 8 verses. The context of this passage is that God has in the previous chapter issued an invitation to all who are hungry and thirsty (for Him) because He will satisfy them: **Listen carefully to Me, and eat what is good, and let your soul delight itself in abundance.** (Isaiah 55:2, NKJV)

---

[8]   See for example Romans chapter 9.

[9] God's covenant with Abraham is recounted in Genesis chapter 15 and Genesis chapter 17. It is further formalised in Deuteronomy Chapter 28.

Having listened to God, they will go away fully satisfied, as this picturesque language shows:

For you shall go out with joy,
and be led out with peace;
the mountains and the hills
shall break forth into singing before you,
and all the trees of the field shall
clap their hands.

(Isaiah 55:12, NKJV)

This promise, it should be noted, is made to the chosen, Hebrew, people. But it will be extended to cover all mankind, as we discover in the following chapter:

Thus says the LORD:
"Keep justice, and do righteousness,
For My salvation is about to come,
and My righteousness to be revealed."
Blessed is the man who does this,
and the son of man who lays hold on it;
who keeps from defiling the Sabbath,
and keeps his hand from doing any evil."
Do not let the son of the foreigner
who has joined himself to the LORD
speak, saying,
"The LORD has utterly separated me from His
people";
nor let the eunuch say,
"Here I am, a dry tree."
For thus says the LORD:
"To the eunuchs who keep My Sabbaths,
and choose what pleases Me,
and hold fast My covenant,
even to them I will give in My house

and within My walls a place and a name
better than that of sons and daughters;
I will give them an everlasting name
that shall not be cut off.

"Also the sons of the foreigner
who join themselves to the LORD, to serve Him,
and to love the name of the LORD, to be His
servants—
everyone who keeps from defiling the Sabbath,
and holds fast My covenant—
even them I will bring to My holy mountain,
and make them joyful in My house of prayer.
their burnt offerings and their sacrifices
will be accepted on My altar;
for My house shall be called a house of prayer for all
nations."
The Lord GOD, who gathers the outcasts of Israel,
says,
"Yet I will gather to him
Others besides those who are gathered to him."
(Isaiah 56:1–8, NKJV)

This is an important prophecy: it promises that salvation in
the broadest sense is not reserved solely for Jewish people.
Godists may take this passage and try to reinterpret it to
mean that all 'religionists' who keep God's laws will be
saved by Him, and/or that He will accept their personal
efforts as a sufficient basis on which an eternal relationship
with Him can be built. If they do so, they are building a
huge 'theology' on a perilously narrow base. What the
passage *does* clearly state is that in the future God intends
to build a relationship with those who are not Jewish but

who nevertheless do truly follow Him. Christians see this as fulfilled precisely and without equivocation in the promise that to all who follow the Lord Jesus, salvation will be assured (John 3:15 in particular, but John 3:1–21 is relevant). We immediately need to add that mere belief in Jesus is not what God has in mind here — after all, even the devil believes in Jesus! So this is a belief which completely transforms and enables Jesus to present such believers before God not only as His disciples, not only as people who have conscientiously tried to live good lives in His power, but also as people who are holy! This is a difficult thing to grasp so we will return to it later in chapter 10. Rather than try to do a detailed examination of the Old and New Testaments, to show the unity between them, which would be better served by a different sort of book, we will simply posit the view that God's personality as revealed in the two Testaments is not split, but is in perfect harmony. So, to look at the key attributes of God that we glanced at in chapter 2, we list them in the table below, which indicates that beautiful harmony and consistency:

GOD'S INNER HARMONY

God's attribute revealed	Old Testament	New Testament
One and only	Is 44:6	Gal 3:15-20
Unchangeable	Mal 3:6	Jas 1:17
Invisible	Deut 4:12	Col 1:15
		Jn 5:37
Infinite	1 Kgs 8:27	Eph 3:18-19
Holy	Is 6:3	1 Pet 1:15-16
Unity	Deut 6:4	Gal 3:20 (& v.16)
		1 Tim 2:5, Jas 2:19
Father, Son and Spirit	Gen 1:26; Is 9:6	Matt 28:19 (name, not names!)
		2 Cor 13-14
		Heb 1:8, 1 Pet 1:2

Eternal pre-existence	Gen 1:1, Dan 7:9, 13, 22	Jn 1:1,1 Jn 1:1
Wisdom	Prov 3:3 Prov 4 (all)	1 Cor 1:25
Sovereignty	Ps 24:1	Rev 6:10
Immensity	Ps 139:7-12	2 Pet 1:3
Independence	Ex 3:14 (I AM)	Jn 8:58
Spirituality	Gen 1:1-2	Lk 1:35, Rom 15:19
Omnipotence	Job 42:2 Gen 18:14	Matt 19:26
Truthfulness	Num 23:19	Jn 14:6
Love	Gen 34:6 Ps 136 (all)	Jn 3:16, 1 Jn 3:11-18 1 Jn 4:8

It is important to state that the texts above are *not* proof-positive of the key claims they make and the author does not expect the reader to accept them slavishly as such. However it is difficult to argue, as Godists seem to, that God's personality is in some way split so that He has to reveal Himself (or has chosen to reveal Himself) in diametrically opposed ways in the various religions. The passages cited here do at least suggest — and this author would claim, suggest beyond reasonable contradiction — that God as revealed in both Old and New Testaments of the Holy Bible is entirely self-consistent. Rather it is for the Godists to prove the point that they are making (whether they acknowledge it or not — and many of them will not!) that 'god' has in fact contradicted Himself by His supposed employment of multiple, fractured and inconsistent 'revelations' (and indeed to prove their claim beyond reasonable doubt).

9

JESUS

Jesus the Messiah

Christians tend to have long memories! We honour the apostles of the New Testament, the prophets of the Old, the church fathers in the early church period, and various notables since: Martin Luther, John Calvin, Charles Spurgeon, Corrie Ten Boom and so on. So it is that Christians read and enjoy, and find valuable books and teaching published perhaps hundreds of years earlier. So literary classics, such as John Bunyan's *Pilgrims Progress*, originally published in 1678, are books still sought by serious Christians as helpful in their own pilgrimage. The author finds Alfred Edersheim's[1] *The Life and Times of Jesus The Messiah*, first published in 1883 to be a useful reference. Written by a Messianic Jew (a Jewish believer in the Lord Jesus) and a man with a truly encyclopedic knowledge of ancient Jewish writings, as well as the Christian Scriptures, Edersheim's book remains generally available today.[2] In

---

[1] Alfred Edersheim (1825-1889) was born in Vienna to Jewish parents. Converted to Christianity as a young man whilst studying in England. He studies theology in Edinburgh and Berlin, and was one of the leading authorities of his time regarding the doctrines and practices of Judaism in the centuries preceding and during the early Christian era.

[2] Republished in 1993 by Hendrickson Publishers Inc, ISBN: 0-943575-83-4.

more than 1,100 pages it traces the background to the New Testament and gives a real sense of the times of Jesus — political, cultural, economic and historical. Edersheim makes the valuable observation that there are in excess of 900 messianic prophecies in the Old Testament. In other words, prophecies that point towards the coming Jewish Messiah, who was always identified also as *the* Saviour, and whom Christians readily recognize as Jesus, their Lord. Appendix 9 to Edersheim's book lists some hundreds of these prophecies. The author has found it both helpful and genuinely exciting to simply mark in his own Bible all references to the future Messiah. Often we find several such prophecies on a single page in the Old Testament, as well as entire chapters that are exclusively Messianic.[3] After a while a diligent student will become attuned to spotting these prophecies and develop a sense of what to look out for. Christians reading this book who have never tried this exercise may want to prayerfully ask the Holy Spirit to open their eyes to perceive such prophecies as they read the Old Testament. The pay-off in this exercise (if we may put it so prosaically!) is that the Christian's confidence in the truthfulness and accuracy of the Bible will be increased, as well as gaining a heightened assurance that the as-yet unfulfilled prophecies will also come to pass.

So what is a prophet and why is this of interest in our exploration of the *empty promise* of Godism? As so often in this book, we find that a challenge must revert to the Godist to give their understanding of the role and limits of prophets and prophecy. This is particularly relevant as Godists usually find they are on difficult ground in determining which prophets they consider to be genuine and which false. So

---

[3] For example, Isaiah chapter 53 which foretells the crucifixion of Jesus.

Godists will generally say that they consider the prophets of the so-called higher religions are genuine, but others very often are written off as false or mistaken. So Mohammed the founder of Islam is considered by them to be a prophet, whereas Joseph Smith the founder of the Mormon religion is not considered to be the genuine article, despite the fact that the lives of Mohammed and Joseph Smith display striking similarities — a matter of simple historical record. Since the Holy Bible tells us of the existence of false as well as genuine prophets (see for example Jeremiah chapters 26 and 28 and Ezekiel 13), we note that it is important to make a distinction between the genuine and the false. If we fail to make that distinction then like many Israelites of old, we risk being led astray. Indeed the New Testament contains a significant number of warnings about a time when false religious teachers will hold sway within society and that this will infect even the Church. The Lord Jesus Himself warned that 'many' deceivers would come masquerading in His name (Matthew 24:5) and that this would be a feature especially towards the end of time, when 'many false prophets' will appear and 'deceive many people' (Matthew 24:11) and that 'many' will turn away from the faith (v. 10). These are sober warnings indeed. As the Lord Jesus made them we are bound, if we are Christians, to take them seriously and to meditate upon them. Readers who want a clearer picture of the world in the end times may want to read the entirety of Matthew chapter 24. Jesus speaks of the love of 'most' growing cold at that time — and when He says this, the context seems primarily to be a reference to the Church rather than to society as whole, which elsewhere He tells us will by then have been fractured beyond repair. The apostle Paul in writing to Timothy his 'dear son' also warns that a time will come **when men will not put up with**

sound doctrine. Instead, to suit their own desires, they will gather around them a great number of teachers to say what their itching ears want to hear. (2 Timothy 4:3). Paul goes on to say that these people will turn away from truth 'and turn aside to myths'. Although there have always been times when the church has faced heresy and demonic assault, it should be a matter of concern that in the early twenty-first century we do seem to see exactly this scenario being played out. So governments and societal leaders gather about them in our own day 'teachers' who tell them that there are many paths to 'god' and that the future lies in the multi-faith agenda. Covered by the fig-leaf of societal cohesion and the desire to be tolerant of all, politicians and 'religious leaders' are at last finding that they can be rid of the 'irksome' and exclusive demands of the Lord Jesus — and of Christianity.

What are the biblical marks of a true prophet, then? Several criteria are set out in the Holy Bible in order to evaluate prophecy and prophets: (1) prophecy must be in continuity with the customs and traditions of Israel as enshrined in the Torah (Deuteronomy 13:1–5; 18:20; cf Romans 12:6); (2) the prophet must speak only that which the Lord commands (Deuteronomy 18:20); and (3) true prophecy will be historically verified (Deuteronomy 18: 21–22; Jeremiah 28:8–9). The author well remembers a wide-eyed and innocent new Christian inviting him to come and hear a foreign speaker to whom her church (one of the smaller house churches) had accorded the status of true prophet, on a par with the prophets of old. I duly went and listened to the gentleman. He said nothing out of the ordinary and appeared to be a sound Christian. However it is impossible for Christians to speak of there being current-day prophets. The era of the prophets is gone. As the apostle Paul reminded the early church (Ephesians 2:20 in particular, but see verses 11 to 22 to acquire the context in which Paul made the assertion) God's household is 'built' upon **the foundation of the apostles and prophets, with Christ Jesus himself as the chief cornerstone**. The era of prophets ended with those in the Old Testament who continued to prophesy about the coming future Messiah. Their role was completed by the apostles and the chief cornerstone, Jesus Christ. The church is built upon foundations already laid. There is no biblical idea of further foundations to be laid, as though we are to build an 'extension' or 'extensions' to the house of God, although this seems to be precisely the position of the determined Godist. The generic subjects of apostleship and of prophecy and prophets is outside the scope of this book, and there is plenty of good material for readers who want to explore these in greater depth. We will leave the subject with this thought: has God sent new prophets? If yes, how do they meet the criteria already set out in the Scriptures? And when will He stop sending these additional prophets — are we to expect more in the future? Or has God been true to His Word, quite literally, in sending prophets to point the way to the Messiah, and concluding that era of prophets with the apostles of the early church? Those who believe in post-apostolic prophets and prophecies will surely find themselves easily led. And one day there will appear an Antichrist who will be so powerful and compelling that he will threaten to lead astray **even the elect, if that were possible** (Matthew 24:24; and see also Mark 13:22). Godists will find themselves especially vulnerable when this prophecy is fulfilled.

Throughout this book we have assumed a certain minimum level of understanding among readers about both Jesus and His role as Messiah. Today both assumptions are dangerous. In what is increasingly a post-Christian culture in the western world, and with education arguably dumbed-down, religious concepts that a reasonably educated person just two generations ago would readily have understood (as a reflection of their basic education) are today largely unknown, as biblical questions in Britain's popular TV quiz show *University Challenge* attests. In this TV show highly educated students from some of the world's top universities reveal themselves to be completely ignorant of the Bible. It is in this ground of general biblical ignorance that Godism as a philosophy finds it so easy to take root. As there will be readers who struggle with the idea of Jesus as Messiah, or indeed may have never encountered this concept, we owe them at least a short exposition of what Christianity is all about.[4]

Yeshua was a common name among Jews of the Second Temple Period, and is believed to be the Hebrew or Aramaic name for Jesus. In modern Hebrew, *Yeshu* and *Yeshua* are in fact the common transcriptions for Jesus. The understanding that this pronunciation and Hebrew spelling accurately represent the original and historic name of the man we now know almost universally in the English speaking world as Jesus remains the subject of some scholarly debate, but the normative view today is that Yeshua is the correct original Hebrew rendering of that name. Messiah is a title derived from Hebrew *mashiach*, a verbal adjective meaning anointed one. Along with its New Testament Greek equivalent *christos* (Christ) it refers to an act of consecration where an individual is set apart to serve God and anointed

---

[4] Some material in this chapter is borrowed from *The Birth of Christ* (Glory to Glory Publications, ISBN 0-9551790-1-7) by Peter Sammons. Readers who want to get an understanding of the birth narratives of Jesus and why Christians consider them to be reliable, as well as a more detailed appreciation of what the author calls *salvation history*, may want to consult this book.

(smeared or sprinkled) with oil.

Jewish hope for the advent of the Messiah developed from David's reign when it was prophesied that his kingdom would continue until the end of time (2 Samuel 7:16). Israel was told that, through David's descendants, his throne would exert a never ending dominion over all the earth (2 Samuel 22:48 – 51; also Jeremiah 33). The New Testament writers discern that He who is the child of supernatural origins (Isaiah 7:14; Micah 5:2) carries the full weight of divinity (Isaiah 9:6; Philippians 2:6; Colossians 1:19) and is both Son of God and worthy to receive the worship of all men (Palm 45:6–7; cf Hebrews 1:8–9). Jesus, fully aware of the messianic focus of Scripture (John 5:46; 8:56) acknowledged Himself to be *the Christ* on numerous occasions. He accepted the title from the crowds on what we think of as Palm Sunday during the triumphal entry into Jerusalem (Matthew 21:9), from blind Bartimeus (Mark 10:46–48), from the children in the Temple (Matthew 21:15) and in other situations as well — see Matthew 16:16 – 18; Mark 14:61–2; Luke 4:21; John 4:25–6. Jesus warned His disciples not to advertise His miraculous acts as those of the Messiah prior to His resurrection (Matthew 17:9; Luke 9:20–21). As Jesus knew that the popular and faulty idea was of a military styled Messiah who would become a political saviour, Jesus avoided the use of the term Messiah and instead used the title Son of Man, which is taken from the prophet Daniel's vision of a heavenly conqueror (Daniel 7:13–14). Jesus consistently employed this less well known title and endued it with the true character of messianic salvation. We now pause to explore some basic Christian theology about God's overall plan of salvation for mankind.

Stages in God's plan of Salvation

It is impossible to appreciate the full meaning of Jesus without recognising that His entry into the world, His subsequent life, death and resurrection from the dead are part of an overall scheme devised by God to remedy human kind's state of enmity with and rebellion against God. The relationship of humans to their God is 'fallen' from the intended state of close friendship and spiritual intimacy so clearly described in the early chapters of Genesis. This condition is usually described by theologians as 'the fall'. The Bible explains that a state of sin separates us from God and spoils our relationship with Him. The Bible teaches that the fall of Satan, an archangel, with certain other angels, took place before the world was created. Jesus himself (probably) referred to this fall in Luke 10:18 — **"I saw Satan fall like lightning from heaven."** A fascinating glimpse of the battle in heaven that preceded Satan's expulsion is found in Revelation 12:7–12. Jesus referred to Satan's character in John 8:44: **"He was a murderer from the beginning, not holding to the truth, for there is no truth in him."** It seems that Satan and other rebel angels, thrown out of heaven, sought to obtain possession of the world shortly after its creation and similar possession of mankind,[5] which had been created for special and intimate fellowship with God. In order to hurt God and to gain a measure of temporary control over His world, Satan induced mankind to rebel against God (or to 'sin'), as set out in Genesis chapter 3, which led to humans becoming *spiritually fallen* beings, their previous intimate and loving relationship with God being replaced by fear and shame.

Whether Genesis chapter 3 is accepted as literal or

---

[5] The Bible always refers to humankind as mankind. We follow this practice.

allegorical, the essential reality portrayed in the Bible remains: humans *are* alienated from a God of love and holiness. Mankind's 'natural' spiritual state is dead, rather than alive. Man's innermost being (or soul) is blinded and perverted from what it was intended to be and our physical body is liable to disease and death. Most importantly, the moral disease of sin (or rebellion against God) is ever-present in the very bloodstream of the human race. So it was that mankind passed under the usurped and limited control of Satan (e.g. see Acts 26:18; Colossians 1:13; Hebrews 2:14). Certainly our broken and often disastrously flawed human relationships, whether they are between individuals, groups or nations, seem to confirm that there is something badly wrong with mankind.

Living, as we do, in an age where self-promotion and self-fulfilment are considered to represent the highest expression of human life, some readers may complain that sin — falling short of God's standards, even rebellion against God — cannot be so serious as to make a full relationship with Him impossible. Among the world's religions only Christianity teaches that sin is serious — so serious that we cannot remedy it ourselves and need to be saved from its power and its effects. It is fair to say that most religions teach that people work and earn their way to a 'right' relationship with God by observing religious ceremonies and by doing things that will appease God. This, emphatically, is not the Christian message. The Bible teaches that sin is so bad that God will not tolerate it at all. He is completely holy and completely righteous. That is how we need to be if we are to have a right relationship with Him. Since we cannot make ourselves holy and righteous, a complete and effective remedy to our condition as *spiritually fallen beings* is necessary. Two things need to be kept in mind:

1. We are all sinful (Romans 3:23)
2. Sin is not just the awful things we easily recognise as sin (e.g. murder, robbery, violence). It is, equally, all the rebellions we have against God's right to be God in our lives. Sin, then, can be simply ignoring God.

Isn't it completely overbearing of God to be so hard on sin? To answer that question we might consider that if sin is not as serious as the Bible tells us it is, God would have found a simpler and less costly way of dealing with it than the way the Bible tells us He decided upon. This way ultimately involved the sacrifice of His Son on a cross of execution — a humiliating, disgraceful, torturous form of death, borne by the one person in history who was without sin.

In order to rescue humans from the power, grip and guilt of sin, to fully restore us to our former position which was lost in the Garden of Eden, and indeed to elevate us to a yet higher position (that of being adopted as children of God[6]) God determined on a plan of salvation. But this plan would be immensely costly because, as the apostle Paul wrote **the wages of sin is death, but the gift of God is eternal life in Christ Jesus our Lord** (Romans 6:23). It was the Lord Jesus who was to pay the price. As the apostle Paul again wrote: **For if, when we were God's enemies, we were reconciled to him through the death of his Son, how much more, having been reconciled, shall we be saved through his life!** (Romans 5:10). The baby born in Bethlehem in 6 to 5 B.C. was born to achieve God's plan of salvation.

Did God make a mistake in allowing the fall of mankind to occur? Did He know it was going to happen and if He did,

---

[6] There are a number of references in the Bible to our adoption as children — e.g. see Ephesians 1:5–7 and Romans 8:15–17.

is He not at least partly responsible for the effects of sin in His world? The Bible does not give us a clear answer as to why God allowed sin to enter His world, but He certainly went to extraordinarily costly lengths to provide for all people an escape route *from* the power and consequences of sin *to* the safety of kinship with His Son. A former Principal of the Birmingham Bible Institute in the UK, H. Brash Bonsall, examined this difficult question in his excellent study book *The Person of Christ*:

'While it is plain from Scripture that God *foreknew* that the Fall of Man would occur, it must never be thought that he *foreordained* it. This would be to regard God as the author of sin, and as morally responsible for the effects of it. He *foreknew* the Fall; but He *foreordained* Redemption. The difference between the two words may be made clear by an illustration. Some years ago the Perth to London express train was travelling near the Boxmoor Tunnel at 70 m.p.h. just before the diversion from the fast to the slow line. These points should have been taken at 15 m.p.h.. The train consequently left the rails and plunged over the embankment. As a result over forty people lost their lives. At the enquiry the signalman stated that he observed the train running too rapidly for safety and testified "*I saw it would happen.*" He *foreknew* there would be a train wreck but he did not foreordain it, indeed he did all in his power to avert it. It was so with God in relation to the Fall of Man. Why He did not prevent it is a problem which the Bible does not explain. We can only take the facts as we find them and as the Bible states them to be — that is, that God's creature, man, has fallen and that he has been redeemed. Until we have clearer light we must trust where we cannot trace.'[7]

[7]   *The Person of Christ*, H. Brash Bonsall, Christian Literature Crusade (1967) p. 22

God's plan of salvation is also referred to as a plan of redemption. When the word 'redemption' or 'redeemed' is used in every day life, it indicates that something has been bought back, or regained by payment of money or by effort. In the theological context, the word 'redeem' refers to God 'buying-back' mankind, by paying the price necessitated by sin in order to return mankind to a right relationship with Himself. The Bible is certain about the fact, the process and the extent of redemption, as the following four quotations make clear:

But now he [Christ] **has appeared once for all at the end of the ages to do away with sin by the sacrifice of himself. Just as man is destined to die once, and after that to face judgement, so Christ was sacrificed once to take away the sins of many people; and he will appear a second time, not to bear sin, but to bring salvation to those who are waiting for him.** (Hebrews 9:26–28)

For he rescued us from the dominion of darkness and brought us into the kingdom of the Son he loves, in whom we have redemption, the forgiveness of sins. (Colossians 1:13)

He [Jesus Christ] **is the atoning sacrifice for our sins, and not only for ours but also for the sins of the whole world.** (1 John 2:2)

. . . if you confess with your mouth, "Jesus is Lord" and believe in your heart that God raised him from the dead, you will be saved. (Rom 10:9)

Christ, then, swapped places with us and paid on our behalf the price of our rebellion against God. We have something to do (confess Jesus is Lord — which action has as much to do with true belief in Him and acceptance of His right to be Lord of every aspect of our lives as it does with using a certain form of words as some religious mantra) and God guarantees that Christ's death in our place is *the* necessary atoning sacrifice, sufficient for the needs of the whole world. The various stages in God's redemptive plan can be described as:

Christ's Incarnation
Christ's redeeming death
Christ's Resurrection from the dead
Christ's Ascension, and His ministry from heaven on behalf of His people
Christ's future return in glory

The Incarnation was an event in history, which began when a baby was born in humble circumstances in Bethlehem some two thousand years ago. The baby grew quite normally to become a man who lived in the world for a total of around thirty-three years. But what of this idea of 'Incarnation'? What exactly does it convey? The term *Incarnation* comes from two Latin words *in*, 'in' and *caro*, 'flesh' and means the doctrine that at a given point in time God took upon Himself human flesh and, with it, human nature. What makes the Lord Jesus distinct from all other human beings, both before and since, is that He was without sin. He never sinned or in any way rebelled against God. He only is good enough to pay the 'wages' of sin — death. How do we know that Jesus was without sin and that therefore His death is completely adequate payment for our sins? Two answers help us here; first, there is nothing in the accounts that we have of the life of Jesus that looks remotely like rebellion against God. Everywhere the opposite is evident — that the Lord Jesus submitted Himself entirely to His Father's will. **"Yet not as I will, but as you will"** (Matthew 26:39) was more than simply a statement of His priorities,

211

it was in every sense the reality at the centre of His being. Second, the Bible itself makes clear that He was without sin: **But you know that he appeared so that he might take away our sins. And in him is no sin** (1 John 3:5–6).

Who Paid the Price? The Baby Born to Die

Staying with the theological aspects of Christ's Incarnation a little longer, we see that the Incarnation — God becoming flesh — is an essential factor in order for God to secure the redemption of mankind. Whilst there are many facets to this doctrine of the Incarnation, in relation to the birth of the Lord Jesus, three are particularly important:

Firstly, *Christ was born to die*. Redemption involves a substitutionary death — someone dying in the place of the guilty one. God the Father cannot die, but Man can. Only if the Son became a man could he die. In this sense the Lord Jesus was 'born to die' as is emphasised in Hebrews 2:9 — **we see Jesus, who was made a little lower than the angels, now crowned with glory and honour because he suffered death, so that by the grace of God he might taste death for everyone**.

It should be noted that there is something in the death of the Lord Jesus which will never be experienced by His children (i.e. those adopted into His family as made clear in Hebrews 2:9–13). When we die, even if we think or feel we are forsaken, God will be there — having promised never to leave or forsake us. But when Christ died, the Father's presence was withdrawn from the Son because He who was without sin was made sin for us (2 Corinthians 5:21). And this separation from God is the ultimate penalty for sin - no wonder Jesus called out from the cross **"My God, my God, why have you forsaken me?"** (Matthew 27:46).

Secondly, *God the Father cannot represent man in*

sacrifice, only a man can do that. The Lord Jesus became a man so that He could, on behalf of all mankind, offer His life. In Romans 5:12–21 Paul writes about the representative nature of Adam's and Christ's acts, the first in bringing sin into the world, the second in providing the gift of righteousness. **If, by the trespass of the one man [Adam] death reigned through that one man, how much more will those who receive God's abundant provision of grace and of the gift of righteousness reign in life through the one man, Jesus Christ.** Because only a man could represent mankind, so it was necessary for a baby to be born into the world, who would become that representative.

Thirdly, *Christ's redemption covers all mankind* — everyone who ever lived — not just those who are saved by accepting His free gift of salvation. This means that the price is paid, but that the free gift of salvation still has to be accepted by each individual. To underline that Christ's redemption is *for all*, we recall that John the baptist said **"Look, the lamb of God, who takes away the sins of the world!" (John 1:29).** Reference to 'the world' in Scripture, and especially in the apostle John's writings, means the whole mass of mankind, loved by God (see John 3:16) and able to be saved, but at present under the domination of the 'prince of this world' — the devil (John 14:30). The Lord Jesus, as God's sacrificial Lamb, is, in John's words, **"the atoning sacrifice for our sins, and not only for ours but also for the sins of the whole world."** (1 John 2:2).

On this latter point of Christ's redemption covering all mankind, for clarity and to avoid any misunderstanding it should also be noted that this redemption is not automatic — in other words not everyone is saved. Such a belief is mistakenly taught by some both within the umbrella of the Christian church and also beyond the church. The idea is that everyone will be saved and made right with God — a superficially attractive idea but one which is dangerous in the sense that it denies God His right (and duty) to see justice done and one which runs counter to the clear teaching of the Bible on this issue. H. Brash Bonsall in *The Person of Christ* casts some light on this:

'The Bible says **"Return to me; for I have redeemed thee"** (Isaiah 44:22). One may be redeemed, but if the conditions of repentance and faith are not fulfilled, if the offer is not closed with, the redemption is without effect. Thus a cancer remedy might be discovered and offered free to all, but not all would thereby be saved. Some would never hear, some would hear and not believe, some would hear and believe but not actually take the remedy; all would die. Only those who, hearing, believed and by an *act* of faith actually took the remedy, would live. James 2:14-16 defines faith as more than an intellectual assent; it is a belief which acts. . . . .)'[8]

The prophet Isaiah provides a clue that it will be a *person* who would be needed to pay the price. And this person would go willingly to be the substitute for the sin — offering.

Sacrifice and offering you did not desire,
But a body you have prepared for me,
burnt offerings and sin offerings you did not require.
Then I said, "Here am I, I have come — it is written
about me in the scroll.
I desire to do your will, O my God;
your law is within my heart."

(Isaiah 40:6–8)

---

[8] *The Person of Christ*, H. Brash Bonsall, Christian Literature Crusade (1967 — p56)

No longer would God be satisfied with symbolic sacrifices of animals in the Temple. The days of the Jerusalem Temple were numbered, in any case. In a few years it would no longer be possible for the priests to sacrifice animals on behalf of the people.[9] Now a permanent and all-sufficient sacrifice was needed, and so God prepared a body of flesh for his Son. The sacrifice was to be made by God Himself, through the person of His Son.

Jesus the Saviour

This title of Jesus, amongst so many titles found in the pages of the New Testament, is one of the most profound. Jesus entered a world where salvation was the deepest desire in the hearts of ordinary men and women. This was a time of immense cruelty of man to man — and particularly, of leaders to their people. There can seldom have been a time of such political insecurity. It was a time of tyrannical rulers who could do what they liked and do it to anyone. The crimes of Herod 'the Great' were so enormous that the slaughter of the babies in Bethlehem (in Herod's vain attempt to kill the infant Jesus) was scarcely seen as abnormal. In the Jewish historian Josephus' works, written a few years after the time of Christ, the slaughter of the little boys is not even mentioned, which some have taken to mean that it never happened, but more probably was simply an indication that this sort of behaviour towards ordinary people was not unusual.

This was an age of informers, where no one, especially in the courts of the kings and emperors, could live in security. The ancient 'gods' were on their way out. 'It was not' writes William Barclay 'a case of men becoming so

---

[9] The Temple was destroyed in AD70 by the Romans during the 'Jewish War'.

depraved that they abandoned their gods; it was a case of the gods becoming so depraved that they were abandoned by men.'[10] The old gods were going and there was nothing to take their place except the worship of rulers, who were as depraved as their 'gods'. It was a time of superstition, when demons were seen to be everywhere waiting to injure men — indeed the number of references to Jesus casting out demons suggests this may indeed have been so. It was a time of astralism, men believing that their fate was sealed by the stars under which they were born. This in turn led to fatalism and hopelessness, a return to which we are perhaps seeing at the beginning of the twenty first century. There was a consciousness of moral failure and moral helplessness — men knew they were sinners but knew no cure for sin. Small wonder, then, that they were searching for a Saviour. The very title 'Saviour' was prevalent at the time — any king, or even pretender to a throne, who could bring a measure of peace and security was often called a 'Saviour'.

God, in the Old Testament, is often identified as Saviour, as a short list of references will illustrate: Isaiah 45:15, 21; Deuteronomy 32:15; 1 Samuel 10:19; Psalm 24:5; 27:9; 65:5; 79:9; 85:4−9; Micah 7:7; Habakkuk 3:18. The Old Testament points towards a state of salvation when God will enter His Kingdom and reign. Having seen the yearning for salvation in the predominantly pagan world into which Jesus was born, we see the word 'Saviour' in the New Testament also applied to God: In Mary's song: **"My spirit rejoices in God my Saviour"** (Luke 1:47); Paul is an apostle by command of God our Saviour (1 Timothy 1:1); God our Saviour desires all men to be saved (1 Timothy 2:3); The living God is the Saviour of all men, especially

---

[10] *Jesus As They Saw Him* - William Barclay - SCM Press Ltd - 1962

those who believe (1 Timothy 4:10); Paul's preaching has been entrusted to him by the command of God our Saviour (Titus 1:3); Everything is to be done in such a way as to adorn the teaching of God our Saviour (Titus 2:10); In Christ there appeared the goodness and loving kindness of God our Saviour (Titus 3:4); In Jude the object of praise is the only God our Saviour (Jude 25)

Now this is an important truth to grasp: in working out God's plan of salvation, there is no tension between the stern wrath of God and the love of Jesus. It was not a case of Jesus doing something to alter the attitude of God to men, to convert the wrath of God into the love of God, or to persuade God to stay His hand, outstretched to punish. God is the Saviour God; Jesus did not live and die to change the attitude of God to men, rather he lived and died to show what that attitude is.

The Lord Jesus, also, is titled Saviour in the New Testament. The message of the angel Gabriel was that He was to be called Jesus, the Greek form of Yeshua, which means 'Jehovah is salvation'. Jesus was given this name, said Gabriel **because He will save his people from their sins.** (Matthew 1:21) Paul, when writing to the Hebrews, stated plainly that Jesus **is able to save completely those who come to God through him, because he always lives to intercede for them.** (Hebrews 7:25). True, the title Saviour is used sparingly in the Gospels: in Matthew and Mark the title is not given; in Luke it is used only once, in the announcement of the angels to the shepherds: **"Today in the town of David a Saviour has been born to you; he is Christ the Lord. This will be a sign to you: You will find a baby wrapped in cloths and lying in a manger."** (Luke 2:12). In John's Gospel the title is, again, used only once. In John 4:42 the Samaritan villagers say to the woman who had spoken with Jesus **"We no longer believe just because of what you said; now we have heard for ourselves, and we know that this man really is the Saviour of the world."**

Readers who are interested in a full survey of the title 'Saviour' as applied to the Lord Jesus are recommended to obtain the book *Jesus As They Saw Him* by William Barclay (referenced in note 10). It looks in detail at forty-two titles applied to Jesus and how these titles would have been understood in Jesus' own day. Regarding the Lord's role as Saviour, Barclay writes:

'No matter from what angle it may be approached the basic and essential idea is the idea of *rescue*, rescue from a situation in which a man is quite unable to rescue himself. It is *rescue from the past*. Through the work of Jesus Christ the penalty which man's sin deserves no longer hangs threateningly over him. The estrangement between man and God need no longer exist. The power and slavery of past sin are broken and man is no longer shackled by the chains which his own sin forged.

'*It is rescue for the future*. Through Jesus Christ, the living and ever-present Christ, man is no longer a slave to his own sin. He can break the habits which have been his fetters, and conquer the sins which conquered him. He is no longer frustrated and defeated; he has found the way to victorious living. He is no longer the victim of temptation; he is victorious over temptation.

'Salvation deals not only with a man's past; it makes him a new man and gives him a new future. It is not merely negative escape; it is positive victory. Jesus is indeed the Saviour for whom men were desperately searching, and for whom the world was waiting, and whom the world still needs.'[11]

---

[11] *Jesus As They Saw Him*, William Barclay (SCM Press Ltd, 1962, p. 227).

10

THE WAY TO THE FATHER

Many mansions

During the years 1962 to 1974 the BBC screened a TV sitcom called *Steptoe and Son*. The 'situation' around which the comedy was built was that of a retired rag and bone man and his son, who now runs the family business. Comedy and pathos meet regularly in this series which pushed the boundaries in the use of expletives, but was otherwise considered widely to have been a comedy triumph. In one episode, *Men of Letters*, first screened in 1972 the local vicar[1] calls to invite these two rag and bone men to write a history of 'totting' (the cockney word for the trade in household rubbish) for the parish centenary magazine. Albert, the older of the two, offers the vicar a drink and comments that today the local Church of England faces stiff competition from the Muslims who 'stream out' from the former local cinema, now a mosque, on a Friday night. The vicar says that he welcomes the presence of other believers in the local community and their contribution to an understanding of the Divine. Christianity, he implies, is not the only way to God and then he quotes from the King James Bible **"in my Father's house are many mansions."**

---

[1] A Church of England minister of religion.

At this the younger son, Harold, who had on previous occasions (the vicar reminded him) expressed his views on religion 'rather forcefully' nods vigorously in agreement with an approving smile on his face.

The phrase used by the Lord Jesus about *many mansions* is one occasionally offered by church attending Godists as demonstrating that all religions belong to God and that Christianity is just one mansion. Before looking in detail at this conclusion, we will comment on the idea of 'Christian Godists'. It seems to the author on the basis of observation that there are at least two currents within this overall mindset when encountered within the setting of the Church. First are those church-attenders who have not really thought through the issues and would rather not bother; we will call them *casual Godists* for the sake of identification. Casual Godists would also include the vast majority of people 'down at the local pub' who also hold the liberal view in a liberal society that there cannot be religious exclusivity as 'this would be unfair'. Second are those church attenders who have noted the obvious claims to exclusivity revealed in the Bible, in the sayings of Jesus, in the history of Israel under the old covenant and in the reality of the church under the new covenant. They have rationalised their desire to harmonise *the religions* in the manner suggested by the Steptoe and Son vicar, by bypassing Christianity's claims to exclusivity and focusing on parts of the Bible (usually taken out of context) that they feel will buttress their view that all religions ultimately lead to the same place. For the sake of identification we will call these *determined Godists*.

We will look shortly at the overall passage from which the *many mansions* phrase is taken (John 14:2) in order to see, overall, what the Lord was revealing in this statement. The many mansions, or *many rooms*, to use the words of modern translations, could be interpreted in this way: in God's house there is room for all. In practice this seems a good explanation, insofar as God's kingdom is not limited and any human being can become a subject in that Kingdom — none need be lost if they are prepared to acknowledge their own rebellion against God ('sin') and to accept the free gift of new life through Jesus by turning away from (repenting of) their former life and turning to Jesus the Saviour, asking Him into their life by faith, to become their Lord and Master — and go on believing in Him.

Some niggardly people have a cramped and narrow view of the house of God, of heaven, and appear to wish and to expect that it is a small place where they and a few kindred spirits will gather, with all the rest being left outside. In the New Testament, however, heaven is a gloriously spacious place, with 12 gates opening in every direction (Revelation 21:12–13) and multitudes pouring in from all nations, peoples and tongues: **After this I looked and there before me was a great multitude that no one could count, from every nation, tribe, people and language, standing before the throne and in front of the Lamb. They were wearing white robes and were holding palm branches in their hands. And they cried out in a loud voice: "Salvation belongs to our God, who sits on the throne, and to the Lamb."** (Revelation 7:9). In that mass of happy people the individual is not overlooked or forgotten or lost — *you* are not overlooked! Each person has his or her own distinctive, personal, exclusive place in the Father's heart, and in the Father's house. No one else can ever fill it.

This is so expansive a conclusion that we need to be cautious in using it. Without caution and reverence this statement of Jesus might well become a danger to us, seeming to sanction individual whimsies. Simply because

Jesus has not expressly repudiated them, He cannot be held to have acquiesced in everything that our foolish hearts choose to desire or to claim. This author would contend that the view that all religions are essentially the same is just such a whimsy — nowhere supported by either the words of Jesus or the Bible as a whole. So, in the Father's house are indeed many rooms, but these seem to be places where we, as individual believers, will feel at home for eternity.

'When an honoured and loved guest is coming, preparations are made which are designed to meet his tastes and likings. The books that will appeal to him are laid where he can find them; flowers which he will remember as favourites are set about the rooms. These preparations are not merely general, but are thought out for very him. And yonder Jesus Christ is so lovingly making ready for our coming; arranging a place, our place; and that with such an exact remembrance of our particular needs and likings that it cannot fit anyone else. It is your place. And it is waiting for you, yonder. We must not fail the Father; leaving him to all eternity with that room designed for us still empty. For God wants all his family to gather home, not one of them missing.'[2]

Commenting on the same passage, another writer said this: 'It is an insult to Jesus to neglect heaven. Just think — He has personally prepared a place for you in His home. What a staggering thought that God the Son has been getting your home ready for you. If he has gone to such trouble to make it possible for you to live in heaven forever, how can we neglect to think of it, to anticipate it and to speak about it to one another? Remember what He has so tenderly said

---

[2] The Interpreter's Bible Volume VIII – 1952, published by Pierce and Smith. Library of Congress Card Number: 51-12276.

— **". . and if I go and prepare a place for you, I will come back and take you to be with me so that you also may be where I am"** (John 14:3). God could have got the angels to prepare a place for us in heaven, after all, they are His servants. He could have given them a general instruction to let us in when we go there. But the deep personal love that He has for us as individuals caused Him to do it Himself! Some Christians have such a high view of God, that they can hardly conceive that God would bother about them as an individual. They reason that the apostle Paul may merit some personal attention from the Most high God, but not them. But Scripture is so plain; Jesus said that He was preparing a place for us. Why not believe it, and enjoy the thrill of it'?[3]

So we can conclude with excitement and gratitude that the new heaven and the new earth (to give it its rightful title from Revelation chapter 21) will have many 'rooms' or 'mansions'. This reflects Jesus' love for His disciples, whom He loves *as individuals* and for whom He will prepare a special place. Other interpreters of this passage, which we provide in full below, have observed that the many mansions may also be a reference to the fact that there will be different kinds of reward for the disciple of Jesus. It seems certain for example that those who have been martyred for the name of Jesus, and those who have been persecuted[4] for the name of Jesus, will in some way be honoured by Him through eternity for the suffering that they faithfully endured. It may be that the world's roles may well be reversed vis a vis all those comfortable and relatively rich western

[3] *Heaven and Hell*, Alex Buchanan, (Sovereign World, 1995, ISBN 1-85240-154-0, p. 16.)

[4] At the time of writing it is estimated that one in ten of the world's Christians face active and serious persecution, including to the point of maryrdom.

Christians and their poor third-world counterparts. Many Western Christians may have bothered little about their faith, perhaps reaching the point of loving Jesus and turning to Him in repentance, and then living quiet and law-abiding lives — but fail to go out truly in faith to serve Him. These Christians may find themselves in some way rewarded with a *smaller mansion* than awarded to those who have suffered for Him. What we can say emphatically, at this stage, is that the passage in John chapter 14 has nothing to do with the multi-faith agenda.

The Last Supper

There are four life histories (or Gospels) of Jesus in the New Testament: Matthew, Mark, Luke and John. In this chapter we focus somewhat on the last of these. At the end of the Gospel of John (21:24), we have an indication of precisely who wrote this book. John is said to be *the disciple whom Jesus loved*. Now of course He loved all the disciples, but for the young John our Lord Jesus had a special compassion. John was one of the first disciples, being among those whom Jesus called by Lake Galilee, and was probably the youngest of all of them. (Matthew 4: 21–22; Mark 1:19–20). Scholars have conjectured that he was the unnamed companion of Andrew when he first followed Jesus (John 1:35–37). That John was part of the inner circle around Jesus is indicated by the fact that he was one of the three who were allowed to be with Him at some special events,[5] for example at the event we call the Transfiguration (Matthew 17:1–2; Mark 9:2; Luke 9:28–29), and when Jairus' daughter was raised from death (Mark 5:37; Luke 8:51). Before Jesus' arrest at the garden of Gethsemane He took this trio to pray

---

[5] The other two being Peter and James. John and James were sons of the fisherman Zebedee. Peter and his brother Andrew were also fishermen.

separately with Him (Matthew 26:37; Mark 14:33). It was into John's hands that Jesus entrusted his mother, at the crucifixion (John 19:26).

The Gospel according to John presents Jesus as the eternal Word of God who became a human and who 'lived among us'. As the Gospel itself says, it was written so its readers might *believe* that Jesus is the promised saviour, the Son of God, and that through their faith in Him they might *have life* (John 20:31). The part that we are about to focus on takes place in what we now call 'the last supper'. Chapters 13 – 17 of John record at length the close fellowship of Jesus with his disciples on the night of his arrest and the words of preparation and encouragement given to them on the eve of His crucifixion. So it is there, at that last supper, as Jesus' heart is so heavy knowing what is about to happen to Him, and probably also the hearts of the disciples who have some dim understanding that a crisis or a turning point is near, that we join them. We join them, if you like, at the table. The text is from John 14:1 – 13. It is the Lord Jesus Who is speaking:

"Do not let your hearts be troubled. Trust in God; trust also in me. In my Father's house are many rooms; if it were not so, I would have told you. I am going there to prepare a place for you. And if I go and prepare a place for you, I will come back and take you to be with me that you also may be where I am. You know the way to the place where I am going." Thomas said to him, "Lord, we don't know where you are going, so how can we know the way?"

Jesus answered, "I am the way and the truth and the life. No one comes to the Father except through me. If you really knew me, you would know my Father as well. From now on, you do know him and have seen him."

225

Philip said, "Lord, show us the Father and that will be enough for us."

Jesus answered: "Don't you know me, Philip, even after I have been among you such a long time? Anyone who has seen me has seen the Father. How can you say, 'Show us the Father'? Don't you believe that I am in the Father, and that the Father is in me? The words I say to you are not just my own. Rather, it is the Father, living in me, who is doing his work. Believe me when I say that I am in the Father and the Father is in me; or at least believe on the evidence of the miracles themselves. I tell you the truth, anyone who has faith in me will do what I have been doing. He will do even greater things than these, because I am going to the Father. And I will do whatever you ask in my name, so that the Son may bring glory to the Father.

It was John Stott, the Anglican writer and Bible teacher, who commented that when the church goes wrong on Christ, it goes wrong on everything. Stott meant the Church's understanding of Who Christ is, and what He has achieved. He was referring to what some people call the Church's *Christology*. If the church goes wrong on the Lord Jesus, in terms of its understanding of Who He was and what He achieved, and His uniqueness, it will simply go wrong on everything else. It will go wrong on salvation, and on sin, and on doctrine. It will go wrong on interfaith 'dialogue'. And on other things, no doubt. We really *do* need to take a special note of what Jesus said about Himself, if we are to encounter the real Jesus, and not one of our own invention. It is always wonderful to read in the Bible what others said about Jesus. Some, to be sure, called him a glutton and a drunkard, and a false teacher. But others got it exactly right as they stated with clarity Who Jesus is. One of the things the author has tried to do over the years as he has read the Bible is to underline the things that others said about Jesus and that Jesus said about himself. If readers don't mind marking their Bible then this is highly recommended as an extended bible study. Some of the comments of others about Jesus will leap off the page. For examples:

Col 1:15 – **He is the image of the invisible God . . . .**

Col 1:17 – **He is before all things and in him all things hold together**

Col 1:18 – He **is the head of the body, the church**

Col 2:9 – **In Christ all the fullness of Deity lives in bodily form**

1 John 1:7 – He **is the atoning sacrifice for our sins, and not only or ours but also for the sins of the whole world**.

So what *did* Jesus say about Himself? And why does it matter? Jesus actually said quite a lot about Himself! There are a series of statements prefixed by the two words 'I am' and it is these statements, perhaps, that give us the fullest theological picture of precisely Who and What Jesus is. Refer to Appendix 2 for a complete listing of the 'I Am' statements of Jesus. Some of the better known I AM sayings of Jesus are given immediately below in italicised text, with simple comments by this author:

I AM

The light — through which men and women can see — to see ourselves in *the* true light, as we really are. There is no other light by which we can see ourselves as God sees us. Without seeing ourselves as we truly are, we are in eternal danger.

The bread of life — of which a man may eat and never die.

It is only by 'feeding' on Jesus that we may have eternal life. Feeding means living for Him. Living by His power. Living in His strength. Living on His words.

The gate — whoever enters through Jesus will be saved. What are we to enter? God's kingdom, here on earth. How do we enter? By true repentance (turning away from) sin and accepting Jesus as Lord and as (all sufficient) Saviour.

The good shepherd — who lays down his life for the sheep. We know that Jesus died for us on the cross. But why did He die? Certainly, we can say because He loves His Father. But also because He loves us. And finally because if He did not die for us, then no one else could do so. No one else is good enough to pay the price of sin.

The resurrection and the Life — it is through Jesus that a disciple of Christ will ultimately be raised and having been raised will find true Life. Life with a capital 'L'. (Revelation 22:1) **"Then the angel showed me the river of the water of life, as clear as crystal, flowing from the throne of God and of the Lamb".** The passage in Revelation 22 goes on to say that His servants will reign with Him 'for ever and ever' (v. 5).

The Way, the truth and the Life — Jesus is *the* way, *the* truth and *the* life. He is not *a* way, *a* truth and *a* life, but *the*..... That remains a stumbling block for many in the so-called multi-cultural, multi-religion Western world today. It is inconvenient, if not downright offensive (to some) to be faced with a Saviour who has said such a thing. But that is precisely what Jesus said. We either accept it or we reject it.

To borrow a rather hackneyed British phrase, 'you cannot have your cake and eat it' as regards Jesus. There are some Godists who will say 'Yes, I believe in Jesus. I believe He was a good man and did some lovely things. I even believe

He was God's Son'. But those same people will go on to say that they also believe in Buddha, and Mohammad, and Hinduism with its 7000+ gods. That is simply not a choice that Jesus has given us. By accepting other religious figures, you have rejected Jesus, no matter what nice things you may say about Him. We repeat, this is simply not a choice that Jesus has left open to us.

An analogy from marriage may help: when a man chooses to have an affair during his marriage, it is in a very real sense, a rejection of the wife whom he married. There are probably some men in this situation who would say 'I still love my wife'. Or even I love my wife *and* my mistress — what a loving man I am! But readers can probably see that to embark on such a course is a rejection. It's a rejection of promises to exclusivity. It's a rejection of the love that, hopefully, the wife has given. Most people can see that unfaithfulness in marriage is a real rejection of the marriage partner, even if the marriage survives. Acceptance of multiple paths to God is *ipso facto* a rejection of Christ, as the Bible itself tells us: **Salvation is found in no-one else, for there is no other name under heaven by which we must be saved.** (Acts 4:12) Readers may also want to check out John 14:6 and Ephesians 4:1–16 in this regard. Reverting to our illustration from marriage, we must again confront this idea of unfaithfulness: in Ephesians 5 the apostle Paul speaks of marriage, in a passage that many have found to be very challenging for a whole host of reasons! In this same passage Paul says this: **After all, no one ever hated his own body, but he feeds and cares for it, just as Christ does the church — for we are members of his body. For this reason a man will leave his father and mother and be united to his wife, and the two will become one flesh. This is a profound mystery — but**

I am talking about Christ and the church. (Ephesians 5:29–32). From the viewpoint of Godism we are bound to note that Chris's invitation is to become *one flesh* — or we might say one body — with Himself, as husband and wife become one flesh together in marriage. To speak of multiple paths to God, or perhaps that should read *multiple partners* to God, is certainly a rejection of the exclusive nature of the relationship that Christ offers by way of salvation. This symbolic picture of Christ marrying His church is completed in Revelation: **And I heard, as it were, the voice of a great multitude, as the sound of many waters and as the sound of mighty thunderings, saying, "Alleluia! For the Lord God Omnipotent reigns! Let us be glad and rejoice and give Him glory, for the marriage of the Lamb has come, and His wife has made herself ready." And to her it was granted to be arrayed in fine linen, clean and bright, for the fine linen is the righteous acts of the saints.** (Revelation 19:6-8, NKJV)

As Christians we are invited to a marriage relationship with our Saviour. It is for the church-based Godist to confirm or deny that Jesus is betrothed to His church. It is for the Godist to prove beyond doubt that a good and holy God intends this to be an *open marriage*, where there are multiple and radically different paths to peace with Him. And if God does indeed mean this (heaven forbid!) then precisely what is the relationship of God to the other faiths if He is married solely to His church? Is God effectively 'double-timing' His intended marriage partner? The mind begins to boggle at this rather horrible idea. Nevertheless, it does seem to be the logical outcome of the overall Godist position when expressed from within the Church.

We revert for a moment to our central theme of Godism: when people invent a religion or a philosophy of religions, or a synthesis or religions, and say that it doesn't really matter what people believe so long as they are sincere and have compassion, they are certainly rejecting Christ. 'Multiple religions and multiple paths' is not a choice that Jesus has left us. Jesus Himself is *the* way, Jesus Himself is *the* gate. A choice in favour of other 'ways' or other 'gates' necessarily implies that Jesus is not an *all-sufficient* Saviour, and that his death on the cross is not *the* all-sufficient penalty for sin. If the cross is not all-sufficient, and living compassionately is somehow the primary duty of a child of God, then this begins to imply that in some way we can assist God to help us into heaven; that we can in some measure earn our way to heaven. When Godism is expressed by church attending people, then they are suggesting that humans can give God a helping hand through their good works, or their faithfulness in prayer and church attendance, or their Bible reading and so on. The Bible, however, is emphatic that God needs no helping hand. Jesus *is* the way. Jesus is *the* way: **Just as man is destined to die once, and after that to face judgment, so Christ was sacrificed once to take away the sins of many people; and he will appear a second time, not to bear sin, but to bring salvation to those who are waiting for him.** (Hebrews 9:27–28)

I AM!

In Exodus 3 we read of that amazing encounter between God and Moses, as God calls him to lead the Hebrew people who were in appalling slavery to the Egyptians. Moses, full of doubts about his own worthiness to undertake the task of rescue, asked God that fundamental question — Moses would need to tell the Israelites who had sent him to free them. What should he say? God Himself provided the answer. **And God said to Moses, "I AM WHO I AM."**

And He said, "Thus you shall say to the children of Israel, 'I AM has sent me to you.'" (Exodus 3:14, NKJV)

Does not that statement by God put a fresh perspective on the things that our Lord Jesus said? We recognise in those great I AM statements of Jesus the attributes of God Himself. God the Light, God the Life, God the Resurrection, God the Truth, God the Bread (of life). The things that Jesus was saying surely must have been recognised by those who opposed Him. And we read, don't we, in John 8:59, that they picked up stones to kill Jesus when He said that He had seen Abraham: **Then the Jews said to Him, "You are not yet fifty years old, and have You seen Abraham?" Jesus said to them, "Most assuredly, I say to you, before Abraham was, I AM." Then they took up stones to throw at Him; but Jesus hid Himself and went out of the temple, going through the midst of them, and so passed by.** (John 8:57–59, NKJV). Ultimately, Jesus' critics recognised what He was saying, and they rejected it. Ultimately, people still recognise what Jesus is saying and the demands that He makes, and sadly many still reject Him. To be sure not always in an atheistic 'God doesn't exist' sort of rejection, but too often in this 'Jesus-Plus' sort of 'do it yourself' theology where there are many avenues to God and you pick out your own personal route to get to God. Mixing, matching, sharing and borrowing from all the so-called 'higher religions' — and possibly some of the lower ones too! That religious *room for manoeuvre* is something that Jesus simply has not given us. A 'DIY' god is no god at all.

Why does it matter what the Lord Jesus said about Himself? Because Jesus reveals all truth — indeed, Jesus is Himself the Truth. The Lord Jesus is *the* way to God, not a way. We accept that, or we reject it. It is as simple and as uncomfortable as that. We leave this section of our study on a real note of hope — indeed a note of triumph! Jesus is believable. He invited the disciples to believe on the *evidence* of the miracles that they saw. Evidence, of course, is a strong word. Many today would say 'I've never seen a miracle, so how can I believe?' Most Christians will have been privileged to see God's hand at work in some startling ways, often in their own lives, and often in the lives of those close to them, especially in the form of answered prayer. As Christians we will have witnessed some amazing things: our own friendship with Jesus, and the Holy Spirit working in our lives and the lives of people known to us. The evidences of answered prayer are often deeply compelling and there are often so many little 'coincidences' (or 'God-incidences' as some people have called them) where we recognise the hand of God in action. These may be evidences that the world at large cannot see, let alone accept. But to a Christian they are indeed evidences of a God who is intimately interested in, and involved in, our lives. What did Jesus say? **Believe me when I say that I am in the Father and the Father is in me; or at least believe on the evidence of the miracles themselves. I tell you the truth, anyone who has faith in me will do what I have been doing. He will do even greater things than these, because I am going to the Father. And I will do whatever you ask in my name, so that the Son may bring glory to the Father. You may ask me for anything in my name, and I will do it.** (John 14:11–14)

We are disciples of a Saviour who responds as we seek His will and His enabling. Jesus promised that anything asked in his name will be answered in the affirmative. Again the author must confess that this statement of Jesus has given him pause for thought, in the past. Sometimes we ask for things we believe to be in accordance with His will, things that we really feel passionate about and where we are convinced we are praying in His Spirit. And yet we seem to have no answer. We need to remember, of course, that Jesus does not always answer our prayers as we want. His oversight of our situations is better than ours. If I pray for a Rolls Royce in the name of Jesus, I'm not going to get it. Why? Because it will not advance the cause of the Kingdom. God's answers to prayer are always answers in accordance with the principle that His name is honoured and that the cause of His Kingdom is advanced. But in spite of the occasions of prayer that is not answered in the way we want or expect, most Christians would also be able to speak of many instances where prayers offered up in humble expectation, and in faith, have indeed been answered — and often answered beyond our wildest expectations.

The Power in a Name

Names can be powerful and meaningful in their own right, even causing strong emotions, as any parent who has had the difficult task of choosing a name can recognise! Many people in history have been given popular titles based on their achievements or their notoriety, titles that have become instantly recognisable as a 'celebration' of the person and what they did. So we have all heard of Alexander *the Great*, of William *the Conqueror*, of *Bloody* Mary, and of John *the Baptist*. Slightly less well known may be the English King Ethelred *the Unready*. From biblical times we encounter Judas Maccabeus — *God's Hammer*, a popular title given because of his stunning victories over the Persians. One of Jesus' own disciples is principally remembered not for what he did but for the simple fact that he was an adherent of a political movement — Simon *the Zealot*.

234

The Lord Jesus was given many titles which can be seen as both affirmations of what He was and confessions of faith in Him. W. Graham Scroggie lists in his *Guide To The Gospels* fifty-two such titles given to Jesus,[6] but it is the simple name 'Jesus' by which the Lord is most often referred to in the Gospels — almost six hundred times, in fact. The name Jesus emphasises the real humanity of the Lord. Whilst to us it has become a sacred name, and we would consider it irreverent to give the name to any child today (though in some Latin societies this is not an uncommon practice), in New Testament times Jesus was one of the most common names for a boy. 'Jesus' is the Greek form by which the Old Testament name Joshua (e.g. as in the Book of Joshua) is translated. Whilst a common name when Jesus was born, by the second century A.D. it was rapidly dying out. Among Jews it had become a hated name whilst among Christians it was too sacred for common use.

Ordinary though the name Jesus was, it was nevertheless a significant name. In the ancient world a name could be seen as being very meaningful, often describing something about the person to whom it was given. The name Jesus was given to our Lord by the direct instruction of God (Matthew 1:21) and indeed this name might have been thought somewhat irregular by people at the time because it was customary to name eldest sons after their father. We would note, in this regard, that Jesus had no biological father, so in His name may be found some clue as to His heavenly Father. The Jewish rabbis had a saying: 'Six persons received their names before they were born, namely, Isaac, our great lawgiver Moses, Solomon, Josiah, Ishmael and the Messiah.' Jewish belief was that God would directly

[6] *A Guide To The Gospels*, W. Graham Scroggie DD (Pickering & Inglis Ltd, 1948) p. 519.

command what the name of the Messiah must be.

In both Hebrew and Greek the name Jesus has a special meaning, being in a sense, a one word summary of the work that the Lord was sent to do. In Hebrew the name Joshua means, variously, 'Jehovah is my help' or 'Jehovah is rescue' or 'the help of Jehovah'. In Matthew 1:21 we read **"you are to give him the name Jesus, because he will save his people from their sins."** The very name Jesus, therefore, marks Him out as Saviour. 'He is God's divinely appointed and divinely sent Rescuer' writes William Barclay 'whose function it is to deliver men from their sins. He came to rescue men from the estrangement and the alienation from God which is the consequence of their past sins, and for the future to liberate them from the bondage to sin, from the moral frustration and the continuous and inevitable defeat which are the result of sin. He came to bring friendship for fear, and victory for defeat.'[7]

To the Greek mind a connection was made between the name Jesus and the verb *iasthai*, which means *to heal*. The connection between the two words is only in the sound, but the Greeks made much of the idea of Jesus as the healer of the bodies and souls of men. Jesus was the only one who could bring health to the body in its physical pain and renewal of the soul polluted by the spiritual disease of sin. It was no accident, therefore, that Jesus was given His name, for it summarises the things He came to do and which *only* He could do. He came to be the divine rescuer of men from the consequences and the grip of sin.

Jesus, Man and God

The traditional Christian view is that the baby born in Bethlehem is both God and Man, an astounding thought and a stumbling block for many, notably the Jehovah's

---

[7] *Jesus As They Saw Him*, William Barclay (SCM Press, 1962) p. 12.

Witnesses in the western world and Muslims in the east. How did this doctrine develop? Is it biblical? What did Jesus Himself have to say? We will try to answer these questions as we evaluate whether anyone other than God, Himself, could ultimately pay the debt owed for rebellion (sin) against Himself.

The first point to make is that Jesus was a real, complete and ordinary human being. He was born like us and developed through childhood to adulthood in a completely normal way. In the Bible we read that he ate, drank, slept, sweated, became tired, felt pain and emotion. He died. He was also tempted to sin as we are, even in a quite unprecedented way by the devil himself (Luke 4:1–13), although Jesus did not surrender to the temptation and so we can say with certainty that He was without sin. Just as He taught His disciples to pray, so Jesus Himself needed to pray, to remain in close intimacy with His heavenly Father. He acknowledged He could do nothing without His Father's power and taught only what His Father had shown Him (John 8:28). In spite of all Jesus' undoubted supernatural power, He was fully dependent on His heavenly Father, so He stated plainly that He did not know the time when He would return — this was known only by His Father (Mark 13:32).

So why do Christians equate God with Jesus? The foundations of the belief are in the Bible itself — indeed it should be said that the doctrine is based on viewing the Bible as an organic whole — the doctrine is alluded to, albeit indirectly, throughout the unveiling of salvation history. It should be added, straight away, that Christians do not claim to have a perfect understanding of this Incarnation — of God becoming flesh. We can, however, say that the evidence is overwhelming as this following short study will illustrate:

What has God revealed about Himself?
One and only — Isaiah 44:6 (and Galatians 3:15–20)
Unchangeable — James 1:17
Invisible — Colossians 1:15
Infinite — 1 Kings 8:27
Holy — 1 Peter 1:15–16
Spirit — John 4:24
His unity
Deuteronomy 6: 4
Galatians 3:20 (see also verse 16)
1 Timothy 2:5
James 2:19
Father, Son and Holy Spirit
Matthew 28:19 (name, not names!)
2 Corinthians 13:14
Hebrews 1:8
1 Peter 1:2
"I AM" Exodus 3:13–15 His name revealed to Moses.
Jesus uses term 'I am' of Himself
John 8:58	before Abraham was born, I AM!
John 6:48	the bread of life
John 10:7	the gate
John 10:11	the good shepherd
John 10:36	God's Son
John 11:25	the resurrection and the life
John 14:10	in the Father and the Father is in me (see also John 10:30)
John 15:1	the true vine

It is plain that Jesus was claiming the divine co-existence of God the Father and Himself, the Son. So it was that the people in His own home town rose up against Him (Luke 4:29) when He compared Himself to Elijah. **"My Father has been working until now, and I have been working."**

238

said Jesus in John 5:17. The Gospel writer continues: **Therefore the Jews sought all the more to kill Him, because He not only broke the Sabbath, but also said that God was His Father, making Himself equal with God.** (John 5:17–18, NKJV). It is true that nowhere did Jesus ever say unambiguously 'I am God' but He nevertheless made some explicit statements leading to this conclusion. Thus **"I and the Father are one"** (John 10:30) is the most obvious, but is reinforced by, for example, **"All that belongs to the Father is mine"** (John 16:15) and **"All authority in heaven and on earth has been given to me**." (Matthew 28:18). So, whilst we read in Acts 10:36 that Jesus is Lord of all, elsewhere we read that **the Lord your God is God in heaven above and on the earth below** (Joshua 2:11) and similarly in Genesis 28:13 we read of God introducing Himself to Jacob as **"I am the Lord, the God of your father Abraham and the God of Isaac."**

Since the earliest days of the church, Christian belief has been that the man Jesus is also God. Not a man with god-like qualities, nor God *appearing* in human guise, but God the eternal Logos who 'became flesh' (John1:14). Four great ecumenical Councils of the fourth and fifth centuries A.D. wrestled with the mysteries of the godhead and each clarified an important aspect of it. The Council of Nicea (A.D. 325) affirmed that Jesus is truly God, and the Council of Constantinople (A.D. 381) confirmed that He is truly man. The Council of Ephesus (A.D. 431) clarified that, although God and Man, He is one person. Finally the Council of Chalcedon (A.D. 451) confirmed that, although one person, Jesus is both God and man perfectly. These beliefs have been reaffirmed both by Roman Catholics and the Reformers down through the centuries.

Critics of the doctrine of the Trinity often ask how God

239

can be in two places at once. We might as well ask how God can create a universe or how he can raise from the dead someone who has been crucified. The very question, perhaps, tries to lock the infinite God into a definition easily comprehended by limited human minds. It has been rightly observed that we can call Jesus God, but we cannot call God Jesus. God continued to control the universe in His omniscience, omnipotence and omnipresence when the man Jesus was on this earth. However, in the man Jesus we meet absolutely and completely God in His personal relationship with men. We see perfectly in Jesus God in His attitude to and in His relationship with men. Although this is in the fullest sense incomprehensible to humans, this is God as He has revealed Himself: as three distinct persons — one in three and three in one.

The Way to the Father

We close this chapter by looking once again at that fundamental statement of Jesus that He is *the way to the Father*. We note that Christians were not originally known as Christians — they were actually known as the people of *the way* (Acts 19:9). It was in Antioch that followers of Jesus were first called Christians (Acts 11:26). There is an entire theology around this concept of *the way*. In summary:

- It is a word used in a moral sense, for conduct (Psalm 1:6)
- 'Ways' are used to describe the laws of the Lord (see Genesis 18:19; Psalm 18:21).
- 'Way' is used to describe customs, manners and the way of life (Genesis 6:12; Jeremiah 10:2).
- 'Way' is used in connection with salvation (see Acts 19:9).

A trawl through a good Bible concordance such as

Cruden's will see the phenomenal power in this idea of *the way*. We should hopefully be able to see that all these ideas are encompassed in what Jesus taught His disciples at the last supper. Let us remind ourselves of precisely what He said: **"I am the way and the truth and the life. No one comes to the Father except through me"** (John 14:6). We remind ourselves once again that He did not claim to be *a* way, or *a* truth, He used the definite article: 'the'. This alone should be compelling as we seriously and reverently consider what Jesus meant in this final statement to His disciples when He was aware that within a short time He was going to be arrested and killed. We must not simply 'write off' what He said. If anyone does so, what other statements are also to be written off? But this writer has certainly heard a determined Godist attempt to dismiss them in this manner: *when Jesus said that he was the way to the Father he did not mean that he was the only way to God. No, he meant that he was the only way to the Father* (full stop!) This is either astonishingly woolly thinking and inexcusably loose logic, or it is malicious. That God is Father is stated often in Scripture. If God is not Father then it is difficult to know to whom Jesus invited all His followers to pray as he taught them to address **"Our Father in Heaven"**. [8] We have explored in chapter 6 that God is good. We have explored in chapter 7 that God is holy. God does not tell lies, nor does He mislead or obfuscate. He desires to have a relationship with all humans and He has graciously made possible a way for that to be achieved — through His Son, who in turn is our Lord if we ask Him into our lives and obey Him. Surely it would not be good to say that Jesus is *the* way if there are others available? Surely Jesus would have said something like: *I am a sure way to peace with*

---

[8] See Ephesians 4:6 and John 17:1 - 3.

the Father, but you know there are other ways, and in the future there will be yet more. But for the time being I invite you to follow me as a dependable way to the Father. Don't worry if you get smashed up on a cross as I am about to. When the Father decides upon other 'ways' to Himself, they won't be so demanding! The very idea is absolutely preposterous!

The author has also heard the 'problem' of John 14:6 explained away thus: *Yes Jesus is the only way to God, but Jesus will willingly admit all genuine God-seekers into eternal union with Himself providing they have not been bad, because His sacrifice on the cross covers all.* This is more subtle. It enables those who hold the view to acknowledge something which is plain from Scripture, that Jesus is God's Son and that following Him is the only way to peace with God, but it neatly sidesteps the issue of other religions. We are back to the vicar from Steptoe and Son back in 1972! By this view God's plan of salvation is so encompassing that virtually all will be saved (sometimes known as *universalism*) and only those most determinedly anti-Christ (Hitler is generally given as an example) will find themselves on the wrong-side of God's judgement. Usually this vector of thinking takes its philosophers into very uncharted waters around precisely who will be saved, and the philosophy usually degenerates into a sort of DIY theology, always with a 'happy ending' of salvation for virtually all — and always far removed from the revelation of Scripture. Rather than pursue these ideas further we will conclude with this: those who think this must inevitably hold a low view of God, as suggested in the diagram in Appendix 1. There is no biblical basis for the idea that those of *the religions* can rely upon Christ's sacrifice for eternal salvation.

11

A GOD OF RELIGIONS?

Religions and the Religious

Readers will have noticed that the author occasionally refers to *the religions*, but in some contexts does not apply this term 'religion' to Christianity. Yet the *Oxford English Dictionary* defines religion as: *the belief in a superhuman controlling power, especially in a personal God or gods entitled to obedience and worship*, thereby implying that Christianity is a religion. Few would argue with that definition at one level, but the 'true religion' revealed in the Bible differs in basic respects from all the other religions in the world, and must therefore be accorded a different categorial status. The key features which mark out authentic Christian faith have to do with the distinctive relationship between God and the believer, marked by faith, love and obedience. In Deuteronomy 6:4–9 we read the Jewish *shema*: **Hear, O Israel: The LORD our God, the LORD is one. Love the LORD your God with all your heart and with all your soul and with all your strength. These commandments that I give you today are to be upon your hearts. Impress them on your children. Talk about them when you sit at home and when you walk along the road, when you lie down and when you get up. Tie them as symbols on your hands and bind them on your foreheads. Write them on the doorframes of your houses and on your gates.**

The command is to love. And that command is to be written upon a person's heart. God looks for *relationship* founded on love, and the love that God demands is total love. The author recognizes that some readers will have difficulty with this concept, especially if they have no real experience of God and have never met pure self-giving love. These readers are encouraged to 'hang on in there' whilst we explore a little more of this God Who gives love and demands love. If we were to love God in the way He demands, by giving Him our first allegiance and our best in everything, then surprisingly our love for our fellow humans, whether 'brothers' or 'neighbours' (there is a biblical distinction[1]) will grow and express itself in ways that will amaze us!

The *shema* love that we are to experience as we worship God is to be so absorbing that we can hardly help ourselves from impressing that same love onto our children, and gossiping about it, and thinking about it regularly as we go about our daily business. The truly pious Hebrews of the Old Testament period did indeed tie God's commandments onto their wrists, and head-dress, and on the door posts of their houses. Symbolically today a Christian (and indeed an observant Jew) would expect to 'wear' the commands of God around their mind so that these commands are foundational to all they think and do. Christians would add that it is through the Holy Spirit that these commands become real to us; we are baptised in the same Holy Spirit and we are to go on being filled with Him.

Jesus affirmed the Jewish *shema* as He spoke about the greatest commandment: **One of the teachers of the law came and heard them debating. Noticing that Jesus had given them a good answer, he asked him, "Of all the commandments, which is the most important?"**

---

[1] See Appendix 3.

"The most important one," answered Jesus, "is this: 'Hear, O Israel, the Lord our God, the Lord is one. Love the Lord your God with all your heart and with all your soul and with all your mind and with all your strength.' The second is this: 'Love your neighbour as yourself.' There is no commandment greater than these."

"Well said, teacher," the man replied. "You are right in saying that God is one and there is no other but him. To love him with all your heart, with all your understanding and with all your strength, and to love your neighbour as yourself is more important than all burnt offerings and sacrifices."

When Jesus saw that he had answered wisely, he said to him, "You are not far from the kingdom of God." (Mark 12:28–34).

We note straight away that true love for God leads to true love for neighbour. The command here is not so much to love our brother or sister (although Jesus elsewhere makes special provision for this),[2] the command is to love all people everywhere and recognize in them the potential for that same love of God (whether or not they presently acknowledge Him). In loving our neighbours as ourselves, we will do them no mischievous harm. Instead we will live peaceably among all men, so far as it depends on us (other men may choose not to treat us peaceably). **"If it is possible, as much as depends on you, live peaceably with all men."** (Romans 12:18, NKJV).

Is the author of this book trying to make an artificial distinction between *the religions* and Christianity? As already noted, most would agree that Christianity matches that basic dictionary definition. But, at a deeper level, the author contends that there is a world of difference between *the religions* and true Christianity. *The religions*, in essence,

---

[2] See Appendix 3.

teach how humans reach up to a god or gods; Christianity teaches about a God Who reaches down to humanity. *The religions* teach about earning god's favour and so earning a right to some sort of paradise experience. Christianity teaches about a gift of life, given by God to penitent sinners — an amazing gift of grace given freely to human creatures who, in the final analysis, do not deserve it.

As we saw in the previous chapter, Christians were first called *the people of The Way*. And what is this 'Way'? We revert to the words of the Lord Jesus in John 3:14: **"Just as Moses lifted up the snake in the desert, so the Son of Man must be lifted up, that everyone who believes in him may have eternal life."** The Way is Jesus. The believing of which Jesus spoke is clearly much more than a simple mental assent or acknowledgement. It is a believing that transforms and a believing that acts, so the believer becomes an entirely new creation; as it continues: **"whoever believes in him shall not perish but have eternal life."** (v. 16). The relationship of believer to God becomes one of parent and adopted (born again) child: **"Yet to all who received him, to those who believed in his name, he gave the right to become children of God — children born not of natural descent, nor of human decision or a husband's will, but born of God."** (John 1:12–13) This new birth leads us to a new life here in this world as we seek to become more like Jesus, our Lord and our Saviour: **"How great is the love the Father has lavished on us, that we should be called children of God! And that is what we are! The reason the world does not know us is that it did not know him. Dear friends, now we are children of God, and what we will be has not yet been made known. But we know that when he appears, we shall be like him, for we shall see him as he is. Everyone who has this hope in him purifies**

himself, just as [Jesus] is pure" (1 John 3:1–3). With this new life comes a new assurance before God, so the apostle John continues: **Everyone who believes that Jesus is the Christ is born of God, and everyone who loves the father loves his child as well. This is how we know that we love the children of God: by loving God and carrying out his commands. This is love for God: to obey his commands. And his commands are not burdensome, for everyone born of God overcomes the world. This is the victory that has overcome the world, even our faith. Who is it that overcomes the world? Only he who believes that Jesus is the Son of God.**

Becoming a disciple of Jesus leads to a completely new identity in Christ. There seem to be three key categories of identity in Christianity as suggested by the following short study, which readers may want to follow through as a separate exercise. These categories of identity are *acceptance* by God, *security* in God and *significance* in God. A true believer then can confidently claim:

I am accepted
I am God's child — John 1:12
I am Christ's friend — John 15:15
I have been justified — Romans 5:1
I am united with the Lord, and one in spirit with Him — 1 Corinthians 6:17
I have been bought with a price and belong to God — 1 Corinthians 6:19–20
I am a saint — Ephesians 1:1
I have been adopted as God's child — Ephesians 1:5
I have direct access to God through the Holy Spirit — Ephesians 2:18
I have been redeemed and all my sins forgiven — Colossians 1:14

I am complete in Christ — Colossians 2:10

I am secure

I am free forever from condemnation — Romans 8:1–2

I am assured that all things work together for good — Romans 8:28

I am free from any condemning charges against me — Romans 8:31

I cannot be separated from the love of God — Romans 8:35

I have been established, anointed and sealed by God — 2 Corinthians 1:21–22

I am hidden with Christ in God — Colossians 3:3

I am confident the good work that God has begun in me will be perfected — Philippians 3:6

I am a citizen of heaven — Philippians 3:20

I have not been given a spirit of fear but of power, love and self control — 2 Timothy 1:7

I can find grace and mercy in time of need — Hebrews 4:16

I am born of God, and the evil one cannot harm me — 1 John 5: 18

I am significant

I am the salt and light of the earth — Matthew 5:13–14

I am a branch of the true vine, a channel of his life — John 15:1,5

I have been chosen and appointed to bear fruit — John 15:16

I am a personal witness of Christ — Acts 1:8

I am God's temple — 1 Corinthians 3:16

I am a minister of reconciliation for God — 2 Corinthians 5:17ff

I am God's co-worker — 1 Corinthians 3:9 and 2 Corinthians 6:1

I am seated with Christ in the heavenly realm – Ephesians 2:6

I am God's workmanship — Ephesians 2:10

I may approach God with freedom and confidence — Ephesians 3:12

I can do all things through Christ Who strengthens me – Philippians 4–13

Readers will see that these are pretty amazing claims to make. Christianity is not so much a religion as a relationship; the relationship of a child to their loving and holy Father through Jesus Christ, the Father's Son. Christianity is not so much *distinct* from *the religions* as *a world apart* from any other religion, and that is why this writer asserts that true Christianity is not a religion at all. It is therefore much more appropriate to speak of *The Way* as compared to *the religions* and that is why in this book we have generally made a distinction by referring to other faith systems as *the religions*. It is a subtle but real distinction we have made. Readers may want to adopt this distinction in their own thinking as it helps us to see the 'clear blue water' between true Christianity and other belief systems. In thinking of the categories of identity we looked at above (acceptance, security and significance) the challenge, as always, reverts to the Godist to explain how *the religions* provide equivalent overpowering assurance to their respective followers.

If God has graciously given Christians these amazing promises and assurances, then what is provided in the so-called 'higher' religions? And how dependable are any such assurances that these religions *are* able to give to their followers? A Christian knows that Christ died an appalling death for them personally, and for love of His Father. A Christian knows that Jesus rose from death to conquer death, and that this was always God's ultimate plan. A Christian knows that Jesus Christ intercedes before the Father for them still (Romans 8:34). As God has lavished these assurances—these *golden promises* — to those who follow Jesus, just what has He done for the other 'paths' that are supposed to lead to Him?

Whilst writing this book the author's attention was drawn to the testimony of an Indian lady in the nineteenth century who was brought up as a pious Hindu but later came to faith in Christ. She was of the Shudra caste (one of the higher castes) and her father taught his children *the way of Moksha*.[3] Moksha is considered to be liberation from the everlasting trouble of reincarnation 'in millions and millions of animal species, and undergoing the pains of suffering of countless millions of diseases and deaths'. Her father lived the life of an itinerant guru, travelling from one sacred place to another, staying in each place for several months, bathing in a sacred river or tank, visiting temples, worshipping household gods and the images of gods in the temples, and reading Puranas in temples and other convenient places.

For the lady's father, the reading of Puranas served a double purpose. The first and foremost was that of 'getting rid of sin' and of earning merit in order to obtain Moksha, and the other to earn a living without resorting to begging. The readers of Puranas ('Puranikas') are popular public preachers among the Hindus. They sit in some prominent place, in temple halls or under trees with their manuscript books in their hands, and read the Puranas in a loud voice. The text, being in the Sanskrit language, may well not be understood by the hearers and the Purikanas are not obliged

---

[3] Notable that Moksha should be considered as 'the way' in the light of our earlier thoughts on this subject

to explain it to them. *'They may or may not explain it as they choose. Sometimes …. the Purikana takes great pains to make his speech as popular as he can, by telling greatly exaggerated or untrue stories. This is not considered sin, since it is done to attract the common peoples' attention.'* After a reading, the pious among the Hindus would prostrate themselves before the Purikana and offer flowers, sweetmeats, garments, money, and other things. *'The offeror knows that his store of merit will be according to what he gives, and he tries to be as generous as he can.'* The Hindu lady engaged in deeper studies after the death of her father. She affirmed: *'While reading the Dharma Shastras I came to know many things which I never knew before. There were contradictory statements about almost everything. What one book said to be righteous, another declared to be unrighteous. While reading the Mahabharata I found the following. "The Vedas differ from each other; Smrities, that is books of sacred laws, do not agree with one another; the secret of religion is in some hidden place: the only way is that which is followed by great men."'*

Most unsettling of all, the lady discovered that the position of women whether of high or low caste was appalling: *'They could not get Moksha as men. The only hope of their getting this much desired liberation from Karma and its results, that is countless millions of births and deaths and untold suffering, was the worship of their husbands. The husband is said to be the woman's god; there is no other god for her. This god may be the worst sinner or a great criminal; still he is her god and she must worship him. She can have no hope of getting admission into Svarga, the abode of the gods without his pleasure, and if she pleases him in all things, she will have the privilege of going to Svarga as his slave, there to serve him and be one of his wives among the thousands of Svarga harlots who are presented to him by the gods in exchange for his wife's merit.'* The testimony continues: *'The woman is allowed to go into the higher existence thus far but to attain Moksha or liberation, she must perform such great religious acts as will obtain for her the merit by which she will be reincarnated as a high caste man .... the extraordinary religious acts which help a woman get into the way of getting Moksha are utter abandonment of her will to that of her husband. She is to worship him with whole-hearted devotion as the only god; to know no other pleasure in life except in the most degraded slavery to him.'* The testimony goes on to note that the lot of the Hindu men is not much better, especially if they are of low caste.

Once again the challenge reverts to the Godist: why does their 'god' reveal 'himself' or 'itself' in such sublime purity and offer such sublime assurance to the follower of Jesus, as we saw above, but gives no *equivalent* assurance within the so-called higher religions. Lack of time prevents us from looking at the other religions, but the same verdict is broadly applicable. And the same question must be answered by the Godists as they seek to defend those other belief systems: why does their 'god' treat people so differently? And to a specifically church-based Godist, how does this treatment square with a God who is good (chapter 6) and holy (chapter 7)? As we shall see later, there are today some church based Godists who say that 'god' is both good and bad at the same time!

We will leave our testimony from India with this interesting postscript: in the mid nineteenth century a new form of Hinduism emerged in India, called Brahmoism. A reader can quickly Google a description of the religion if they are so inclined. The female witness we have followed simultaneously looked into Brahmoism as she explored

Christianity. She wrote this: *'The Brahmo religion was not a very definite one, for it is nothing but what a man makes for himself. He chooses and gathers whatever seems good to him from all the religions known to him, and prepares a sort of religion for his own use. The Brahmo religion has no other foundation than man's own natural light and the sense of right and wrong which he possesses in common with all mankind.'* This, surely, is a very apposite description of Godism!

Are atheistic political ideologies such as communism religions? Thinking 'outside the box' a little, our definition of 'religion' may go wider. We noted earlier the definition of true Christianity as a *relationship rather than a religion* — a relationship like that of a child to his parent; a relationship of trust and total dependence by those who acknowledge their need and acknowledge their dependence on a completely righteous and completely holy God; a relationship with God who loves His adopted children, in spite of their unworthiness, with the tender love of a parent to his child. Some have defined religion rather more widely as *any systemised belief in 'god' where 'god' may be a supernatural deity, or may be mankind himself.* All such belief systems involve a measure of collaboration with their 'god' in 'earning' his respect and his reward. This way of viewing religions suggests that they all have human founders, have their special writings and believe in the utter rightness of their particular 'revelation'. By this definition we can easily include communism, fascism and even fundamentalist evolutionism. All religions share the foundation stone — or *cornerstone* if you prefer — of making man the measure of all. Of making man into 'god' or a sort of co-god alongside the deity. So we think of Adolf Hitler and *Mein Kampf*, of

Karl Marx and *Das Kapital*, and even Charles Dawin and his *On The Origin of Species*. Few would bracket Charles Darwin with Hitler and Marx, but evolutionism at its most fundamental also sees man as the measure of all — not created man, but evolved man. It must then be noteworthy that each of these — communism, fascism and evolutionism, alongside the other more obvious religions — persecute those who follow Jesus solely as Lord and as Saviour. This world, it has been wisely observed, is not anti god. This world is anti *Christ*. We have religions and belief systems literally everywhere, but they all preach something radically different to the *righteousness of God*, who shouldered our guilt as Jesus died on the cross at Calvary.

Looking at just one of these belief systems, we quote from H.G. Wells, the British writer and essayist who is best known for his science fiction writings such as *The War of the Worlds* and *The Time Machine*. Wells was an outspoken socialist, but one who had no time for communism. He wrote this in chapter 15 of his massive 1936 tome *The Work, Wealth and Happiness of Mankind* — a sort of hymn to a socialist utopia:

> Perhaps the most vital contemporary religion is embodied in the disciplines of the communist party.... The Communist prides himself upon his implacable materialism. He is resolved not to fall away from the intense practicality which all other religions have so conspicuously lost . . . .
>
> The sense of the danger of 'weakening off' haunts the Communist and produces, just as it produced in other religions, a heavy stressing on orthodoxy. The [Communist] religion is fighting hard for great ends, and there is a heavy strategic disadvantage in any modifications of doctrine.

Communism clings to orthodoxy, the true and only faith, and already there have been heresy hunts in the Communist body . . . . Eminent officials are accused; they are subjected to rigorous enquiries, they confess and submit gratefully to discipline . . . . For the edification of the weaker brethren there are now prophets and saints, Marx and Lenin to begin with, whose intelligence and character must no longer be questioned, whose every utterance was divine.

And there is even a mystical communism, affecting the art and literature of Moscow profoundly, whose aim is self-identification with 'the Proletarian'. 'The Proletarian' is a superhuman entity with whom the devout Marxist seeks and attains spiritual communion. The individuality of the worshipper is merged therein.... From our present point of view Communism is only the latest and not the last of the world religions.'

Although he did not mention it, Wells may have had in mind Fascism, which in the Nazi manifestation also had its mystical ideals: of swearing allegiance to the military, of the *Volk* as the counterpart to the Proletariat. Both communism and fascism[4] worship the state as 'god' and see mere mortals as necessarily subsumed into the greater good of the state. It is not difficult to find precise counterparts in *the religions* of today.

Some basic Godist arguments with Christianity

In recent years the Godist philosophy has posited its own 'objections' to Christianity and especially to the exclusive claims of Christianity. It may be a surprise to some readers

---

[4] Communism and fascism also have their sacred 'hymns' — large numbers of patriotic songs, of which the most famous communist example is *The Internationale*. Google 'communism' and 'internationale' for the words.

that these objections emerge generally from within the church itself, which is where *determined Godists*, as opposed to *casual Godists*, are often to be found. As we noted in the Foreword to this book, Hinduism in most of its sub-categories certainly makes room for multiple gods, but Hinduism is not overall Godist in complexion. Islam is certainly not Godist, but can use the multi-faith agenda to promote its political objectives in the West.[5] Post-modern Judaism, in its 'liberal' manifestations, will certainly have some sympathy for the philosophy of Godism. It is sometimes commented that when a 'multi-faith initiative' or even a 'multi-faith service' is planned, it is usually church-based people who are the instigators and organisers. It would not be possible to list all Godist objections to Christianity because, as we noted elsewhere in this book, Godism is a malleable thing. However there are several key 'arguments' deployed, so it is worth considering these in turn:

- Jesus never commented on the 'other religions' of His day.
- Jesus never asked anyone to convert or change their religion.
- 'The Troubles' in Ulster prove that Christianity is just like the other religions — as regards warfare.
- God is ultimately responsible for His creation and therefore as He allowed sin to enter the world, it is His obligation to provide the remedy: so it was that Jesus (as God) 'deserved' to die on the cross.
- It would be unfair of God to 'damn' people of *the religions*, who had not had the opportunity to hear the saving good news of Jesus.

[5] See for examples *Islam and Dhimmitude* by Bat Ye'or, Fairleigh Dickinson University Press 2002, ISBN 0-8386-3934-7, especially chapter 10. Also *Faith, Power & Territory* by P Sookhdeo, Isaac Publishing ISBN 0978-0-9547835-8-7.

- All religions are the same once you take out 'fund-amentalism' and it is fundamentalism that the primary danger, not the alternative 'paths' offered.
- Religions are part of God's providence for all people.
- All religions contain truth and all contain error.
- Belief in *the religions* (as opposed to *The Way*) leads people closer to God, and so enables them to lead more godly lives, even if they fall short of the beauty of true Christianity.

Before we address these questions from a specifically Christian viewpoint, it is worth reminding ourselves of a few key biblical passages that have a bearing on this. It will be noted, in any case, that if the Godist as a church attender (as opposed, for example, to *the average man in the street*) has a low view of the Holy Bible — in other words considers Scripture to be tainted and unreliable — then there is little room for agreement or indeed any shifting of positions, because there is no dependable 'court of appeal' upon which both Godist and Bible believing Christian may agree. Acting as a *final court* has traditionally been one function of Holy Scripture, enabling the peaceful and authoritive resolution of differences within the church. We appeal to Holy Scripture once more as we try to discern the pathway that God has set apart for those who put their trust in Jesus. So just what is the 'great salvation' in which humans are invited to put their faith?

We must pay more careful attention, therefore, to what we have heard, so that we do not drift away. For if the message spoken by angels was binding, and every violation and disobedience received its just punishment, how shall we escape if we ignore such a great salvation? This salvation, which was first announced by the Lord,

was confirmed to us by those who heard him. God also testified to it by signs, wonders and various miracles, and gifts of the Holy Spirit distributed according to his will. (Hebrews 2:1–4)

So there we are reminded that we should be wary of drifting away from the true path. In the previous chapter (at 1:3), it is already stated plainly that Jesus **is the radiance of God's glory and the exact representation of his being**. Jesus had already spelled out what that salvation is, as he spoke to the crowds that had followed Him:

"Do not work for food that spoils, but [instead] **for food that endures to eternal life, which the Son of Man will give you. On him God the Father has placed his seal of approval."**

Then they asked him, "What must we do to do the works God requires?"

Jesus answered, "The work of God is this: to believe in the one he has sent."

So they asked him, "What miraculous sign then will you give that we may see it and believe you? What will you do? Our forefathers ate the manna in the desert; as it is written: 'He gave them bread from heaven to eat.' "

Jesus said to them, "I tell you the truth, it is not Moses who has given you the bread from heaven, but it is my Father who gives you the true bread from heaven. For the bread of God is he who comes down from heaven and gives life to the world."

"Sir," they said, "from now on give us this bread."

Then Jesus declared, "I am the bread of life. He who comes to me will never go hungry, and he who believes in me will never be thirsty. But as I told you, you have seen me and still you do not believe. All that the Father gives me will come to me, and whoever comes to me I will

258

never drive away. For I have come down from heaven not to do my will but to do the will of him who sent me. And this is the will of him who sent me, that I shall lose none of all that he has given me, but raise them up at the last day. For my Father's will is that everyone who looks to the Son and believes in him shall have eternal life, and I will raise him up at the last day." (John 6:27–40)

These were wonderful promises that Jesus gave to those who would follow Him. The apostle Paul reaffirmed the same point in his letter to the Roman church: **If you confess with your mouth, "Jesus is Lord," and believe in your heart that God raised him from the dead, you will be saved. For it is with your heart that you believe and are justified, and it is with your mouth that you confess and are saved. As the Scripture says, "Anyone who trusts in him will never be put to shame."** (Romans 10:9–11)

And similarly in his letter to the Ephesian church: **As for you, you were dead in your transgressions and sins, in which you used to live when you followed the ways of this world and of the ruler of the kingdom of the air, the spirit who is now at work in those who are disobedient. All of us also lived among them at one time, gratifying the cravings of our sinful nature and following its desires and thoughts. Like the rest, we were by nature objects of wrath. But because of his great love for us, God, who is rich in mercy, made us alive with Christ even when we were dead in transgressions — it is by grace you have been saved. And God raised us up with Christ and seated us with him in the heavenly realms in Christ Jesus, in order that in the coming ages he might show the incomparable riches of his grace, expressed in his kindness to us in Christ Jesus. For it is by grace you have been saved, through faith — and this not from** yourselves, it is the gift of God — not by works, so that no one can boast. For we are God's workmanship, created in Christ Jesus to do good works, which God prepared in advance for us to do. (Ephesians 2:1–9)

The apostle John made a similar point: He is the atoning sacrifice for our sins, and not only for ours but also for the sins of the whole world. (1 John 2:2)

Paul reaffirmed these basic truths: For he has rescued us from the dominion of darkness and brought us into the kingdom of the Son he loves. (Colossians 1:13.)

And in the Epistle to the Hebrews we read: For Christ did not enter a man-made sanctuary that was only a copy of the true one; he entered heaven itself, now to appear for us in God's presence. Nor did he enter heaven to offer himself again and again, the way the high priest enters the Most Holy Place every year with blood that is not his own. Then Christ would have had to suffer many times since the creation of the world. But now he has appeared once for all at the end of the ages to do away with sin by the sacrifice of himself. Just as man is destined to die once, and after that to face judgment, so Christ was sacrificed once to take away the sins of many people; and he will appear a second time, not to bear sin, but to bring salvation to those who are waiting for him. (Hebrews 9:24–28.)

By now we should be beginning to see the power and consistency of the affirmations of the New Testament writers, confirming what the Lord Jesus had already claimed — that He is the way, the truth and the life, and that no one comes to the Father except by Him (see John 14:6). With these thoughts informing us, let us now consider those typical Godist arguments in turn:

'Jesus never commented on the other religions of His day.' As the Lord Jesus did not come into this world in order to found a religion but rather to fulfil the Law of God[6] (and in that sense to delineate the end of 'religion') there was no reason for Him to refer to or to comment upon *the religions*. There were many religions in His own day, so the Lord would have had plenty of scope for comment had He chosen to do so. Jesus stayed singularly within the geographical precincts of ancient Israel. The Romans, who actually governed the lands, brought their many 'gods' with them. Why on earth should Jesus concern Himself with rather vacuous arguments about *belief systems* when His singular purpose was to fulfil the Law? Jesus' actions and teachings were already controversial, without the added difficulty of engaging in debate about religions — the figments of men's minds.

A subsidiary argument is also deployed by the Godist:

'Jesus never asked anyone to change their religion.' That surely is to miss the point entirely. In a very real sense Jesus *did* ask people to change their religion, by following God in spirit and in truth, rather than in religious observances. The 'religious' leaders of Jesus' day were in large measure (although it must be stated clearly that there were good and faithful priests and rabbis) leading ordinary people astray. Rather than acting as shepherds and protecting the flock, they were heaping religious burden upon burden onto those unhappy people, who had nowhere else to turn. Jesus was an observant Jew, but He plainly knew that His followers would be expelled from the organised Hebrew religion. He also knew that the Old Covenant was to be extended as a New Covenant and offered to all mankind,[7] and so He

---

[6] This is explored further in chapter 12.

[7] e.g. Hebrews 8:8–13 and 9:15.

commanded that the good news of Jesus (of Himself) should be preached to the ends of the earth.[8]

It would hardly be logical to command that the good news of freedom in Christ should be taken everywhere, to the very ends of the earth, if everywhere people were expected to remain within their religions. How then could people find peace if, for example, they were to continue to carry the burdens of their religions? It is disingenuous to claim that the Lord expected people to remain as they were, yoked to religions with all their incessant demands, all their burdens and all their uncertainties. How could the prince of peace give people peace if they were to remain wedded to religions that afford no peace? And we ask again, what on earth is meant by the marriage feast of the lamb, if people were to remain married to their religions?[9]

The incessant demand of the whole Bible is for people to 'come out and be separate' — to 'repent, for the kingdom of heaven is near'. Where Jesus lived there was only Judaism, though there were different factions, and their leaderships combined to persecute Him. The relationship with Jesus that He planned for His followers was one where He would indwell them by the Holy Spirit, so that His disciples would be conscious of Jesus' power within them.

Jesus never travelled outside of Judea, Samaria and Galilee (except of course when He was taken to safety by Joseph and Mary, in the *flight to Egypt*). His mission was solely to the Jewish people, hence in Matthew 10:5–6 Jesus gave clear instructions that His disciples should seek only the lost sheep of Israel (the covenant people); as their Messiah this was Jesus' sole mission (Mathew 15:2) for He had come to fulfil the law (their law). (See also Romans

---

[8] e.g. Matthew 28:19–20.

[9] Revelation 19: 7–10

1:16.) But we know from pre-history that God's plan was that a new covenant would be given to the benefit of all who follow Him, and would be sealed in His blood.[10] It must then be noteworthy that Jesus predicted that the disciples would be thrown out of the synagogues and a time was coming when those who follow *the religions* would kill disciples and think they were doing God's will.[11] That was true in apostolic times and remains the experience of Christians today as they encounter religious persecution.[12]

Christians are called to come out and to be separate — the call of the old covenant (to be separate) is extended into the new — which is why a true disciple must leave *the religions* in order to follow Jesus as Lord. It is also noteworthy that in the earliest discourses Paul noted the futility of religion (= circumcision) and the fact that religion places those who follow it straight back under Law.[13] When Christ-believing (Messianic) Jews and other believers were thrown out of their religions in the first century AD, that enabled them to become the true body of Christ. That was true then — and remains true today. The *body of Christ* is what we call the church. It is argued by this author (once again) that the church is not a religion, it is the body of Christ in this world today and for all time.[14]

'Jesus never asked anyone to convert.' No, but he told people to come and follow Him. He invited them to tread a narrow path that leads to life and to leave the broad road that leads to destruction.[15] He still does. It is interesting,

---

[10] Jeremiah 31:31–34.

[11] John 16:2.

[12] See Appendix 6.

[13] Galatians chapters 4 – 6 allude to this. Especially 4:9; 4:17 and 5:1.

[14] 1 Corinthians 12:12–30, especially v. 27.

[15] Matthew 7:13–14 and Luke 13:23–24.

then, that those who have been under the yoke of religion usually adopt a Christian name when they follow the Lord Jesus. Having a foot in both camps is simply not an option for a true disciple.

Lastly, it is noteworthy that the body of Christ (the church, the saints, by whatever name they are known) is grafted in to the root stock — the root being Israel. (See all of Romans 11, but especially verses 17, 19, 23 and 24.) God's elect constitute a good tree that cannot bear bad fruit — for this reason *the religions* cannot be in-grafted. The reality is, then, that a true follower of Jesus must convert — not as it happens from one religion to another religion, but to convert from death to life.[16] One of the practical out-workings of that is that they must come out from the yoke of religions as they come into His Kingdom.

Jesus told His followers quite plainly something that would have amazed them: unless their righteousness exceeded that of their religious leaders and *teachers of the law*, they would never enter the kingdom of heaven (Matthew 5:20). That was the bad news. But the good news was, and remains today, that Jesus had Himself come to fulfil the Law,[17] since no other human could. Rather than found a religion, Jesus came to change men's hearts, so that they could begin to lead God-honouring lives in this world *and* have assurance of being with Him forever as they remained rooted *in* Him. Jesus instituted those things that would enable men to follow Him and be identified as His disciples — meeting together for prayer, the universal call for repentance, the rite of baptism and the mutual breaking of bread as they remember Him. Jesus was not founding a religion, but these things were to become the hallmarks of

---

[16] John 5:24 — see also chapter 12 and the section headed *Life's Basic Choice*.

[17] Matthew 5:17.

Christianity — *The Way*.

'Jesus never asked anyone to leave their religion.' True, but His earthly ministry was solely to the Hebrew people. Since He came to fulfil their Law — to satisfy it forever — there would be no logical reason to ask Hebrew people to leave it. It is clear that He foreknew that His disciples would in any case be forced out of the synagogue and out of the fellowship that went with it. He did not need to invite what He knew would happen after He returned to heaven. But the critical need to come out and be separate, to follow Jesus single-mindedly and of not hiding our light under the table means that a parting of the ways between a follower of Jesus and *the religions* is quite inevitable, sooner or later. Jesus knew that the New Covenant would be available to all mankind — so, again, continuing within Judaism under the Old Covenant was no longer an option. Indeed, as observant Messianic Jews of the first century battled with this whole issue of continuing within Judaism, they found that it was impossible to remain within the synagogue without coming back under the 'Law'. And so the parting of the ways between Jesus' disciples and the Jewish religious hierarchy became permanent.

As it is the Godists who have raised this issue we must thank them for encouraging clarity in this: we focused earlier on a nineteenth century Hindu lady who yielded her life to the Lord Jesus. What did she have to say on this matter?

'I shall not attempt to describe how and what I felt at the time when I made an unconditional surrender, and knew I was accepted to be a branch of the True Vine, a child of God by adoption in Christ Jesus my Saviour . . . . How very different the truth of God was from the false idea that I had entertained from my earliest childhood. That was that I must

merit to earn present or future happiness, the pleasure of Svarga, or face the utterly inconceivable loss of Moksha or liberation. This I could never hope for, as a woman has no hope of Moksha . . . .

'How good, how indescribably good! What good news for me a woman, a woman born in India, among Brahmans who hold out no hope for me and the like of me! The Bible declares that Christ did not reserve this great salvation for a particular caste or sex . . . . No caste, no sex, no work, and no man was to be depended upon to get salvation, this everlasting life, but God gave it freely to any one and every one who believed on His Son Whom He sent to be the 'propitiation for our sins'.

'I had to give up all pride of ancestral religion being old and superior, which is preventing many of my country-people from finding Christ although they know they have not got the joy of salvation. They can never have it except in Christ . . . . Do not therefore lose time through pride or because of any other difficulty. The caste may put you out, your near and dear ones perhaps reject and persecute you, you may very likely lose your temporal greatness and riches; but never mind. The great salvation which you will get in Christ by believing on Him and confessing Him before men, is worth all the great sacrifices you can possibly make. Yes and more than that, for all the riches and all the gain, and all the joys of the world, do not begin to compare with the JOY OF SALVATION.

'I would urge you, dear brother or sister, to make haste and get reconciled with God through Christ. For the great day of judgement is fast coming on us, so make haste and flee from the wrath of God, which you and I have justly merited. God is love, and He is waiting patiently for you to accept His great salvation. So despise not 'the riches *of His goodness and forbearance and longsuffering', and know 'that goodness of God leadeth thee to repentance' (Romans 2:4).*

'The "Troubles" in Ulster prove that Christianity is just like the other religions.'

This is a singularly British issue, but similar comments might be made of the tensions and animosities that have sadly afflicted (for example) the Roman Catholic and Greek Orthodox traditions. Presumably as people make this comment they also have in mind that *if God cannot keep 'His own' in order then what is the point of following Him*? Since at least some of this reasoning (or lack of!) is rather disingenuous, one suspects that the objection is offered up as a neat excuse rather than as a genuine stumbling block to seriously considering the claims of Jesus. Nevertheless, as it is a widespread objection in the UK we will answer it in relation to the Ulster problems. But the answer we proffer is likely to be of relevance where similar animosities have been found in the past. So, the Irish Republican Army (IRA) is sometimes offered as an example of 'Christian extremists' who, it is claimed, are on a par with (for example) Muslim jihadists. But they are not and cannot be: the Ulster 'troubles' owed a lot to 'right versus left' politics, with the Protestants being broadly right and the Catholics broadly left. The IRA owed much of its political theory to communism and it is not surprising it lost a great deal of political and military support with the final demise of communism in Europe. That seems to have been one of the reasons why the IRA/Republican leadership became more interested in 'peace' in the late 1990s. Also, of course, there was a reduction in financial support due to the reduction in US (Catholic) support after the 9/11 terrorist attack in New York. As far as the author knows, no one has ever claimed in Eire or Ulster that they were doing God's will in the terrorist 'Troubles'. The fact that the Roman Catholic church was muted in its condemnation of the IRA and widely perceived to have failed to condemn IRA violence may require a commentary from Roman Catholics rather than this author, but could reflect the readiness with which Catholicism historically appears to perceive itself as a political as well as a spiritual instrument.

A true Christian will be recognised by their gifts (1 Corinthians 12:4–11 and 28) and by the fruit in their lives (Galatians 5:22–6). Since this fruit was singularly lacking in the main armed factions, it is fair to conclude that they did not comprise true Christians (i.e. people who were born again). What are called 'Christian' belligerences, if they exist at all, are in direct contradiction of the clear teaching of Jesus. Violence, by contrast, under Islam, is specifically legislated for in the Koran. It is for Godists to explain why their 'god' so completely changed His mind on peace and war as between Christianity and Islam.

The final nail in the coffin of this idea of IRA having been 'Christian militants' comes from the former *Red Army Faction* terrorist Astrid Proll, a German terrorist of the 1970s (active, coincidentally, at the height of the Ulster Troubles). The Red Army Faction was linked to the Baader Meinhof gang in Germany. Trained by Fatah (Palestinian organisation) in use of guns and terrorist techniques, they caused much bloodshed and heartache in West Germany, as it then was. She was interviewed by the Times Newspaper in its 12 November 2008 edition. Remembering as we have said, that communism bears the hallmarks of man-made religion, Proll's comments on the IRA, spoken as an expert in the field of left wing militancy, are instructive. She fled to England after release by the German authorities and said that she met many left wing people in the UK, but that they were not so hysterical and morally rigorous as the ones she knew in Germany. And this most pertinent comment of all — *there was no space for an armed left-wing group in the UK, because the IRA already held that role*. The IRA were not religious terrorists. They were left wing terrorists. No doubt some will continue to cite the IRA as being a 'Christian' terrorist group. A few no doubt in sheer ignorance, others in a disingenuous way.

'God is ultimately responsible for His creation and therefore as He allowed sin to enter the world, so he must provide the remedy: so it was that Jesus (as God) 'deserved' to die on the cross' We review that claim exhaustively in chapter 13.

'It would be unfair of God to 'damn' people of **the religions,** *who had not had the opportunity to hear the saving good news of Jesus.'* We will leave this question for the time being as it is dealt with exhaustively in chapter 13.

'All religions are the same once you take out 'funda-mentalism' and it is fundamentalism that the primary danger, not the alternative 'paths' offered. Religions are part of God's providence for all people' If readers have been following this book systematically, it should by now be abundantly clear that whatever *the religions* are, they are not the same! This book is not a comparison of religions, but even the most cursory and casual glance reveals phenomenal differences and contradictions between *the religions*. Even if they could all be wrong, they could not all be right! Godists may claim *the religions* are the same but they delude only

themselves. We revert to the question about the nature of a 'god' who decides to reveal 'himself' or 'itself' in markedly different ways, indifferent to the potential for harm and conflict that this entails.

'All religions contain truth and all contain error.'

The background in which all religions operate is that of the created order, in which the one true God has given man the basic insight that He (the Creator God) exists, and in which man knows right from wrong, good from evil. (See Romans 1.) So it need not surprise us if we find traces of that basic human awareness cropping up here and there in human life and culture. These basic insights are the reason why man is *without excuse* for sin. But *truth*, as we have seen, is not merely a set of propositions, it is a person, for the Lord Jesus stated plainly that He *is* the truth: **"I am the way the truth and the life. No one comes to the Father except through me"** (John 14:6). The Lord's statement requires no elaboration. You either accept it or you reject it. A middle course is not possible — although many continue to try to 'find' one, as for example in Godism. Whilst individual Christians and even some churches may fall into error, the Lord will guide us into all truth; and God's Word, the Bible, remains the standard by which truth claims are to be tested.

'Belief in the religions (as opposed to The Way) leads people closer to God, and so enables them to lead more godly lives, even if they fall short of the beauty of true Christianity.'

If belief in *the religions* enabled people to lead better lives, then most would consider that to be at least a benign side-effect. However the various religions do seem to entail belief systems and practical outworkings that are often injurious to their followers, or to those who refuse to follow. The Christian's focus should be on *salvation*. We are not called to live 'slightly better lives'. We are actually called to be holy (1 Peter 1:15). It is the Lord Jesus who is able to present us to God as 'without fault' (or holy) as we read in Jude 24. In order to avoid God's righteous and just judgement we must either fulfil the Law or be saved from the Law. Religions may have the (unintended?) consequence of deluding their followers into the idea that they are earning their 'salvation' when in fact they remain entrapped by sin, and without anyone to plead on their behalf. Instead of focusing on religious beliefs and their various burdens, Jesus comments in Matthew 11:30 quite simply that His burden is 'light'. And His 'yoke' is easy — giving us the impression of a well-fitting harness, one that does not chafe or hurt us. For those of us who are wearied by the burdens of *the religions*, we do well to heed Jesus' words rather than try to harness ourselves to those religions:

"Come to me, all you who are weary and burdened, and I will give you rest. Take my yoke upon you and learn from me, for I am gentle and humble in heart, and you will find rest for your souls. For my yoke is easy and my burden is light."

Remember, salvation ultimately is a gift, as we see in Titus 3:5 — **". . . he saved us, not because of righteous things we had done, but because of his mercy. He saved us through the washing of rebirth and renewal by the Holy Spirit."** The New Testament makes it clear that the gift of salvation is received through faith. **By grace you have been saved through faith; and this is not your own doing, it is the gift of God.** (Ephesians 2:8)

The Religions, it must be remembered, may lead people to live worse lives! The Bible's contention is quite clear: it is only through Jesus that people might be saved. We nailed Him to the cross by our sins, as the apostle Peter stated before the Sanhedrin (Acts 4:10, as Peter was forced to explain the miraculous healing of a crippled beggar) but in a very real sense he addresses us as well: **". . . then know this . . . . It is by the name of Jesus Christ of Nazareth, whom you crucified but whom God raised from the dead, that this man stands before you healed. [Jesus] . . . is 'the stone you builders rejected, which has become the capstone'. Salvation is found in no one else, for there is no other name under heaven given to men by which we must be saved."**

Case proven?

It is hoped that readers will begin to see that there are sound arguments that address the basic Godist objections to Christianity. There comes a point at which we have to ask just how much we are entitled to expect in terms of 'answers' to our specific questions of God. He has been plain enough in all that He has said. There is a limit, surely, to what we can expect in terms of our somewhat insubstantial questions about the way in which God has chosen to offer us the gift of salvation. When we incessantly find objections and difficulties, are we like lumps of clay trying to have an argument with the potter? **You turn things upside down, as if the potter were thought to be like the clay! Shall what is formed say to him who formed it, "He did not make me"? Can the pot say of the potter, "He knows nothing?"** (Isaiah 29:16)

The church welcomes honest questioning and honest doubts. But there must come a point at which people will have to make a decision about the evidence given. We think again of our *Oligarch's Game* described in the Foreword to this book, although we recognise that the analogy has its limitations. Ultimately, people need to make a decision if they are to be enriched immeasurably by the love of God and know for themselves the saving power of Jesus. To fail to make any decision is ultimately a 'vote against' Jesus. When so great a salvation has been revealed it must be the ultimate insult to God to reject it — to throw back in His face a gift that He has gone to such extraordinary and costly lengths to provide.

Some readers may object that the answers provided still do not satisfy them personally: if so, then that is their ultimate choice. God does not force Himself on anyone. Jesus does not barge in, and He graciously gives us time and opportunity to respond with repentance and faith in Him. But time for decision must inevitably one day run out, and that is why we suggest that to fail to make any decision as regards Christ is the same as casting a vote against Him. How shall we escape if we ignore such a great salvation? (See Hebrews 2:3) This salvation has been confirmed to us by those who actually saw Jesus, and at the end we are bound either to accept or reject their testimony.

The world generally casts its vote against Jesus (at least in the sphere of *the religions* and in the popular media and amongst Western intelligentsia), rejecting His claim on their lives and effectively declining the offer of forgiveness, salvation, eternal life. Some readers may be shocked and consider this is just too harsh a conclusion, but we repeat: God has graciously allowed us time to decide which side we are on, and no-one knows when they will die and have to face judgement. Others may object: surely to be neutral as regards this great salvation cannot be construed as a rejection? Jesus was emphatic that it could: **"he who is not with me is against me"** he said (in Luke 11:23).

Knowledgeable readers will immediately pick up the apparent contrast with Luke 9:50. Let us close this debate with a few words to see how Jesus' two statements do *not* conflict. To understand the deeper meaning of Jesus' words, we need to know the context. What did Jesus say, to whom did He say it and why? There are four occurrences which look relevant. In Matthew 12:30 and Luke 11:23, Jesus says: **"He who is not with Me is against Me; and he who does not gather with Me scatters."** But, in Mark 9:40 and Luke 9:50, He makes two statements that seem to say the reverse. In Mark 9:40, Jesus said: **"For he who is not against us is for us."** And in Luke 9:50, He says: **"He who is not against you is for you."** We encounter the first occurrence of our negative statement (not with me is against me) in Matthew 12, which taken in context spans verses 22 to 32: **Then they brought him a demon-possessed man who was blind and mute, and Jesus healed him, so that he could both talk and see. All the people were astonished and said, "Could this be the Son of David?"**

But when the Pharisees heard this, they said, "It is only by Beelzebub, the prince of demons, that this fellow drives out demons."

Jesus knew their thoughts and said to them, "Every kingdom divided against itself will be ruined, and every city or household divided against itself will not stand. If Satan drives out Satan, he is divided against himself. How then can his kingdom stand? And if I drive out demons by Beelzebub, by whom do your people drive them out? So then, they will be your judges. But if I drive out demons by the Spirit of God, then the kingdom of God has come upon you.

"Or again, how can anyone enter a strong man's house and carry off his possessions unless he first ties up the

strong man? Then he can rob his house.

"**He who is not with me is against me, and he who does not gather with me scatters. And so I tell you, every sin and blasphemy will be forgiven men, but the blasphemy against the Spirit will not be forgiven. Anyone who speaks a word against the Son of Man will be forgiven, but anyone who speaks against the Holy Spirit will not be forgiven, either in this age or in the age to come.**"

This account is repeated in Luke 11:14–28. It is interesting to note that the two negative accounts were given to the Pharisees when they accused Jesus of casting out demons in the name of Beelzebub. The account in Matthew leads into a warning about the unforgivable sin of blasphemy against the Holy Spirit. The negative account in Luke leads into a discourse about an unclean spirit leaving a man only to return later with seven spirits far worse than itself. We can see that in these two negative occurrences, Jesus is speaking out against the Pharisees. Let us take a look at the same basic phrase in its positive context (he who is not against us is with us). In Mark 9:38–41 we read: "**Teacher," said John, "we saw a man driving out demons in your name and we told him to stop, because he was not one of us.**"

"**Do not stop him," Jesus said. "No one who does a miracle in my name can in the next moment say anything bad about me, for whoever is not against us is for us. I tell you the truth, anyone who gives you a cup of water in my name because you belong to Christ will certainly not lose his reward.**" The same episode is recorded in Luke 9:49–50. We see that the positive occurrence was communicated to the disciples, as they questioned the authority of other people casting out demons in Jesus' name.

This phrase is the same one that, when reversed and spoken in context to the other group of people (the Pharisees), meant something entirely different. Jesus' words signified: these men whom you would like to turn away actually believe although they lack knowledge. The Pharisees, though they have full knowledge of the sacred writings, still profane that which they know to be truth. To put this another way, the men who are *for* Jesus (though they may seem, at first glance, to be rather far away), walk faithfully in the light they have available. The Pharisees, who present themselves as devout and dedicated to God, are actually far from Him, perverting the light that they do have. To the hard-hearted and unbelieving Pharisees, Jesus spoke words they needed to hear: 'You are not with Me.' Conversely, to the disciples, He spoke the words they also needed to hear. In effect: 'Do not judge people who work in my name; they are with us.' The Pharisees did not believe in Jesus; the disciples did believe but were limiting His power.

Some church-attending Godists might say that, irrespective of their unbelief in all that the Bible has to say, and their belief in multiple religions, they too are acting in Jesus' name. However, there must be a huge danger that, like the Pharisees, they too are deeply hard-hearted and stiff-knecked. With the clear knowledge of Jesus Who has declared Himself to be the way, the truth and the life (not *a* way, *a* truth and *a* life), and supposedly a knowledge of the gospel of Christ, they persist in saying that God has revealed Himself in multiple and contradictory ways. How sad! And they are determined to keep others subject to the burdens of *the religions*. How selfish!

12

LAW AND GRACE:
THE BASIC CHOICE IN LIFE

A Titanic Mistake?

We begin to draw this exploration of Godism to a close. Through this book we have looked at various ideas that underpin Godism, which itself reduces to the view that all the 'higher' religions lead to God, although we note that Godism does not clearly define what constitutes a *higher* religion. We noted early in our study that Godists, whether of the *determined* variety, or the *casual man in the street* sort, all share a 'god'-focus, to the extent that they acknowledge that there exists a 'god' or 'gods' and that this 'god' is presumed to have an obligation to 'save' the majority of people in this world. Early in the book we asked whether the Godists' 'god'–focus or 'god'–centric, 'god'–positive but (selectively) religion–negative view of the deity is correct, and indeed whether this view honours God. We suggested that this is a question that must be faced by anyone with any real integrity in this debate. In chapter 8 we posited a pseudo formula to describe Godism (Godism is **G + R[N] + RI + AK − TS**) but throughout we have noted that Godism is a malleable philosophy that resists simple classification. Although not yet a religion, it seems entirely possible that

Godism will spawn either a new religion or religions in the future. Christian writers concerned with eschatology have well developed views on this latter thought, so interested readers will have no problem finding useful biblical material on the subject. The Holy Bible certainly indicates an end-time global religion emerging — one that is fundamentally anti-Christ. We repeat an earlier assertion: this world is not anti-God; it is anti-Christ.

Whenever there is a discussion about religions and the simple claim of the Lord Jesus, *I am the way the truth and the life, no one comes to the Father except through me* (John 14:6), there is an explicit or implicit accusation that Christians are 'damning' those of other faiths. In polite company this is seen as the 'ace card' with which either to trump believing Christians and silence them or to 'prove' that their God is unfair, and therefore unworthy of worship. In impolite company this is seen as hectoring by Christians and bordering on the social sin of something called 'religious hatred' — although precisely why it might be hateful to suggest that there may truly be ONLY one way to peace with God, allowing that there must be (at the very least) a prospect that this view is actually correct, is never adequately explained. Others argue in contrast that it is, in fact, loving to warn people of the sedative effect of *the religions* that may well lead their unknowing adherents into error and into conflict with God. When the RMS Titanic ploughed at top speed through a mill pond North Atlantic ocean on an inky-black moonless night on 14 April 1912, on a direct heading to a large iceberg, would it have been 'hatred' to have warned its passengers who were so sure of their security? To have warned that, in spite of the age and 'higher' status of the White Star shipping line, in spite of the strength of the ship, in spite of the grandeur and experience of captain Smith who saw no danger, in spite of the excellent crew and the 'unsinkable' nature of the ship — that it was a ship on a course that would lead it to utter disaster? 'God Himself could not sink this ship' was a reported comment of one of the deck hands to Mrs Albert Caldwell.[1] Even if the prospect that God has uniquely revealed Himself through Jesus, and made only one provision for salvation, through His blood, were considered to be only a remote possibility, then because of the nature of the issues at stake, it would surely be prudent to take a candid and calm look at the claim, no matter how uncomfortable it might at first seem.

The question about the eternal destiny of non-Christians is often sincere, so we must explore the issue *from a biblical perspective*. First, however, we need to set the scene to ensure we are asking the right question, and finding the right answer. Readers who really want to get to grips with this difficult issue will find a wealth of material available. Of course, Godists themselves say quite simply that all religions lead to God, and they proffer what they consider to be the similarities between them, carefully ignoring the glaring differences. In Appendix 1 we note that the underlying belief that 'there are multiple paths to God' ultimately reveals a dismissive attitude to the Almighty. We noted that 'god' is seen by some as being a sort of CEO (chief executive officer) of a global religious conglomerate, a CEO who is not too concerned about brand loyalty because He owns all the brands and has a monopoly on the supply of salvation. Elsewhere in this book we have challenged whether such a CEO type 'god' could be either good or holy — and in chapters 6 and 7 we looked at these matters exhaustively from the biblical perspective, where God is indeed revealed

---

[1] *A Night to Remember* by Walter Lord, chapter 3.

as being both good and holy. Is it not unbelievable that a supposed 'god' of the Godists' would present 'himself' in multiple guises, with no clear message except perhaps, a rather vague 'Golden Rule' (see chapter 1) which people are supposed to discern amongst all the 'noise' and 'clutter' of religious belief systems and sacred writings?

In the preceding paragraph we spoke of a wealth of material available to help readers to get a grip on the underlying issues. The author has in mind two key biblical concepts: *law* and *grace* — massive subjects that have spawned myriad volumes, but which we must now refer to in summary form. If readers feel that the author has not explained himself adequately, or possibly has mis-represented the case, then they are urged to review these two concepts exhaustively as their own separate study.

By 'law' here we mean primarily the law of Moses (*torah*) which observant Jews have endeavoured to follow, though there is a second important usage, which focuses on God's basic laws for all mankind. That all men, including Gentiles, should know the latter is made clear by Paul in Romans. Under the Mosaic covenant, 'righteousness' was conditional on obedience to the law, accompanied by faith. Under the law, man failed, because people tried to obtain righteousness by fulfilling the legal requirements only, but so often without faith. (Further study will be helped by looking at: John 7:19; Galatians 3:11–12, 22, 24; Exodus 20:1–26; 24:12 and 31:18; Deuteronomy 6:6–9; Psalm 1:2; 19:7–8 and 37:31; Psalm 40:8 and 119:1.)

Under law, men failed. Christ came to bring a better hope (see Hebrews 7:19) which was a new way of grace in a new covenant. (Cf. Isaiah 1:13–18; 5:24; Jeremiah 9:13–16; Ezekiel 22:26; Daniel 9:8–13; Matthew 5:17 and 22:36, 37, 40; Luke 1:6; John 1:17; Acts 13:39 and 15:5, 10–11,

28. Romans 2:12–14; 3:20; 4:15; 5:13–14; 8:3–4 and 13:8–10; Galatians 3:21; Philippians 3:4,6; James 2:10.)

The freedom of grace (God's gift) has been bought with the blood of Christ. Therefore any Christian who relies on outward observance of the regulations of the Mosaic law comes again under the judgement of God[2] (see Acts 15:1, 2, 5, 19; Galatians 3:10, Galatians 5:3–4). The early church background to this was twofold: 'Judaisers' were commending circumcision as a legal requirement for Gentile converts; and Jewish messianic believers might be tempted to go back to the synagogue and renounce Christ in order to come under the protection afforded to Jews against persecution by the Roman authorities, who began at a certain point to require emperor worship by non-Jews. It has been observed that requiring 'tithing' today is not dissimilar to the early efforts of the Judaisers.

'Grace' is God's gift: He has exercised unmerited favour toward us by providing the way of salvation through repentance and faith in Jesus Christ, not by any 'works' or righteousness of our own. The messianic covenant of grace began in this world with the death and resurrection of Christ. See Titus 3:4–5; John 1:17; 1:12–13 and 3:36; Romans 3:24–27; 5:2, 15–21 and 6:14; 2 Corinthians 6:1–3 and 8:9; Galatians 1:3–15; 2:21 and 5:4.

Law demands, grace gives (see Deuteronomy 5:17–20; cf 1 John 4:19; John 1:12 and 3:16; Romans 3:21–24; Romans 8:3 and 10:4–10; Philippians 3:9 and 4:13; Hebrews 7:19; cf Psalm 51:11; Ephesians 5:18.) Grace saves sinners as they repent and believe (see Ephesians 2:1–9). The law of God

---

[2] Readers may want to check 1 Timothy 1:6–11. Here we are reminded that some had come into the church as false teachers, had wandered away from the command to love and instead wanted to teach the law which, Timothy tersely notes, they did not understand.

was revealed to men; they failed to repent and believe, and they ended up by crucifying Christ. At the end there will be much apostasy, and the judgements that the Bible foretells will take place. But it is vital to note that it is mankind that fails, not God's plan of grace. (See 2 Corinthians 4:3–4; 2 Timothy 3:1–8; 1 John 4:1–3; 2 Peter 2:1; Jude 4:8, 11–13, 16; 2 Thessalonians 2:11–12; Revelation 3:14–16. The freedom and simplicity of the gospel is God's final plan of salvation. Any other gospel is anathema. (See Galatians 1:8–9; cf John 10:1.)

Life's Basic Choice

Mankind has made his so-called 'case' against God in many and diverse ways, some of which we have explored in this book. It may be a discomfiting surprise for many to learn that, in a very real sense, God has His own case against mankind. Everyone has a basic choice: to attempt to satisfy God with one's own attempts at righteousness or to live under the new covenant, having responded with repentance and faith in Jesus Christ. No other way has been provided by God for relationship with Him. It is useless to trust in our own righteousness, only in the righteousness of Christ and His sacrifice for our sins. We have contrasted law and grace, but we must qualify that at once by noting that God's purpose in revealing His will is of course always wholly good. The law showed man how to live, but man did not reach its perfect standard. The new (messianic) covenant, under which a righteousness from God is made available, is all too often rejected. We humans are found wanting unless we repent (turn away from sin and turn back to God in sincerity), believe (and go on believing) in Jesus Christ, and live in the power of the Holy Spirit.

God's case against mankind is explicit, as we have seen,

but He has also gone to extraordinary lengths to redeem mankind. So He sent prophets to teach and to warn, as well as to give the promise of a permanent Saviour. Jesus lived a life of perfect holiness. He, the innocent, died in place of the guilty. His death was substitutionary (He died in your place and mine).[3] His death was fully effective *and was final*. As our resurrected Saviour, He has defeated death, which is our ultimate enemy. All humans, then, have a basic choice, *to live* (in Him) or *not to live* (in Him): to accept His sacrifice on the cross as the penalty for our sins, and to turn to Him and follow Him as His disciples. This is the concept of new birth, about which the Lord Jesus was quite plain in his conversation with the Pharisee Nicodemus (John 3:1–21; text is generally from the NKJV, except that a rendering of the correct continuous present tense as regards 'belief' has been added by the author):

There was a man of the Pharisees named Nicodemus, a ruler of the Jews. This man came to Jesus by night and said to Him, "Rabbi, we know that You are a teacher come from God; for no one can do these signs that You do unless God is with him."

Jesus answered and said to him, "Most assuredly, I say to you, unless one is born again, he cannot see the kingdom of God."

Nicodemus said to Him, "How can a man be born when he is old? Can he enter a second time into his mother's womb and be born?"

Jesus answered, "Most assuredly, I say to you, unless one is born of water and the Spirit, he cannot enter the kingdom of God. That which is born of the flesh is

---

[3] A Greek Orthodox friend who read this in draft form reminded the author that although Christ has died in our place, we too are to die – but we are to die to sin. See Romans chapter 6.

flesh, and that which is born of the Spirit is spirit. Do not marvel that I said to you, 'You must be born again.' The wind blows where it wishes, and you hear the sound of it, but cannot tell where it comes from and where it goes. So is everyone who is born of the Spirit."

Nicodemus answered and said to Him, "How can these things be?"

Jesus answered and said to him, "Are you the teacher of Israel, and do not know these things? Most assuredly, I say to you, We speak what We know and testify what We have seen, and you do not receive Our witness. If I have told you earthly things and you do not believe, how will you believe if I tell you heavenly things? No one has ascended to heaven but He who came down from heaven, that is, the Son of Man who is in heaven. And as Moses lifted up the serpent in the wilderness, even so must the Son of Man be lifted up, that whoever *[continues to believe]* in Him should not perish but have eternal life. For God so loved the world that He gave His only begotten Son, that whoever *[continues to believe]* in Him should not perish but have everlasting life. For God did not send His Son into the world to condemn the world, but that the world through Him might be saved.

"He who *[continues to believe]* in Him is not condemned; but he who does not *[continue to]* believe is condemned already, because he has not *[continued to]* believe in the name of the only begotten Son of God. And this is the condemnation, that the light has come into the world, and men loved darkness rather than light, because their deeds were evil. For everyone practicing evil hates the light and does not come to the light, lest his deeds should be exposed. But he who does the truth comes to the light, that his deeds may be clearly seen,

that they have been done in God."

Key verses for our present study are probably vv.14–15. These foretell what would happen to the Lord Jesus at Golgotha, and follows with the promise that those who believe in Him will have eternal life. As the correct tense of the original Greek passage (where indicated above) is the *present continuous tense* (and modern English translations seem to miss this[4]) we have included in the passage above the idea of *going on believing* in Jesus, which suggests that there are circumstances in which a believer can cease to believe and so lose their relationship with Him. This should be a wake-up call to Godists where they are found within church settings and consider themselves to be orthodox believers. Note, too, that God 'loved' the world and the tense in this case is singular, not continuous, and it refers to the unique event when the Son of God was given, providing the way of salvation like that event recorded in the Old Testament when sick Hebrews could look at a bronze snake on a stake, and live (see John 3:14, cp. Numbers 21:4–9). It does not mean that God loves the world (continuously); His 'agape' love here is in providing (once) for our greatest need: a Saviour, who alone can save from sin and give life.

Whilst some churches are called 'broad',[5] there must come a point at which it becomes clear that Godism ceases to be in any meaningful way Christian, as we suggested in the Foreword to this book, when we used the analogy of a politician of one political party constantly sitting and voting with a rival party. In that secular analogy we have

---

[4] The interlinear transliteration of the New Testament published by Zondervan (ISBN 0-310-40160-7) renders this more correctly as 'everyone believing in him' and 'the one believing in him' – thus correctly capturing the present continuous tense in the original Scripture.

[5] This is perhaps more a statement of fact than a statement of God's intention!

no difficulty in seeing that at some point, in spite of any protestations to the contrary, such a politician would cease in any meaningful sense to be a true member of their party. This lesson is quite easy to comprehend in the case of secular politics and it is difficult to see why the same point cannot be made with regard to Christianity.

The straightforward choice for all people can be summarised in this way: to live, or not to live? To be forgiven, to be made new, to be born again, to be saved from the power, the grip, the guilt and the consequences of sin? To be saved from an eternity without God? Or to live without God here, and to be conscious of that loss through all eternity? These are serious matters, indeed. The Godist mentality is all too often one of surrender to the philosophy of the day in which it lives. We heard in chapter 1 of a religious *Council of Sages* meeting at the time this book was being written, with the objective of discerning a so-called 'Golden Rule' among *the religions*. Well meaning men and women will, with the active support and funding of agencies like the UN, tell us that religions are in fact all one, and that religious differences are merely illusory. This, of course, may be the counsel of a spiritual Captain Smith and risks a religious catastrophe of Titanic proportions. We can only observe once again that the view that all religions are essentially one (a) ignores the inconvenient and self-evident truth that they are not, and (b) runs the very real gauntlet of the wrath of God to Whom we will all one day have to give an account (e.g. 2 Corinthians 5:10 and Revelation 20:11–15). It must surely be of some significance that the very first reference in the Holy Bible to heterodox religious beliefs is quite early on, in Genesis chapter 31:19, where Rachel (the wife of Jacob) steals her father's *household gods*. In chapter 35:2 Jacob commands his household to get rid of the foreign 'gods' and to purify themselves for true worship of Almighty God. It must be of real symbolic importance that the first reference to belief in other 'gods' is met with Almighty God's uncompromising demand for purity.

Although we may assume that there were other 'gods' being worshipped at the time, the Bible is silent about them. On the Godist's argument, in the interests of 'diversity', and of giving people more than one chance to get right with Him, surely God would have made at least some comment upon the positive value of other belief systems and of a need for respect and understanding of other peoples' 'gods'? He does not. The call remains one of purity. Has God changed His mind and decided that purity is no longer necessary? Irrespective of the gravitas of today's politicians or religious leaders who say otherwise, the Holy Bible is quite clear that purity remains the central requirement of Christianity. As regards Godism, then, the choice seems to be: full steam ahead, to the iceberg of religious syncretism, or chart a safe course by keeping our eyes fixed upon Jesus? (See Hebrews 12:2).

What is Christianity?

Christianity has become such a broad term that its meaning is today blurred. Most people, however, will understand that it truly means to be a sincere and faithful follower of the Lord Jesus, and to worship God Who sent His Son into this world. Appendix 4 seeks to answer the question of what Christianity is from a biblical perspective, and especially the idea of the Gospel, the *good news* of Jesus. There are today 'Christian Democrat' political parties in Western Europe. The media's news reporters occasionally cite terrorists, or dubious celebrities, or modern cults, as 'Christian'. People will talk about having a *Christian attitude* when they mean to behave in a kindly manner towards other people. Extreme right wing parties in Western countries will sometimes style themselves as 'Christian', not in a religious but in a cultural and racial sense. We can see, then, that the term is just too wide and too open to misinterpretation to be really adequate. So some Christians prefer to call themselves quite simply *believers* as they feel today's church is becoming just too broad. Endeavouring not to be overly prescriptive and divisive, the author offers a description of Christianity in Appendix 4, but recognises that there will be some Christians who have difficulties with some aspects of it. It is unlikely, however, that any serious Christian would quibble too much with the summary in the Appendix. Similarly, such Christians would probably recognise and agree the central thrust of this book, and its message about the emptiness of the Godist 'promise' of 'salvation' through religions.

True Christianity represents freedom from the dominion of the law (signifying here detailed requirements of the Mosaic regulations). The law had to be satisfied, but has been satisfied once and for all in and through Jesus. We are reminded in the epistle to the Hebrews that the law demanded sacrifice by priests year after year, but that Jesus had fulfilled the law by offering Himself as the perfect sacrifice (see Hebrews chapter 10), so His disciples are purified from sin through His body (10:10). The message of the first apostles, and indeed the believing church through the ages, is simply this: repent, believe in Jesus, be baptised, and follow Him. God the Father loved us with a love we did not deserve (or earn) when He gave Jesus for us. He loved us in and through Jesus, His Son. It is not God's will that any people should be lost, but rather that all should be saved (2 Peter 3:9). But God does not force Himself upon us. (And Christians cannot 'force' anyone who is unwilling to know

Him to accept His gift.) God desires a relationship of love and trust with us, where our love of Him is real.

A human being's love for God does not always manifest itself in strong 'feelings', but most Christians will affirm that as the years go by they do indeed love God, Father, Son and Holy Spirit, more and more. 'Love' here is not just about feelings, anyway: at the heart of it is our obedience. We must do what Jesus commands, and we must go on believing in Him.

Before we consider how God views the genuine followers of *the religions*, as opposed to followers of *The Way* (Jesus), we need finally to get to grips with this idea of the law. The apostle Paul's letter to the Roman church contains clear teaching about the law, from the perspective both of God's promises to Israel in the Old Testament and in the messianic Covenant (God's promises to those who are in Christ, believers in Jesus). After initial greetings, Paul writes of the gospel that it is: **the power of God for salvation to everyone who has faith, to the Jew first and also to the Greek. For in it the righteousness of God is revealed through faith** (Romans 1:16–17, NRSV). Both the Jewish and the Gentile believers in Rome had needed to be put right with God because all had been under the power of sin. People are put right with God through faith in Jesus. Paul goes on to describe the new life in union with Jesus, where the believer has peace with God and is set free from the power of sin and death. In chapters 5 to 8 Paul focuses on the law and the power of the Spirit in the believer's life. God is not indifferent to the sin of the world and He will in the end deal with it. So what, precisely, does Romans teach us?

The wrath of God is being revealed from heaven against all the godlessness and wickedness of men who

suppress the truth by their wickedness, since what may be known about God is plain to them, because God has made it plain to them. For since the creation of the world God's invisible qualities — his eternal power and divine nature — have been clearly seen, being understood from what has been made, so that men are without excuse.

For although they knew God, they neither glorified him as God nor gave thanks to him, but their thinking became futile and their foolish hearts were darkened. Although they claimed to be wise, they became fools and exchanged the glory of the immortal God for images made to look like mortal man and birds and animals and reptiles. (Romans 1:18–23).

These six verses are key to an argument we will consider later, so readers may want to note them. God is not mocked and will eventually judge all rebels against Himself. What may be known about God is plain to 'men'. It has been plain from the beginning of time and will be plain until the end of time. When we see the beauty of creation (this world in which we live) and all the good things that it has to offer, and when we see the beauty of love between human beings — and by this we mean true love, not the erotic kind so favoured by the world at large, but love as exemplified in the self-giving love of a mother to her newborn child — then we know in our heart of hearts that in practice there really *is* a good 'design' behind the whole. Despite any theories about evolution, mankind will be absolutely without excuse when one day we all kneel before the judgement seat of Christ. In spite of what we know, all too many of us neither thank nor glorify God. Instead we live in opposition to Him, demanding for ourselves the 'right' to be 'god' of our own lives. All too often this stiff necked rebellion manifests itself in the worship of idols. Readers should not be mistaken, however. Modern idol worship is not restricted simply to the Dharmic and similar religions. As has been wisely observed: *an idol can be anything that you allow your thoughts and ambitions to focus on in your idle moments*. For some ambition and success, for others money, for yet others land and conquests and warfare, and inevitably in the modern world – sex – can be idols. Anything that displaces God can become a very real idol in our lives, so we should be under no illusions about this. Idolatry can also be worship of the created order itself, or any part of it. We note the resurgence of forms of paganism in which created objects in the universe — including, but not limited, to sun, moon and angels — are worshipped, and 'new age' thinking in which the earth itself is accorded worship. Moreover, whilst we recognize that exercising wise stewardship of this God-given earth is right, and indeed goes along with love of neighbour (I am scarcely exercising love toward neighbour if I pollute my neighbour's food and water supplies), Christians involved in environmentalist movements must avoid any tendency to allow earth itself to take the place of our Creator God. Christian believers worship only the Creator, not His creation, and this is a crucial distinction.

Idolatry takes many forms, and we must not forget the original meaning: idol worship. Many Christians believe that it extends to according 'worth' to deities, for example by removing shoes at temples and other *places of worship*, or accepting marks or symbols of various kinds. Many, too, on being filled with the Holy Spirit, have been led to remove from their homes and destroy 'graven images' and objects which could carry particular symbolism in *the religions*, such as statues they may have picked up whilst travelling overseas or purchased as supposedly harmless

291

'ornaments', masks, and other things they used to consider were merely works of art without spiritual significance. The Spirit gives a sensitivity and discernment about what is going on spiritually, and of course this accords perfectly with what is revealed in the Word of God. Word and Spirit work together!

Paul concludes (in v.28): **Furthermore, since they did not think it worthwhile to retain the knowledge of God, he gave them over to a depraved mind, to do what ought not to be done.** The eternal power of God the Creator, and His nature, have been revealed to all mankind from the very beginning. When man turns away in rebellion from God's general laws, He reluctantly allows us to go our own way, permitting us to exercise the free will He has given to us.

The apostle begins to develop his theme of law: **All who sin apart from the law will also perish apart from the law, and all who sin under the law will be judged by the law. For it is not those who hear the law who are righteous in God's sight, but it is those who obey the law who will be declared righteous. (Indeed, when Gentiles, who do not have the law, do by nature things required by the law, they are a law for themselves, even though they do not have the law, since they show that the requirements of the law are written on their hearts, their consciences also bearing witness, and their thoughts now accusing, now even defending them.) This will take place on the day when God will judge men's secrets through Jesus Christ, as my gospel declares.** (Romans 2:12–16)

We should note the above carefully. Those who live under the law will be judged under that law. All who sin apart from law (here Paul means those who are Gentiles), will be still be judged because, as Paul has already explained in v.14, *when Gentiles, who do not have the law, do by nature things required by the law, they are a law for themselves, even though they do not have the law.* Again, any excuse people may have that they were unacquainted with God's general law simply disappears, because God has revealed enough to all mankind, endowing man with conscience. The key aspects of God's law, summarized in the ten commandments (see chapter 3) are known 'naturally' to all humans. We know it is wrong to steal, to lie, to murder, to be adulterous, to be jealous of others, and so on.

The apostle reminds us in Romans 3:11–12 that all alike are rebels against God. He quotes from Psalm 14 as he declares: **. . . there is no one who understands, no one who seeks God. All have turned away, they have together become worthless; there is no one who does good, not even one**. Paul emphasizes the same thing in v. 23, as we shall see shortly. So what is the answer? The law in itself does not provide righteousness before God. So Paul says in vv. 19–20: **Now we know that whatever the law says, it says to those who are under the law, so that every mouth may be silenced and the whole world held accountable to God. Therefore no one will be declared righteous in his sight by observing the law; rather, through the law we become conscious of sin**. The existence of the law, then, makes us aware of sin. People sometimes act as if by ignoring God's law they can forget about sin, but their consciences tell them otherwise, and this all too often leads to genuine spiritual distress. So what is the answer to the dilemma? Paul provides the answer at 3:21, **But now a righteousness from God, apart from law, has been made known, to which the Law and the Prophets testify. This righteousness from God comes through faith in Jesus Christ to all who believe. There is no difference, for all have sinned and fall short of the glory of God, and are**

justified freely by his grace through the redemption that came by Christ Jesus. God presented him as a sacrifice of atonement, through faith in his blood. He did this to demonstrate his justice, because in his forbearance he had left the sins committed beforehand unpunished – he did it to demonstrate his justice at the present time, so as to be just and the one who justifies those who have faith in Jesus.

It is in Jesus that righteousness may be obtained. Readers are encouraged to read all of Romans chapters 4 through 6 to get the full sense of God's amazing life-giving gift through Christ. If they have not read this before then a simple prayer to God to quicken these chapters to your own spirit would be both wise and honouring to God. We follow a few key verses from Romans chapters 4 and 5. Hopefully these will be largely self-explanatory. Paul has already asserted in chapter 3:28 that a human is justified [6] by faith and apart from observing the law. God, Paul points out, is not the God of the Jews only but of Gentiles as well. And both Jew and Gentile will be saved through faith in Jesus.

For if those who live by law are heirs, faith has no value and the promise is worthless, because law brings wrath. And where there is no law there is no transgression. (Romans 4:14–15)

If we could live by the standards of God's Law, then faith would indeed be unnecessary. The trouble is that humans just cannot live free of sin. Where there is no Law there is

---

[6] The terms 'justification' and 'justified' are usually understood to mean the process whereby a sinner is presented before God spotless and free of sin. It is therefore 'just as if I'd' never sinned in the first place. Note however there is a difference in emphasis with for example, the Eastern Orthodox tradition which understands this as a more dynamic rather than legalistic accomplishment of God.

no transgression (sin) as Paul rightly points out. The trouble remains that even where mankind has never heard the name of Jesus, nor even heard of the Ten Commandments, they have still become a law for themselves (Romans 2:14). Where there is no law, plainly there can be no 'transgression' against it. The awkward fact however is that nowhere, absolutely nowhere, is Man free of Law. And the answer?

. . . just at the right time, when we were still powerless, Christ died for the ungodly. Very rarely will anyone die for a righteous man, though for a good man someone might possibly dare to die. But God demonstrates his own love for us in this: While we were still sinners, Christ died for us. (Romans 5:6–8)

This is the awesome truth. God sent His sinless Son to die for sinners (see again John 3:14–18). We observed in chapter 6 of this book that God is good, at a deep level that we cannot totally comprehend. We noted that the word 'good' is over-used and cheapened in this world, where we so easily talk about a 'good day at the office' or a 'good meal'! In v. 7, Paul states that we would rarely consider giving our lives for a righteous, upright person, but we might possibly dare to do it for a 'good' man. But Jesus surrendered His life *for us* – wicked sinners.

Since we have now been justified by his blood, how much more shall we be saved from God's wrath through him! For if, when we were God's enemies, we were reconciled to him through the death of his Son, how much more, having been reconciled, shall we be saved through his life! Not only is this so, but we also rejoice in God through our Lord Jesus Christ, through whom we have now received reconciliation. (Romans 5:9 – 11)

So we have been justified by the blood of Jesus, as and when we put our faith in Him and truly determine to follow

Him [7]. We will be saved from God's righteous wrath through Jesus and, even more, will become completely reconciled to God. For the sake of clarity we should note that this does not mean that Christians will not sin (see Appendix 4) and nor, sadly, that we will always be obviously Christ-like people. But God does graciously and perceptibly make us more Christ-like as we become His disciples and as we walk humbly in His ways.

. . . for before the law was given, sin was in the world. But sin is not taken into account when there is no law. (Romans 5:13)

This is another important verse and one that is sometimes mis-interpreted. Even before the Ten Commandments were given, sin was abroad in the world. Mankind is an incorrigible sinner; he has been from the beginning of time and will be until the end. Where there is no Law sin is not taken into account – at least not in the same way that it is measured by God today. The earliest humans may (and we would emphasize *may*) be judged by a somewhat different yardstick than people who have lived since the time of Moses (to whom the Law was first given – see Exodus chapter 20). This verse does not imply, as some have disingenuously said (taking it completely out of its context) that if we fail to preach Jesus then people are free of sin and will not be punished. Paul has already stated quite plainly that all who sin apart from Law will perish apart from Law (Romans 2:12) but that even Gentiles

---

[7] Again it is worth noting a slight difference in emphasis with the Eastern tradition which notes that being justified refers to an on-going state of righteousness and not 'merely' a one time event. The Eastern tradition makes the useful point that faith in Christ makes us justified as an ongoing state of communion with Jesus. Because of this ongoing communion we have peace with God which is also on-going. The Greek word *pistis*, they point out, which in Western tradition is translated as 'faith' can also be rendered as 'faithfulness' —leading to the pertinent idea of ongoing faithfulness.

have become a Law for themselves, and so will also face judgment (2:14). We are not entitled, therefore, to assume that people are better off not hearing the good news of Jesus as some Godists are wont to say. One Godist wrote to this author that he does not suggest to those of *the religions* that they should follow Jesus. These religionists, he said, would be judged against their law in the same way that Christians will be judged against our law, and that Jesus will save us all! This, however, is both wooly and wishful thinking. God will judge mankind against His perfect Law as summarized in the Ten Commandments, not against a whole raft of strange, conflicting and mutually exclusive religious rules and regulations. The slur against God (and it must be added against the Lord Jesus) is plain to see: we should not 'trouble' religionists with salvation through Christ. Ignorance of Christ, to at least some Godists, is bliss.

We opened this section by asking *what is Christianity?* We have, it is hoped, gone some way to answer as we have begun to look at the Law of God. The apostle Paul has already stated that, **we know that whatever the law says, it says to those who are under the law, so that every mouth may be silenced and the whole world held accountable to God. Therefore no one will be declared righteous in [God's] sight by observing the law; rather, through the law we become conscious of sin.** (Romans 3:19) The Law, besides judging us, helps us to understand what sin is. To avoid judgement under the Law we must be found to be righteous – and righteousness comes through faith in Jesus. We will consider how God loves those who have never even heard the name of Jesus in the next chapter but will conclude this section with further thoughts from the apostle Paul. The Law ultimately could not save us, but Jesus can: **. . . what the law was powerless to do in that it was** weakened by the sinful nature, God did by sending his own Son in the likeness of sinful man to be a sin offering. And so he condemned sin in sinful man, in order that the righteous requirements of the law might be fully met in us, who do not live according to the sinful nature but according to the Spirit.

Those who live according to the sinful nature have their minds set on what that nature desires; but those who live in accordance with the Spirit have their minds set on what the Spirit desires. The mind of sinful man is death, but the mind controlled by the Spirit is life and peace; the sinful mind is hostile to God. It does not submit to God's law, nor can it do so. Those controlled by the sinful nature cannot please God. (Romans 8:3–8)

The sinless Jesus was sent to be an offering on our behalf – the only offering that can meet the righteous demands of the Law. When we reject God, either as religious people who will not yield, or as irreligious people who will not yield, we remain in both cases people living under Law. The one under God's righteous Law; the other under the 'Law' that we have made for ourselves. Readers are encouraged to read the whole of the sublime Romans chapter 8 which reveals so much about life in the Spirit of God. The apostle Paul tells us in 8:15 that *we have received a spirit that does not leave us as a slave to fear, because we have the spirit of sonship*. Once again this must be a challenge to the Godist position, where so many of *the religions* leave their adherents with no clear sense of the future, no clear sense of being a 'son' of God. (In this politically correct age we must straightway deal with this issue of 'sonship' as opposed to 'daughtership' – it is quite deliberate on the part of Paul! A son had full inheritance rights within his family. Females did not. A true follower of Jesus has full inheritance rights before God, whether they are male or female – their full inheritance being eternal life and a place with God here on earth and there in heaven, a place that is assured. *The religions* demand that their adherents lead certain types of life which, if they fail, will leave them cut off from their reward – and possibly punished forever, into the bargain. And it is in this position of fear that (some) Godists want people of *the religions* to remain. Some Godists certainly believe that people should *not* be invited to follow Jesus, but instead should remain in their religions. And in this they connive with those religions, which are jealous of the continuance of their co-religionists within their way, often in outright defiance of Article 18 of the United Nations Universal Declaration of Human Rights.

We proclaim Christ crucified, said Paul in 1 Corinthians 1:23, **a stumbling block to Jews and foolishness to Gentiles**. (NRSV) Jews thought that, as inheritors and guardians of the Law, they could 'earn' their way to a right relationship with God. A crucified Christ was seen as an absolute scandal to a Jew. Indeed to a pious Jew today it still is. To the world at large, a crucified God is utter foolishness. It was seen this way when Paul wrote to the Corinthian church, and still is today – utter folly. The New Testament Greek word that is translated above as *stumbling block* is better translated as an 'offence' or even, more literally, a 'scandal'. The Greek word in the New Testament is *skandalon*, and is the root from which we derive our modern word. It is scandalous that a human can be brought to a right relationship with God simply by believing in Jesus, not by being religious, or by an amazing prayer life, not by church attendance or zealous Bible reading. This is, it might be added, a scandalous thought to some orthodox Christians as well! Before however, readers say 'well, I believe, then!' and put down this book, we need to add something important: as is suggested in Appendix 4, the life of faith is rather more than mere belief. The position that God demands of a Christian is a complete regeneration – or a re-birth. After all, the devil believes in Jesus but that does not make him a Christian! In practice the life that a Christian leads will take on a new character after trusting in Jesus and as they go on trusting in Jesus, and although works are not demanded (as though we can earn any rights before God) yet *they will inevitably follow* in a life dedicated to Jesus. This is one of the paradoxes of Christianity.

Although in Romans Paul is writing to believers in first century Rome, his words are applicable to Christians today. Referring to the need for righteousness before God, Paul comments that, **when a man works, his wages are not credited to him as a gift, but as an obligation. However, to the man who does not work but trusts God who justifies the wicked, his faith is credited as righteousness** (4:4–5). When a man 'works', his wage is an obligation. But the man or woman who has (true) faith will find that, on account of that faith, they will be considered by God as righteous. Paul cites the patriarch Abraham as a man who had faith (in God's promise) and that his faith was not only credited to him alone but also to us: **The words 'it was credited to him' were written not for him alone, but also for us, to whom God will credit righteousness — for us who believe in him who raised Jesus our Lord from the dead. He was delivered over to death for our sins and was raised to life for our justification.** Later (in 5:6) he writes, **You see, at just the right time, when we were still powerless, Christ died for the ungodly. Very rarely will anyone die for a righteous man, though for a good man someone might possibly dare to die. But God**

demonstrates his own love for us in this: While we were still sinners, Christ died for us.

Since we have now been justified by his blood, how much more shall we be saved from God's wrath through him! For if, when we were God's enemies, we were reconciled to him through the death of his Son, how much more, having been reconciled, shall we be saved through his life! Not only is this so, but we also rejoice in God through our Lord Jesus Christ, through whom we have now received reconciliation.

Without over-simplifying what is a complex subject, we can claim with certainty that God credits true faith in Jesus to us as righteousness. Becoming a disciple of Jesus in the sense that Jesus Himself demanded (our repenting, believing, being born again) leads to a radical new life because: **... by dying to what once bound us, we have been released from the law so that we serve in the new way of the Spirit, and not in the old way of the written code**. (Romans 7: 6)

... for what the law was powerless to do in that it was weakened by the sinful nature, God did by sending his own Son in the likeness of sinful man to be a sin offering. (Romans 8: 3)

There are some who think that all they have to do is to believe, albeit sincerely, and that this will satisfy God forever. The normative Protestant position of justification through faith (and it must be readily acknowledged that this view is not entirely agreed with by, for example, the Eastern Orthodox tradition) is that the evidence of true faith is true works. Whilst acknowledging the primacy of faith (the Protestant position) it is impossible to ignore the apostle James' comment that **a person is justified by what he does and not by faith alone** (James 2:24). That seems to deal with any idea that all we have to do is to 'believe' once, with no real change to the way we lead our lives.[8] We are to *go on believing*; *abide* in Jesus; go on being filled with the Spirit; go on allowing him to produce fruit in our lives.

God's Grace

The concept of grace, more than any other theme, distinguishes Christianity from *the religions*. It is unsurprising, perhaps, that grace should be ignored or sidelined by Godists of whatever persuasion. The apostle John wrote **God gave the law through Moses, but grace and truth came through Jesus Christ.** (John 1:17, GNB). Again it should be stated for clarity that the law of God and the grace of Christ are not contradictory. At the event we call the transfiguration, Jesus was seen conversing with Moses and Elijah: the presence of Moses shows Christ as the fulfilment of the law; the presence of Elijah shows Christ as the fulfilment of the prophets.

When the Lord gave to Moses and Israel the law, He spoke as *the Lord*, their God. Moses spoke to Israel in the name of the Lord their God, and not in his own name (Exodus 20:22). When Jesus was born into this world as a human, as the incarnate Son of God, He continued to speak to Israel — now directly, and not through any prophet. In spite of His works of great power and self-authenticity, and speaking in words of wisdom and grace never before (or since) matched as He spoke to Israel, the chosen nation, as their Messiah, Israel in large part refused Him. To those Jews who did believe, Jesus gave the right to become children of God (John 1:11–12). Christ extended this right to believing

---

[8] The author recalls visiting a website where a grinning 'evangelical' preacher on podcast invited people to say a prayer to God inviting Jesus into their lives, and told them that this would guarantee their salvation for all eternity. He mentioned not one word on sin or repentance from sin!

Gentiles as well. Note that the Lord had already made it plain through Moses and the prophets that the Gentiles would also be included in the promises made to Israel (e.g. Genesis 12:1–3; Isaiah 49:5–6). The good news is for all mankind.

As the Lord is the lawgiver, it is no surprise that He is also the One who fulfilled the law and so made it obsolete (see Matthew 5:17 and Hebrews 8:13). As Christ said He came not to destroy the law, should we still observe those Old Testament laws? We have seen that Christ fulfilled (*completed*) the requirements of the Mosaic law. When we review all of Scripture, in context, it is clear that Jesus spoke of his death as ensuring that the law has no more condemnation over us. So, in Matthew 5:17–18 Jesus said **"Do not think that I have come to do away with the Law of Moses and the teachings of the prophets. I have not come to do away with them, but to make their teachings come true. Remember that as long as heaven and earth last, not the least point nor the smallest detail of the Law will be done away with — not until the end of all things"** (Matthew 5:17–18, GNB). By fulfilling the law, Jesus satisfied its requirements on our behalf. So the apostle Paul could exclaim: **Death gets its power to hurt from sin, and sin gets its power from the Law. But thanks be to God who gives us the victory through our Lord Jesus Christ!** (1 Corinthians 15:56, GNB). And he emphasises this elsewhere: **There is no condemnation now for those who live in union with Christ Jesus. For the law of the Spirit, which brings us life in union with Christ Jesus, has set me free from the law of sin and death** (Romans 8:1–2, GNB). The (*torah*) law cannot condemn a true disciple of Jesus (whether Jewish or Gentile) because they are made free in Christ, in Whose righteousness they stand.

None of this licenses impurity or disobedience to God's will, of course, and such antinomianism (denial that any rules apply to believers) was a problem as serious in its way as the legalism of the Judaisers who wanted the Gentiles circumcised and back under the old regulations of the observant Jews. Christianity stands in the revelation that the Messiah came to fulfil the law, or to make complete, or to accomplish what was required, so that those laws will not condemn us. The Lord Jesus brought the law to completion, having stood in for us a substitute, so that the strength of sin (which comes through the Law) will not condemn us.

If readers have stayed with the debate up to this point (and they should not be unduly worried if a great deal of this is difficult to understand, especially if the concepts are new to them), then it is hoped that two points should by now be understood at least at a basic level. Firstly, before we can answer the genuine question of many about the eternal destiny of those who have never even heard the name of Jesus, we need to understand that *all* humans in their natural state, are alienated from God and stand condemned under the general law of God for all mankind (see again Romans 1). Huge numbers of people do not acknowledge or thank God, and do not obey His laws — and not one of us matches up to His holiness, goodness and perfection so that we could stand in His presence depending on the strength of our own supposed righteousness. No-one! We may feel comforted that He is just, but this means that in our natural state we would die in our sins and at the judgement seat of Christ we would be condemned. So, secondly, the really vital question is: how can people be rescued from their ways of rebellion and disobedience, and saved through the great atonement achieved by the Lord Jesus? It is this subject we will begin to address in the next chapter.

13

FURTHER IMPLICATIONS OF GODISM

The Promise of Godism

In chapter 1 we explored the claim that by aligning *the religions*, peace and goodwill between them might be achieved. But we posed the question whether this 'promise' is in fact an empty one and whether politicians, in particular, who pursue this agenda as part of their societal 'cohesiveness policies' will create a religious chimera (a Greek mythological monster with a lion's head, a goat's body and a serpents tail – otherwise defined as a grotesque product of the imagination) that ultimately satisfies no one but still manages to draw people away from Almighty God. Throughout this book we have looked at the nature of God as revealed from the pages of the Holy Bible. It is in fact the Bible that most challenges the Godist position. Certainly some religions lend themselves very readily to the syncretistic thrust of Godism. Others may do so where it is seen as convenient.

This book has contained a number of challenges to the Godist position. We have looked at the nature of a good God Who is simultaneously holy, righteous, truthful, wise, and in love has opened the Way by which anyone can be saved from the penalty of sin, through Jesus Christ. It is this righteous God Who is revealed throughout the pages of the Holy Bible. In chapters 3–4 we addressed some problems people have with parts of Scripture they find difficult to understand. The self-revelation of this one true God is clear and consistent in the Bible. The hard evidence for the resurrection of Jesus Christ is immensely powerful; His claims to divinity could only mean that He is truly God as well as truly man. His claim is that the Father has committed judgement to the Son, so He will judge all men who have ever lived on earth. All will bow the knee to Him. It has been rightly observed that anyone who has made such a claim is either God or mad or bad. The testimony of the saints is that He is alive, He is divine, and all His promises are true. All this means that orthodox, biblical Christianity cannot possibly be part of some multi-faith enterprise in which there are different ways of salvation. That would be completely incoherent at every level of understanding and experience.

To Godism, all this is an extremely troublesome problem that will not go away. The universality of Jesus' claims; their particularity; the historicity of the resurrection and its witnesses, who were willing to die rather than renounce the One who they had seen risen from the dead — every aspect of the Christian claims challenges the syncretist, at every turn. It may well be that a new religion will emerge from the ambitions of Godism, if not from the philosophy itself. We can readily imagine situations where warfare, economic dislocation, ecological disaster and uncontrollable disease might give birth to a widely-held (if erroneous) view that religion is part of the problem and that a harmonised religion must be part of the solution. But only by denying or even outlawing the Holy Bible and its message of the Cross of Christ, could such a religion be imagined. Time will tell if this scenario will emerge in our lifetimes, but the Bible seems to point towards a day when a new global religion will emerge. This is seen by many Christians as part of the interpretation of the Old Testament books of Ezekiel and Daniel, and above all, of course, the book of Revelation. This will be the time of the *Lawless One*, otherwise called the *Antichrist*. There are many competent studies of this important subject, so we will comment no further except to observe how the *Lawless One* will deceive. Again we allow the words of the Bible to speak. Readers may want to read the short second letter of Paul to the Thessalonian church, or just focus on chapter 2 where we read this: **The coming of the lawless one is apparent in the workings of Satan, who uses all power, signs, lying wonders, and in every kind of wicked deception for those who are perishing, because they refused to love the truth and so be saved. For this reason God sends them a powerful delusion leading them to believe what is false, so that all who have not believed the truth but took pleasure in unrighteousness will be condemned.** (2 Thessalonians 2:9–12 NRSV).

Notice that there will be counterfeit miracles, or 'lying wonders' (NRSV). With the advance of technology we can anticipate how such 'miracles' might be staged. The new religion(s) will pander to evil, and perhaps not surprisingly this will be attractive to many. God will therefore give people over to a 'powerful delusion'. If people want to believe in this new religion and its politico-religious leader, then God will allow this. It will be perhaps the ultimate, and final, consequence of that first rebellion in the Garden of Eden, where mankind first determined that he wanted to be like God. **"Did God really say to you ....?"** chided the devil (Genesis 3:1). Did God really say to you that there is only one Saviour and only one path to God? Did God really say that, or are you being narrow-minded in believing that approach? Are you being intolerant? Readers might query whether a truthful God would 'send' a powerful delusion. Does God delude? The point is that God eventually allows us to have our full rein when we harden our hearts against Him. We should be amazed that God mercifully restrains our evil so much: that is His mercy and patience at work. But a day of wrath will come. We may believe whatever we want, but not without either (a) completely ignoring the Bible, the position adopted by all too many both within and outside the church; or (b) twisting what the Bible actually says —and this, it is submitted, is the position of that oxymoron 'Christian Godism'. The Lord Jesus, needless to say, will not submit to such misrepresentation. Having been nailed to a cross once, He is not going to be put there again. He reigns in glory now, and one day He will put all His enemies under His feet. **God made you alive with Christ. He forgave us all our sins, having cancelled the written code, with its regulations, that was against us and that stood opposed to us; he took it away, nailing it to the cross. And having disarmed the powers and authorities, he made a public spectacle of them, triumphing over them by the cross** (Colossians 2:13–15).

Jesus has fulfilled the law, that *written code*, and nailed it to the cross. The *powers and authorities* that He has disarmed are spiritual powers that are further described by the apostle Paul in Ephesians 6:12, and indeed readers may want to reflect upon Ephesians 6:10–18 in this regard. Jesus has not submitted to the spiritual *powers* in the past. Nor will He do so in the future. Rather He has defeated them.

We learn of Christ's supremacy over powers and principalities, as well as over His church in the same letter of Paul to the Colossian church: **He is the image of the** invisible God, the firstborn over all creation. For by him all things were created: things in heaven and on earth, visible and invisible, whether thrones or powers or rulers or authorities; all things were created by him and for him. He is before all things, and in him all things hold together. And he is the head of the body, the church; he is the beginning and the firstborn from among the dead, so that in everything he might have the supremacy. For God was pleased to have all his fullness dwell in him, and through him to reconcile to himself all things, whether things on earth or things in heaven, by making peace through his blood, shed on the cross. Once you were alienated from God and were enemies in your minds because of your evil behavior. But now he has reconciled you by Christ's physical body through death to present you holy in his sight, without blemish and free from accusation — if you continue in your faith, established and firm, not moved from the hope held out in the gospel. This is the gospel that you heard and that has been proclaimed to every creature under heaven, and of which I, Paul, have become a servant (Colossians 1:15–23).

This is the gospel that has been proclaimed. As Christ is supreme it is incoherent to suggest His supremacy could be 'shared' with other religions. Those of *the religions* and/ or Godists and/or Western politicians may consider such a sharing of power to be a 'natural' religious development in the interests of fairness or justice. Their belief, however (*if* they truly believe this!) begins to look like a powerful delusion —a self-delusion! Readers should note in v.23 above, there is an implicit warning specifically to Christians. It is the great 'if' word. We will be presented holy in the sight of God *if* we remain firm in the gospel. There must be a danger that churchgoers who begin to adopt other faiths, or consider other faiths to be co-equal with Christianity, or simply consider *the religions* as alternative paths, will ultimately lose their salvation. This must be an especial danger where their dalliance with Godism is done in stiff-necked defiance of what the Holy Spirit has said on this issue.

Did Jesus 'deserve' to die?

This might sound slightly puzzling, especially when taken in context with all that we have explored so far in this book. The Godist philosophy, when expressed from within the church, clearly has some major biblical obstacles to overcome. 'Christian Godists' recognize this and have been forced therefore to develop their own 'theology' in order to circumvent what the Bible so clearly states. Jesus said **"I am the way, the truth and the life, no one goes to the Father except by me"** (John 14:6 GNB). Some have quibbled as to whether when Jesus said this He meant *God* the Father. Their argument runs along the lines: 'Jesus only said He was the only way to the Father, not that He was the only way to God!' This is inventive, but quite disingenuous. It is perfectly clear what Jesus meant. Another objection from the Godist philosophy is this: because God allowed sin into the world, then He is either fully to blame for its effects, or is at least a co-defendant alongside mankind. Using an ostensibly 'logical' extension to this argument, the Godist concludes: *God is ultimately responsible for His creation and therefore, as He allowed sin to enter the world, so He must provide the remedy: so it was that Jesus (as God) 'deserved' to die on the cross.* We have been happy to use logic elsewhere in this book in deconstructing the Godist philosophy. But we must also note that logic has its limitations, and this may be just such an occasion! Indeed we could go further and observe that this Godist argument represents faulty logic. God has given mankind freewill and there can be little doubt that most humans prefer it that way! Precisely why God allowed sin to enter the world is not given a definitive answer in Scripture.[1] Rather than speculate, most orthodox Christians trust that God knows what He is doing. The key point is that God has gone to extraordinary lengths to rescue humans from the power, the grip, the guilt and the consequences of sin. The ultimate cost to God was the life of His dear Son, who became sin for our benefit. But God did not undertake this rescue mission because He was guilty. He undertook it because He is merciful. We are the guilty ones; we humans are the sinners, and we choose to be that way. God did not 'have' to provide any remedy at all. He could have left us wallowing in the mire of sin. But He has chosen to rescue us. From an orthodox Christian viewpoint it must be added that where the view that *Jesus is guilty* is expounded from within the church or outside it, it is simply blasphemous. It accuses the holy and good God of being like us – a sinner. This is a gross lie.

As the sinless one, Jesus certainly 'deserved' no punishment. But can God be so indicted in the court of public opinion? God allowed freewill and therefore, having foreseen the consequence (sin), was it at the very least a failure not to have prevented it? We must again remind ourselves just how much we would 'rail' against all the strictures that any lack of freewill would place upon us. We would not be able to talk as we wanted. We would not be able to think or act as we wanted. We would be religious-robots in thrall to a God who controlled our minds as well as our

---

[1] See Peter Sammons *The Birth of Christ* (ISBN 0-9551790-1-7, Glory to Glory Publications 2006) chapters 1 and 2 for more background on this subject.

bodies. God could certainly not develop a real *relationship* with us, and certainly not a love relationship, if we were merely spiritual automata. When people rail against God for 'allowing' man-made disasters and crimes, they never stop to think what their demand for God's daily intervention would entail in terms of loss of human choice. And of course one day God *will* create a new heaven and a new earth in such a way that natural disasters, war, pestilence, hunger and poverty will no longer exist.[2] That will happen after Christ has returned as Judge.[3] If people want that sort of a world to be delivered say, tomorrow, then they would have to meet Jesus as Judge tonight. Are they ready? Of course they are not! It is by God's mercy that He continues to give us time to change — but one day that time will run out.

A second and rather more common charge levelled against God runs something like this: *It would be unfair of God to 'damn' people of* the religions, *who had not had the opportunity to hear the saving good news of Jesus.* This is closely aligned to the idea that God has a 'duty' to 'save' all people. This is a genuine concern, so we should tackle it head-on. Some have said that there is no 'obvious' correct path, and so people generally remain wedded to the religion (or lack of religion) into which they were born. As a sociological observation, we can agree that many people remain with the religion of their forefathers, although it should be noted that today large numbers are turning to Christ from *the religions*. From a biblical perspective it is simply wrong to say that there is no obvious path. There *is* an obvious path. That path is Jesus, Who said: **"Enter through the narrow gate. For wide is the gate and broad is the**

---

[2] See Revelation chapter 21.

[3] See Revelation chapter 20.

road that leads to destruction, and many enter through it. But small is the gate and narrow the road that leads to life, and only a few find it" (Matthew 7:13-14). Elsewhere Jesus affirmed "I am the way" (John 14:6). So there *is* an obvious way, and there is an exclusive way. But just how 'obvious' is that Way, if people have never even heard the name of Jesus? Surely people cannot be held accountable if they not even heard that wonderful name?[4]

We begin to answer this objection by recalling the ideas of a well known liberal Christian, Lesslie Newbigin (1909 – 1998). He commented in his book *The Gospel in a Pluralist Society*[5] that it had become customary to classify views on the relation of Christianity to the world religions as either pluralist, exclusivist or inclusivist. His position was *exclusivist* in the sense that it affirmed the unique truth of the revelation in Jesus Christ, but was not exclusivist in the sense of denying the possibility of the salvation of the non-Christian. It was *inclusivist* in the sense that it refused to limit the saving grace of God to the members of the Christian church, but it rejected the inclusivism which regarded the non-Christian religions as vehicles of salvation. It was *pluralist* in the sense of acknowledging the gracious work of God in the lives of all human beings, but rejected pluralism that denied the uniqueness and decisiveness of what God has done in Jesus Christ. Many church-attending Christians, evangelicals as well as liberals, concur. His analysis may have been deficient or incomplete, but it did affirm the reality of salvation only through Jesus, which is,

---

[4] The name of Jesus (Yeshua/Joshua) is significant, meaning broadly 'God is my help' or 'God is rescue'. See Peter Sammons, *The Birth of Christ* (Glory to Glory Publications – ISBN 0-9551790-1-7) chapter 6 for more on this subject.

[5] Lesslie Newbigin, *The Gospel in a Pluralist Society*, pages 182-83 (ISBN: 9780281057023).

it must be said, a cornerstone of true biblical Christianity. On that basis the Newbigin analysis continues to have a following. However it is our view that it is just too close to the Godist position.

We have taken some pains in this book to uncover and understand the self-revelation of Almighty God, so far as we can do so in our mortal and necessarily limited way. We have learned, it is hoped, that God *is* good and holy. In chapter 12 we challenged whether our question can ever be reduced to a simple, formulaic 'does Jesus condemn religionists and those of no religion'? We began to see that the real question is about law and grace, and how people choose to live in this world. And we saw that men will still have no excuse before the judgement seat of God: they will need to have at that point the righteousness that comes from God, to be 'in Christ' — to rely on their own 'righteousness' would be insufficient for their sins to be covered.

The God revealed in the Bible (and speaking for himself, the God known to the author of this book) is a God of utmost love, utmost holiness, and utmost righteousness. He alone is God. He may judge as He sees fit. Countless millions – probably billions – of people down through the ages as well as today, who have real and intimate experience of this God have found that they can trust Him and love Him completely. The God who loved me enough to give His Son for me has surely revealed beyond doubt His mercy. We can trust God absolutely to do the right thing as regards 'judgement': He will be perfectly just and fair for He is perfectly holy and perfectly just and He *will* do the right thing. It may be quite impossible for humans to know what the right thing is in regard to this question of judgement, but we get many clues to God's character throughout the Scriptures. It is not for us to tell Him what He should do.

Many people hold the view that 'good' people will be saved by God. And so they will (John 5:29). The word 'good', however, is grossly over used. The world's understanding of what is good and bad is utterly different to God's overruling on this matter. It is deeply sobering to note that the *very best* things that we do look like filthy rags to God (Isaiah 64:6). We simply have no idea how serious sin is, nor the vast gulf that truly separates us from God — a gulf that is caused solely by sin. When this truth was given to the prophet Isaiah, the image that we are to keep in mind is one of rags covered in faeces – in other words, what people wiped their bottoms with! And that is the very best that we can do! To start to speak of 'good' in almost any context only shows how little humans comprehend of what good is. Men bluntly delude themselves that their conduct is ultimately acceptable and justifiable before God, but God's standards are immeasurably higher (see Proverbs 16:2). He alone can weigh true motives, and that fact should be both a comfort and a warning to us. Who is good? We remind ourselves that Jesus answered the question of the rich young ruler (Matthew 19:17). There is only one who is good, and that is God Himself, Father, Son and Holy Spirit. Whatever we think of as good from our worldly perspective — well, we're back to those filthy rags! So if anyone *is* good, then God will certainly 'save' them. The trouble is, absolutely no one but Jesus is good! Not in the biblical sense, at any rate.[6]

This takes us back then to the only known remedy for

---

[6] This idea of what is truly 'good' helps to put in perspective that otherwise puzzling comment by the apostle Paul in Romans 5:7. He comments that 'very rarely will anyone die for a righteous man, though for a good man someone might possibly dare to die'. It is true that Christians will sometimes be called upon to lay down their lives for the one Man Who was truly good — the Lord Jesus Himself.

sin — the blood of our Lord Jesus. We all fall short – big sinners and 'little' sinners alike — but God does not turn His back on us. We can think of the example of King David — murder and adultery followed by forgiveness and restoration — to demonstrate this reality. Would the Father have sacrificed Jesus if there was *any* other way? Human love and God's love again are poles apart. As with the word 'good', so we over-use and misuse the word 'love'. All too many people think of God as being a sort of elderly *uncle in the sky* who looks down over our sin and winks as He says 'tut, tut; but that's all right. I will see you saved in the end, in spite of yourself.' That is not the God revealed in Scripture. More important still, that is not a 'god' who would have any claim to be considered moral. Sin *is* serious and *must* be dealt with, and it will certainly be dealt with at the final judgement! The seriousness of sin is indicated in the remedy God chose for it — the life of His dear Son. But God's love is awesome – and a million miles from ours! We read about God's true love for His children in 1 John 4:7–21. But we should not go away with the idea that God's love is some cheap love, or can be demonstrated in *any number of guises* (the Godist position?) His love, known by those He has redeemed, is indivisible:

Dear friends, let us love one another, for love comes from God. Everyone who loves has been born of God and knows God. Whoever does not love does not know God, because God is love. This is how God showed his love among us: He sent his one and only Son into the world that we might live through him. This is love: not that we loved God, but that he loved us and sent his Son as an atoning sacrifice for our sins. Dear friends, since God so loved us, we also ought to love one another. No one has ever seen God; but if we love one another, God

lives in us and his love is made complete in us.

We know that we live in him and he in us, because he has given us of his Spirit. And we have seen and testify that the Father has sent his Son to be the Savior of the world. If anyone acknowledges that Jesus is the Son of God, God lives in him and he in God. And so we know and rely on the love God has for us. God is love. Whoever lives in love lives in God, and God in him. In this way, love is made complete among us so that we will have confidence on the day of judgment, because in this world we are like him. There is no fear in love. But perfect love drives out fear, because fear has to do with punishment. The one who fears is not made perfect in love.

We love because he first loved us. If anyone says, "I love God," yet hates his brother, he is a liar. For anyone who does not love his brother, whom he has seen, cannot love God, whom he has not seen. And he has given us this command: Whoever loves God must also love his brother. (1 John 4:7–21)

How do we truly know and have assurance that God loves us? **"This is love — not that we loved God, but that he loved us and sent his Son to be the atoning sacrifice for our sins."** (1 John 4:10, NRSV). Wonderful! Marvellous! Our hearts should overflow with joy and love and gratitude! How unloving it would be to send religious 'gurus', 'teachers' or 'prophets' who could not achieve what Jesus achieved, who could add nothing to what Jesus has already done for us on the cross of execution, and whose sole contribution seems to be to confuse and to take people away from their Saviour. This is simply incompatible with love.

In point of fact nowhere in the Bible does it say that God loves the sinner but hates the sin. His love is shown to those who repent and follow His Son. If readers can find

God's love expressed in a different way anywhere in the Holy Bible, then they may feel that this point is *not proven*. God's love is dangerously misunderstood — sometimes by the 'church' and very often by the world at large. The verses so often used as the 'love' demonstration, John 3:16 – is too often misrepresented. The point has well been made that the gospel is NOT John 3:16, which people have in the past 50 years (in particular) used as a sort of shorthand to underline God's purposes. Rather, a good shorthand of God's purposes would be John 3:15! The wonderful words on love in 1 John 4 are addressed to believers rather than the world at large – we who are to love one another (John 15:12) are the followers of Jesus. The Lord commended this sort of love as He told His followers to love one another, so that the world would know Whose disciples they are.[7] We do well to note the point: the context of love when mentioned in the Bible is almost always within the Christian family (and in the Old Testament in the context of the chosen people God had rescued, the Hebrews). God's love is displayed to the whole world in John 3:16, but what that love means is specific and singular: the giving of His Son in order that those who go on believing in Him will not perish (be ruined for ever) but have eternal life; that they would be saved from hell (that their sins would otherwise lead to at the day of judgement). This kind of agape love is not about feelings but about God's unique and merciful provision for our greatest need. It is not unconditional, it is conditional. The world broadly rejects that love. The Bible also makes clear that the pull of sin ensnares many.

To accept any faith other than Christianity or alongside Christianity is to say that the cross was really unnecessary.

---

[7] For clarity, we are not solely to love our brethren. We are also to love our neighbours as ourselves – Mark 12:31.

It is to say that, in fact, we can 'earn' some or all of our salvation. To accept a faith other than true Christianity or alongside true Christianity is to imply a measure of self justification — something that is frankly intolerable to God as it shows yet again the ugly human face of pride raising itself towards God. The very best things we do even as Christians are morally paltry — we are back to those filthy rags! A true Christian recognises his position as a sinner, saved by grace through faith (from the penalty of sin) *and being saved* (from the power of sin), and one who 'naturally' is a creature of wrath who deserves nothing, absolutely nothing, except God's judgement. A creature who can only plead the blood of Jesus in his defence. All other religions involve earning some, or all, of their 'salvation', however they define that concept. Christianity asserts that the price of our salvation has already been paid — by someone else!

If God has changed his mind and allowed people to earn some or all of their salvation, then the cross has been devalued, if not made irrelevant. Thinking again upon the fully developed Godist argument that because God gave us freewill He is said to be 'responsible for everything including sin, suffering and evil' we must observe that, where this 'theology' is propounded from within the Church, it is manifestly a heresy. Where it is propounded in the world at large, it perhaps reflects that overriding desire to make God a co-defendant alongside man, thus relieving us of our sole responsibility for sin. We are back to that idea that God will 'wink' at all our wrong-doing, except perhaps for those 'very serious sins' such as murder and rape, where God may actually trouble Himself to judge. People who hold this idea of serious versus minor sins forget the impossibly high standards that the Lord Jesus has already set out. For example, that a man who even looks upon a woman lustfully has committed adultery with her in his heart — the moral equivalent of committing that sin in the flesh (Matthew 5:28). And similarly that anyone who is so much as angry with his brother guilty of murder! (Matthew 5:22).[8] All sin is serious. It must remain profoundly sad that any person, whether of Godist or any other religious persuasion, should truly believe in this idea of a good/evil God who is fully, or even partly, culpable for the sins of the world. It is sad because it is so terribly wrong, and leads those who hold the idea into a whole morass of moral relativism. If God is to blame then He cannot be sinless. If He is not sinless our sins are not atoned for. If He is sinful then the Bible is a pack of lies from beginning to end. In trying to indict God, Godists only raise more questions than they answer.

We return to our question: *It would be unfair of God to 'damn' people of* the religions, *who had not had the opportunity to hear the saving good news of Jesus.* It is not of course for Christians or any human being to 'judge' in these matters, but God does graciously allow Christians to explore them, even so. What follows here is the author's understanding, but has the virtue of being consistent with what Scripture has revealed at all points. The 'problem' posited by Godists has two facets: (1) *what happens to the souls of those who died before the time of Christ?* – or, more accurately, before the era of grace – and (2) *what happens to those who die, never having heard?* The author keeps an open mind on (1) although he believes that there

---

[8] Many readers will be familiar with and understand these two teachings of Jesus. For anyone to whom they are new, we would add this clarification: when Jesus spoke of 'looking lustfully' or 'being angry' He surely meant in both cases an absolute determination on the part of the sinner to pursue the sin in his or her mind: it is unlikely that Jesus was referring for example to a momentary physical attraction. But we should also warn that all too often small beginnings can lead to ugly conclusions, so we must be wary — of ourselves!

are biblically sound arguments on the subject. The answer to (1) is probably broadly the same as the answer to (2) in this author's opinion.

A young missionary once had a disarmingly simple answer to this question, which he shared with the author and which we do well to keep in mind: as God is omniscient He may simply judge people on how they *would* have responded *had* they heard the gospel and had a genuine opportunity to become a disciple of the Lord Jesus. God knows, we do not. As an answer the author finds this completely satisfactory. But without in any way undermining it, more can be said. Firstly, God is a God of utmost justice. He will simply not do what is wrong. Of course our ideas of right and wrong are (once again) far, far from His verdict on this subject. It seems therefore to be entirely congruent with the reality of a holy, righteous, morally perfect and loving God that all little children, before the age of maturity and who die in their innocence will be saved by God. The Bible does not explicitly say this, and if it did, weak minded people would no doubt develop all sorts of philosophies around it. But the author suspects that this is so, and it should be a comfort to those who have sadly lost a child in infancy.[9]

The Bible gives no explicit answer to the question of the eternal destiny of those of *the religions* down through history. That there are some 'nice' people of all religions – as well as among atheists and so-called agnostics is a fact we readily recognise. But we do not know how deep their niceness goes. And it certainly cannot go far enough to earn their salvation — *for all alike have sinned...* (Romans 3:23). The author can only observe that, as a Christian, he is more than happy to trust the Lord Jesus to do the right thing as

---

[9] See also Mark 10:13–16 and Matthew 18:1–11 to get a sense of God's heart in this matter.

He deals with those of *the religions* and, indeed, those of no religion. We do however have strong clues about God's attitude, clues that are congruent with the reality of a good God (and now we use the word good in its truest sense, a sense far, far removed from the world's idea of 'good') Who has demonstrated His goodness by His provision of the beauty of the created order, as well as in the person of Jesus Christ, His Son. There is a partial answer to question (1) relating to those people who died before the gospel was preached: it seems clear that between the crucifixion and the resurrection, the lord Jesus preached to the souls of the dead (1 Peter 3:19). Just as in this world, so in the 'prison' where Jesus preached, we may be sure that not all accepted His offer of salvation. Their acceptance or rejection would surely have been in broad agreement with the manner in which those souls had already lived their lives.

Let us turn to consider question (2), relating to those who never hear the good news or who are beguiled by *the religions* in such a way that they cannot or will not hear about Jesus. There are two obvious (and biblically consistent) possibilities, and in fact both may be true. It is simply not for humans to know, and nor is it for politicians or churchmen to preach multifaith religion in the assumption that they do know! But it *is* for us to trust a completely holy, righteous, omnipotent and loving God. God may, in His omnipotence and omniscience, judge people on how they *would* have responded *had* they heard the gospel; because only He knows. We repeat, it is possible that the answer to question (1) applies also to question (2). It is *not* for us to know. But those who put their faith in *the religions* are already on their way to living their lives in the stiff-necked pride (and pride precedes a fall as Proverbs 16:18 reminds us!) of attempting to earn their 'salvation'. The good news is that many, even under the yoke of *the religions*, are still deeply aware of their own abject sinfulness. Some break free by turning to Christ. Most become confirmed in their religion, which always in practice seems to have an outworking of hatred towards Jesus. We repeat what has been said elsewhere in this book: this world is not anti God – this world is anti Christ; an observation that hits the nail squarely on the head. What can be said beyond doubt is that the God revealed in the Bible is absolutely just, and we can therefore rely on Him not to treat anyone unfairly.

Everything we have shared up to this point does not really touch upon theology at the deepest level. From a normative Christian perspective it can be said that *the religions* do not offer salvation, in the sense of enabling their adherents to meet the exacting laws set out in the Pentateuch/Torah of the Holy Bible. *The religions* cannot offer salvation, and God has not offered a *package deal on salvation*, in the same way that you might switch your airline ticket if your carrier cannot take you on a particular day. To assume that all religions can 'do the trick' is simply a vain fantasy, far removed from what any of them actually say. Some Godists (as well as people of no faith, and indeed some of *the religions*) may complain that the God of the Holy Bible is a narrow god, whereas their understanding of 'deity' is much broader and more inclusive than that traditionally linked to Christianity. This is not as profound as may at first appear. Their 'understanding' of deity is precisely that — it is *their* understanding and *their* 'god'. It is a 'god' of their own imagining, but not the God revealed in Scripture. This 'god' is a sort of googled-god, cut and pasted from bits and pieces of *the religions* and of Christianity; bits and pieces that are only half-understood and that are considered by the Godist to back-up their views. As we have already begun to see, this cut-and-paste approach to religion poses rather more questions than it answers!

Theology

Readers will no doubt want to refer across the New Testament in which so much that is prophesied in the Old actually happens. All the New Testament aligns in this – that the Lord Jesus is, as He said, the way the truth and the life (John 14:6). He said this plainly although some today try to 'spiritualise' His simple statement so as to make it mean different things. As always we should look within the context of any Bible verse to ensure we are not simply taking it out of its context. We should always bear in mind 'a verse taken out of context is a pretext!' When Jesus said He was the way, He was comforting His disciples at the last supper. He knew He was about to die and His disciples were perplexed, unable at that point to grasp the reality of what was about to happen. Jesus told them, as He tells us, not to let our hearts be troubled, but to trust in God. Jesus will go ahead of us to that heavenly house where there are many rooms, and He will prepare a place for his disciples. Perplexed about where Jesus was going, His disciples asked Him where He was going and what was the way there – to which Jesus gave that timeless response that *He* is the way. At the profoundest level Jesus and all that He taught is the way. We think back over His three years of ministry, at His parables, His teachings, His miraculous interventions for good, and we begin to see what that way is. John 3:14 tells us that the son of man must be lifted up (literally onto a cross) so that (see v. 15) everyone who believes in Him may have eternal life. Believing Him inevitably means becoming His disciple and treading His pathway. Remember that the devil believes in Jesus but this does not make him a Christian!

Jesus is the way, the truth and the life. At the end of the day you accept it or reject it — but you cannot modify it. We consult once again Paul's amazing and wonderful letter to the Roman church for some deeper theology on this: Look in Romans 2:12–16, but especially vv. 14–15.

All who sin apart from the law will also perish apart from the law, and all who sin under the law will be judged by the law. For it is not the hearers the law who are righteous in God's sight, but the doers of the law who will be justified. When Gentiles, who do not possess the law, do instinctively what the law requires, these, though not having the law, are a law to themselves. They show that what the law requires is written on their hearts, to which their own conscience also bears witness; and their conflicting thoughts will accuse or perhaps excuse them on the day when, according to my gospel, God, through Jesus Christ, will judge the secret thoughts of all. (Romans 2:12-16, NRSV)

God's law is written onto people's hearts. They know when they sin, and all too often their consciences are calloused on such a way that they no longer care, no matter what is revealed to them about God. But when they do by nature the things required by the law, they have become a law for themselves and they prove at the deepest level that God exists, because His law is 'hard-wired' into their consciences. Humans must live in the perfect law as revealed by Jesus,[10] but they fall short and are found wanting. If they choose to live under grace, enjoying mercy and divine forgiveness for sin, then they must faithfully believe and follow Jesus, quite simply, as His disciples —not following

---

[10] And, it might be added, perfectly fulfilled by Jesus.

or owing partial allegiance to other religions. No-one who sins (Jew or Gentile) has any excuse (Romans 1:19–20). This is truly deep theology! In Romans 4:15, Paul reminds us that **where there is no law, there is no transgression** [sin]. Very true. If there was no law, men would have an excuse, but we reiterate there is *no* excuse, whether people are of *the religions* or not. All alike have sinned, and all alike must ultimately be judged. And unless they have accepted the gift of God in Christ they will have no defence.

A Googled God?

We have probably explored sufficiently for the present purpose what Holy Scripture reveals about law and grace. We have seen that all mankind will be judged by Christ, all have sinned, falling short of God's standards, and we all need Christ, who alone can save us. We have observed that God is, by definition, just and merciful, and that we can therefore confidently leave aside questions about the salvation of infants and how God will meet the 'problem' (to us) of those who have never even hear of the name of Jesus. God is holy and He *will* do the right thing. Old and New Testaments lead to the same conclusions. What we cannot do is to point to *the religions* as God's 'also rans', alongside His gift of grace in Jesus Christ. They oppose and contradict each other, both in their general thrust and their detailed claims. If God made them to lead us in different directions then, it is submitted, He could not be good. Such a 'god' would be two-faced; or would not know 'his' or 'its' own mind; or would be evil. The Godist notion that a deity would reveal Himself in many different, inconsistent, self-contradictory ways is obviously completely untenable. But it is precisely this sort of a 'god' that the Godists invite us to trust! If people want to believe in such a 'god' then ultimately that must be their choice in this world of freewill that God has so graciously given to us, but they should be under no illusion that this is not the God of the Holy Bible. It is another 'god', a different 'god'. The God revealed in Scripture however is completely holy, completely righteous and when He saves us we can experience His love for ourselves. God is light. In Him there is no darkness at all. (See 1 John 1:5).

At the very end of the Bible (Revelation 22:18), God has given a powerful warning against addition to and subtraction from scripture. This makes it clear that any Godist claim made on behalf of the writings of other religions is wholly incompatible with the Holy Bible. The one true God, the God of Abraham, Isaac and Jacob, the God and Father of our Lord Jesus Christ (Himself true God and true man), the Holy Trinity of Father, Son and Holy Spirit, is perfectly consistent. His self-revelation is clear, complete and sufficient for salvation. Man is not to add to or take away from what He has revealed. His glory will never be shared by any other 'god'. The God revealed in the Bible and in the person of Jesus Christ is true to His own Word. He has given us a narrow road that leads to life and He has warned us about a broad road that leads to destruction. We remind ourselves once again what Jesus said: **Enter through the narrow gate: for the gate is wide and the road is easy that leads to destruction, and there are many who take it. For the gate is narrow and the road is hard that leads to life, and there are few who find it.** (Matthew 7:13–14 NRSV).

The multi-faith agenda seems to proffer a broad path and is now promoted by the state as well as institutions such as the United Nations. Much more could be said about this desire to create a 'god' in a comfortable, worldly, image, but readers are encouraged to search the Holy Bible on their own to establish in their minds the truth in this matter. As they do so, they should ask the Holy Spirit of God to guide them. He will delight to do so (see John 16:13). In that exploration, along with any other issues they want to search out, the reader may wish to ask: Is God consistent? What is His attitude to sin? How has He remedied the eternal problem of sin? Some helpful pointers can be offered here:

For since in the wisdom of God the world through its wisdom did not know him, God was pleased through the foolishness of what was preached to save those who believe. (1 Corinthians 1:21) We are reminded that those used to speculation and philosophy find the particularity and historicity of the gospel a difficulty they will need to overcome. God has revealed Himself in the person of Jesus, not in mere worldly theories and abstract constructs.

How great is the love the Father has lavished on us, that we should be called children of God! And that is what we are! The reason the world does not know us is that it did not know him. (1 John 3:1) This, addressed to Christian believers, helps us to see something of what it means to be an adopted child of God when we have repented and are believing. Unbelievers cannot see this. As we explored in chapter 9, it is God's good purpose to extend His family and His invitation is given to all people, everywhere who will respond in repentance and faith. To ignore such an invitation is not only tragic, it is also foolish. To present all religions as co-equal, or even as God's *also-rans* is to suggest, falsely, that there are different ways in which we might be forgiven and saved. When this view of the co-equality of religions is expounded from within the church, we are reminded of the words of Jesus in His letters to the churches (in the book of Revelation). His indictment of those who were teaching falsehood is devastating, and it is inconceivable that His words to churches teaching a false message would be any different today!

Of those within the churches today who hold the Godist position, we can say that that their beliefs are heretical. It must be observed that their heterodox views will be held with different levels of conviction depending on the individual concerned. This is not to suggest that Christians get everything right all the time. In secondary matters of biblical interpretation in many areas, there are differences in exegesis which need not lead to break in fellowship. But this is no secondary, minor matter we are concerned with. Godism is aimed at the very heart of the gospel. If Godism were true, there would be no gospel at all; no possibility of the forgiveness of sins; there would have been no need for the cross, the saving death of Jesus; all that suffering for us would have been utterly pointless; Christianity would be offering no hope whatsoever to anyone; the claims of Jesus to divinity would have been manifestly untrue. The matter is a serious as that.

It is the view of many in this world that all religions lead to God in their distinctive ways. Once Godists have considered, as this book has sought to encourage, the full implications of their superficially comfortable belief, they ought to be shocked, and ought to realign their views to be consistent with the great gospel that Christ has given. Some Godists simply will not do so, and will continue to lead astray others who allow themselves to be beguiled into accepting a relativism which is utterly destructive.

We are reminded of an incident in Acts, where a man called Simon sought to buy his way into the leadership of the church. The apostle Peter was blunt with him: **"You have no part or share in this ministry, because your**

heart is not right before God" (Acts 8:21). It would be so tragic if church-based Godists become so hardened in their attitude that in reality they lose any share in God's work. The danger is real, and the call of the gospel should be neither overlooked nor diluted by people who claim to be Christians. Jesus' warning below is salutary for all who aim to teach, lead or prophesy to His people, and it has great relevance for His flock too, who need to be vigilant against false teaching and faithful in their own witness to the true gospel:

"Watch out for false prophets. They come to you in sheep's clothing, but inwardly they are ferocious wolves. By their fruit you will recognize them. Do people pick grapes from thornbushes, or figs from thistles? Likewise every good tree bears good fruit, but a bad tree bears bad fruit. A good tree cannot bear bad fruit, and a bad tree cannot bear good fruit. Every tree that does not bear good fruit is cut down and thrown into the fire. Thus, by their fruit you will recognize them.

"Not everyone who says to me, 'Lord, Lord,' will enter the kingdom of heaven, but only he who does the will of my Father who is in heaven. Many will say to me on that day, 'Lord, Lord, did we not prophesy in your name, and in your name drive out demons and perform many miracles?' Then I will tell them plainly, 'I never knew you. Away from me, you evildoers!'" (Matthew 7:15–23)

The author considers to be perhaps the most chilling words in the entire Bible the final verse in that quotation. There are people who claim to know Jesus but who are in fact unknown to Him — unknown in the sense that they have no part with Him notwithstanding their public religiosity. Earlier in this book it was suggested we would eventually look at clues as to where a person truly stands before Christ, and with particular reference to those who are in church contexts but 'preach' a gospel other than Christ. There is nothing really difficult about this: if people claim to be Christians but bear bad fruit, then in all probability they are not true disciples of Christ. This is not to say that Christians will be sinless — sadly we will continue to sin from time to time even after 'receiving' Christ into our lives (John 1:12), but these sins are not the *bad fruit* that Jesus seems to have had in mind. What the Lord was referring to was persistent and determined behaviour that runs counter to His clear teaching and to the revelation of Holy Scripture. Where someone claims to follow Christ but opposes Him, despite warnings and despite God's ever gracious opportunity to repent, then it is not unreasonable to conclude that they are false in their faith profession. It would be wrong to be definitive about the eternal standing of all Godists when found in a church context. Only God really knows. Yet in the light of the clear teaching of Scripture and what we know of the nature of God, which nature we began to explore earlier in this book, it would be wrong not to remind them of the purity of the gospel, and to remind them with pleading that God is jealous of His reputation; He will not share His glory with other 'gods' or with other 'gospels'.

Some Godists in church contexts, and indeed some outside the church context, may react to the foregoing in this way: what really matters is not the finer points of what you believe, it is how you live your life that counts. This argument is closely associated with that *golden rule* that is said to run through all religions, of 'doing to others as you would want them to do to you', and of demonstrating compassion. Some Godists would say, perhaps with a shrug, that strict belief in Jesus may or may not be important, but

God will ultimately recognize them for their works. They argue in fact that: **You have faith, I have works** (James 2:18). This seems to have been the attitude that Jesus warned against in Matthew chapter 7. There will always be false religiosity. Tragically there will be people who in a stiff–necked way continue to try to 'offset' their sins against their so-called 'good works'. But Jesus will not be fooled: see again Matthew 7:21-23. This is all so tragic. We hear the echo of that classic Godist position, whether expressed from within or outside of the church: 'My God is completely merciful. My God is completely loving. All people (or nearly all!) will be saved by my God. Your God is unmerciful!' Throughout this book we have attempted to understand something of God as He has revealed Himself. The world's attitude that there are multiple paths to God is neatly summarized in our mind map in Appendix 1. This attitude is dismissive of God. God is revealed by the Bible as being holy, righteous, merciful, loving and compassionate, and all these qualities are best expressed in the ministry and achievements of Jesus, the Son of God, about Whom we read:

He is the image of the invisible God, the firstborn over all creation. For by Him all things were created that are in heaven and that are on earth, visible and invisible, whether thrones or dominions or principalities or powers. All things were created through Him and for Him. And He is before all things, and in Him all things consist. And He is the head of the body, the church, who is the beginning, the firstborn from the dead, that in all things He may have the preeminence.

For it pleased the Father that in Him all the fullness should dwell, and by Him to reconcile all things to Himself, by Him, whether things on earth or things in

heaven, having made peace through the blood of His cross. (Colossians 1:15–20, NKJV).

It is in Jesus that we find the atoning sacrifice for our sins, and not only for ours, but also for the sins of the world at large (1 John 2:2). We might also ask, as we consider the extraordinary claims that the Bible makes of Jesus: Who else has added a NEW commandment? (John 13:34). Who else has authority to forgive sins? (Matthew 9:6 and Mark 2:7).[11] Who else is heir of all things? (Hebrews 1:2). Who else is the Word made flesh? (John 1:14). Who else is in very nature God? (Philippians 2:6–11).

With Godists operating in churches there may have to be a *parting of the ways*, especially where such heterodox views are expressed by those who exercise positions of leadership (Titus 3:10).[12] With sorrow and prayer we must warn 'Christian Godists' that there must arrive a point at which their beliefs cease to be Christian. In pursuing these beliefs in stiff-necked defiance of what the Bible teaches, both in its overall thrust (the need to remain pure from *the religions*), and in the specific teaching of the Lord Jesus that He only is the way, He only is the truth and He only is the life, such people run the very real risk of losing their relationship with Him. Trusting in their religiosity, and possibly in their *extreme* religiosity to the extent that they put trust in religions alongside Christ, and trusting in what they see as the evidence of their works, we can only repeat that such people run all too great a risk that one day

---

[11] Jesus graciously delegates His authority to forgive sins to His disciples. See John 10:21–23. This is a great responsibility for Christians.

[12] False teachers style themselves as Christian pastors, teachers, and evangelists (cf. Jude 4) who *secretly bring in destructive heresies*. Their self-designed religious teachings lead to division and faction (cf. 1 Cor 11:19, Gal 5:20) and ultimately spiritual weakness in churches that make a virtue out of tolerating unscriptural teachings and ideas in the name of love and unity.

they will find themselves excluded. There are, said Jesus, some who will be amazed at their exclusion. Jesus used the symbol of a wedding to illustrate His relationship to His church. We think again of the five foolish virgins who were unable to wait faithfully for their bridegroom to return. Jesus uses the same symbol in Matthew 22:1–12, the parable of the wedding banquet of the King. The chosen people had rejected their Messiah (22:5), and sadly did not deserve to attend the feast (22:8). So the King calls for others to be invited to His wedding feast, and in this we see the covenant of salvation being extended to all nations, not just to the Jewish nation. But some people manage to slip into the feast uninvited: **But when the king came in to see the guests, he noticed a man there who was not wearing wedding clothes. 'Friend,' he asked, 'how did you get in here without wedding clothes?' The man was speechless. Then the king told the attendants, 'Tie him hand and foot, and throw him outside, into the darkness, where there will be weeping and gnashing of teeth'** (Matthew 22:11–13). The uninvited guest, who presumably thought he should attend the wedding feast on his merit, was speechless. There must be a similar danger for Godists within the church, that they have so determinedly set their faith in religions and the 'good works' of *the religions*, that they cannot understand that the bridegroom has ceased to recognize them.

334

14

DIALOGUE

We have sought to analyse and deconstruct ideas that travel under the title of Godism, as we have defined it. This may seem to some readers to have had a negative tone, yet it is hoped that it has been positive insofar that we have looked at the beautiful nature of Almighty God, and have begun to explore the wonderful attributes of God and how these attributes combine perfectly and sublimely in the person and works of Jesus the Messiah. It is hoped that readers have themselves been blessed by looking to God, for ultimately there is no better place to fix our gaze. The focus of our book shifts in this final chapter to explore a subject that must have been at the back of the minds of many readers. Given that Jesus is, as He has said, *the* way, *the* truth and *the* life, then precisely what should a Christian's attitude be to the 'great faith systems' of the world? It is this author's view that Christians need to begin by recognizing that Jesus commands that we should love all people, even our enemies, and the apostle Paul taught that we should live peaceably with all men so far as the initiative lies with us (see Romans 12:18). After all, God has been very patient with us — He patiently waits for us to become more like His Son. He patiently takes us through the long process that theologians call sanctification which, in New Testament terms, has in mind the truth that at conversion a believer is 'set apart' and then, insofar as we are yielded[1] to the Holy Spirit, we are progressively made holy by God. This is not, it should be added, a self-reformation, rather it is an activity of God with which we are to co-operate. So there is an initial sanctification when we are born again, followed by a progressive sanctification through which we become more like Christ and our lives become more holy. In a 'normal' Christian life this process will be ongoing.

The challenge of interacting with other cultures and other religions is not as new as we might think. Certainly in the Roman world, where our New Testament was given to us, there were many religions and many 'gods'. It is noteworthy that the Christian religion, that *Way* referred to by Jesus, was not accepted alongside *the religions* of the early New Testament period as just another set of religious people with just another 'god'. From the beginning, Christianity was perceived as something different, both by its adherents and by its persecutors. Suffering through persecution would become a hallmark of the Christian church and the Christian life (see Appendix 5 in this regard). It is in the book of Acts that we see how the early *body of Christ* — His church — was persecuted, almost from the very beginning. Attacks against the church began in Jerusalem but were, from the antagonists' viewpoint, ultimately counterproductive and merely scattered the church far and wide throughout the Roman Empire. In this, Christians see God's providential hand at work. The gospel message continued to be preached, and the good news of peace with God through Jesus who

---

[1] 'Yielded' is a very passive term. By 'yielded' we simply mean the openness of the Christian to the Holy Spirit and our associated determination to work with Him and not to grieve Him. Christians should be daily asking for the infilling of the Holy Spirit so that we can live, quite simply, Spirit filled lives.

is Lord of all (see Acts 10:36) was paramount. The apostle Peter affirmed that all the [Hebrew] prophets testify about Jesus, and everyone who believes in Him receives forgiveness of sins through His name (Acts 10:43). In Acts 17, having experienced persecution, the apostle Paul has been escorted to Athens, that most cosmopolitan of ancient cities. Waiting for friends to join him, Paul was 'greatly distressed' to see that the city was full of idols (see Acts 17:16). No doubt today some Godists would be pleased to see a city full of idols and shrines as 'valid' expressions of their deity!

Paul's reaction to this 'distressing' situation is instructive to the church of today. Monotheism would be at the very heart of Paul's (Jewish) mind and teaching, and rightly so. Idol worship is forbidden in the Scriptures.[2] But rather than beginning by berating the clearly false religions of his day, Paul invited his listeners and critics to consider Jesus. Today, a Christian's task and mission is to preach the gospel of righteousness: repentance, and faith in Jesus, crucified for us, and risen from the dead. We really have little to say about religions except, perhaps, to examine where they differ from the Way. We must start, as did Paul, from where people are and not from where we might want them to be. In wishing that circumstances were different, 'we are where we are' is a phrase often heard (with a sigh) in business and government as people face awkward situations, often with a history of mishap behind them! The same idea is used by Paul in Acts 17. Invited to speak at the Areopagus (Athenians loved new ideas and debate, and were happy to have Paul present his case in this important public debating chamber) Paul opens his address with the pertinent observation that the Athenians

---

[2] We explored in chapters 3 and 4 of this book God's condemnation of idol worship.

are in every way very religious people. They had many 'gods', each with their own set of shrines but, worried that they might have failed to discern some deity that needed to be assuaged, the Athenians had an altar dedicated TO AN UNKNOWN GOD. Paul focused on this idea of an unknown deity as he said: **"That which you worship, then, even though you do not know it, is what I now proclaim to you"** (Acts 17:23, GNB). He went on to tell his listeners of the Creator God who needs nothing from human beings. This God, he told them, is not far from any of us: **God, who made the world and everything in it, is Lord of heaven and earth and does not live in temples made by human hands. Nor does he need anything that we can supply by working for him, since it is he himself who gives life and breath and everything else to everyone.**

From one human being he created all races on earth and made them live throughout the whole earth. He himself fixed beforehand the exact times and the limits of the places where they would live. He did this so that they would look for him, and perhaps find him as they felt about for him. Yet God is actually not far from any one of us; as someone has said, "In him we live and move and exist." It is as some of your poets have said, "We too are his children." Since we are God's children, we should not suppose that his nature is anything like an image of gold or silver or stone, shaped by human art and skill. God has overlooked the times when people did not know him, but now he commands all of them everywhere to turn away from their evil ways. For he has fixed a day in which he will judge the whole world with justice by means of a man he has chosen. He has given proof of this to everyone by raising that man from death!" (Acts 17:24–31, GNB)

Crucially, Paul was honest about the fact that in the past God had overlooked the ignorance of humans worshipping in pagan religions. No doubt a Godist today would want to assure the Athenians that their beliefs and shibboleths were valid expressions of deity which would help to instil godly values and help them to discern a godly concept of compassion. Indeed this passage in Acts is sometimes proffered by 'liberal' Christians as evidence that Paul was reconciled to 'other religions'. That interpretation reads too much into what is recorded of Paul's speech, however. Starting from where they were in terms of spiritual understanding, Paul simply pointed to the Creator God, of Whom the Athenians also wanted to be known as sons and daughters. 'We too are his children' was their assessment — but it was not necessarily God's assessment![3] Either way, the offer of new life was made by Paul, based on the proof of Jesus' body having been raised from the dead.

We need only to look again at the sublime teaching of Jesus to know that dialogue and gentleness are hallmarks of true Christianity. No one is forced into the Kingdom of God. The choice for all men remains today as it has been for 2,000 years: *to live* (in Him) or *not to live* (in Him). Blessed are the meek, said Jesus in Matthew chapter 5, for the meek will inherit the earth. Being meek does not mean lacking in courage to share the truth of Jesus, and its attendant choice to live (in Him) or not to live (in Him) which all humans must make. Meekness does not involve a failure to share truth because of a fear of causing offence! Blessed are the merciful, for they will be shown mercy, said Jesus. Christians are to be merciful with those of *the*

---

[3] All humans are made in the image of God, but they are, it is suggested, *not* His children until adopted into His family by grace, through faith in Jesus, God's Son.

religions as much as to those of no religious beliefs, for all these alike are made in the image of God. Blessed are the peacemakers, said Jesus, for they will be called sons of God. We are to witness to all people who will accept it concerning the peace that passes all understanding — that peace which only Jesus, the Prince of Peace, can impart. Blessed, said Jesus, are those who are persecuted because of righteousness. 'Righteousness' is not a word much loved by this world (with its false idea of self-righteousness and all that flows from that). Those who follow Jesus will face persecution. Those who persecute only serve to show that Jesus was right.

Christian believers have the great commission to make disciples. It is hard to see how that could be achieved without talking with those of the various religions (as did Paul). Clearly, Paul had an accurate idea of what their idol worship amounted to. He would have had no illusions! But we noted above that in Athens Paul did not engage his hearers with an immediate, direct discussion about all the false religion he found. Rather, his witness was to what God had done in creating all things and in raising Jesus from the dead. Paul's focus is on the mighty acts of the only true and living God. That proved to be challenging for Paul's hearers who could quickly work out that their idols or deities had no voice, had never created anything, and certainly had no connection with resurrection! To find the right starting point for witness will require great sensitivity to the Holy Spirit, a clear understanding of what God has done for us, and a love for the person who is in the grip of another religion or belief system. Sometimes personal testimony is appropriate. Intellectual 'head to head' debate, though, is rarely fruitful unless, like Paul, one has a special call and (spiritual) gifting for teaching scriptural truths.

Sometimes people will genuinely ask serious questions about how Christian beliefs differ from those of *the religions*. If this is genuine seeking for the true God, then it has to be a good thing and Christians should wisely and politely explain what the Bible has to say. In the post-Christian culture of the West, and particularly in the UK with its so-called 'religious hatred' legislation, there seems to be a willingness on the part of (mainly left-wing) central and local government and increasingly politically correct business corporations to muzzle any expression of orthodox Christianity, on the dubious pretext of protecting people from 'offence'. Strangely, it seems that others can offend Christians with impunity, and this is because, it is said, Christians are a dominant majority who need no protection! Christians need to be wise, then, in interpreting questions and conversation from at least some quarters, as there is increasing evidence of the willingness of people with a *hidden agenda* to engage in normal discussion about current affairs, invite discussion on religious matters, conduct and conclude these discussions on friendly terms, and later to return and claim they have been offended or feel harassed! In the UK of the early twenty-first century, Government advice on the interpretation of such difficulties appears (at the time of writing this book) to confirm that the perceptions of the person claiming to have been offended or harassed 'shall be paramount'. It is sad that Britian's once proud claim to be a nation of free speech is genuinely under threat from what some observers have suggested is a shift from a democracy to a 'victimocracy'.[4]

Still, in spite of the foregoing, Christians should be will-

---

[4] For example, see David Green's short book called *We're Nearly All Victims Now! How Political Correctness Is Undermining Our Liberal Culture* (Civitas – ISBN 1-903386-53-5, 2006).

ing and pleased to tell others about Jesus, for that is what He wants of us. We are to be His *witnesses*. We remember again the *great commission* of Jesus to His church, to go and make disciples of all nations, baptizing them in the name of the Father and of the Son and of the Holy Spirit, and teaching them to obey everything that Jesus has commanded (Matthew 28:19f). Note that the Lord Jesus said we were to teach people to obey *everything* He had commanded. This seems to preclude any idea that we tell people only what they want to hear or things that will not offend them. We remind ourselves once more that the Christian gospel is a 'scandal' to some (see chapter 12) and that, through the witness and preaching of believers, the good news of Jesus will spread everywhere. To some that gospel will be a fragrance of life. To others it will be the stench of death (2 Corinthians 2:14–16). To those who *are perishing*, the good news of Jesus will be fearful, and will have about it the stench of eternal separation from God (death). We can readily see that the good news can be to some people an absolute scandal! Yet it is that very uncomfortableness, that notion of a God Who has died for each one of us, if only we accept it, that encourages so many people to respond by undertaking those three basic steps of 'A, B and C' — to recognize or Admit their need of Jesus, repenting before Him for their sins; to Believe in Him; and to Commit their lives and futures to Him. From scandal to joy in three easy (or, in reality, not so easy) steps!

So talking to others of whatever religion can be good. It is essential for witness and communicating the word of truth. Without it, people often live with fears, uncertainties and misconceptions about their neighbours. They may well be living with erroneous views of the Christian gospel. How can faulty perceptions be corrected if people are unable and unwilling to converse? This has to be done in love. Scripture uses a number of different words which are translated in English 'love'. Here we mean 'agape' love, which has the very best eternal interests of the other person at heart. In humility but with confidence that we know the One of Whom we speak, we are to have compassion on those who know nothing of the life we have been privileged to begin to experience for ourselves. If people will not accept the good news of Jesus, then ultimately that is their decision. But if our witness can help even one lost soul to come into the kingdom, with all its benefits and promises, any embarrassment, discomfort or inconvenience (or even persecution) is worthwhile.

Jesus gave His *great commission* to His church, and this of course begins with your own life: your primary responsibility is to go on believing in Jesus and go on walking in obedience to Him, your Lord and Saviour. Jesus' invitation, His teaching, His promises are always personal — addressed to you, His disciple and witness! The apostle Peter affirmed the personal responsibility of each human to respond as he told he crowds in Jerusalem in Acts 2:40 to save themselves from their sinful generation. That clarion call has come down with the church for the past two thousand years. To some, the call is a fragrance of life. To all too many it is a fragrance of death. We still need to tell the good news of salvation and the bad news of eternal loss and hell. (Jesus spoke as much about hell as He did about heaven.[5]) Jesus' disciples in this dark world must point to the one true Light; they must highlight the truth that the (only) way to the Father is through Jesus, warn of eternal

---

[5] It is important to note that our Lord's warnings were often addressed to his disciples, as much as to the world at large. Protestant Christians often fail to note this, presuming that all is well and will continue to be well in their relationship with God.

dangers, and proclaim the joyful possibility of eternal life. A Christian's task is to witness to and preach Jesus, crucified and raised from the dead. God the Father draws people towards Jesus (see John 6:44f.) and God the Holy Spirit will convict the world of sin, and of righteousness and of judgement (see John 16:8).

Questions and answers

We have already noted that it is not always appropriate for Christian believers to tackle head on the beliefs of *the religions* or those of no faith, but that sincere questions should be welcomed when they come from the genuine seeking of someone who really wants to know God. The Gospels provide examples of those who were genuinely seeking God. They asked Jesus questions, which He handled with the very greatest wisdom and understanding. He knew where people really are (or, as is often said today) where they were 'coming from'. Other questions, though, were mere trickery, designed to set traps, and they got some very different (but again, of course, immensely wise) answers which challenged their twisted, wicked opposition to the Lord. Had those questioners been open to the truth, they could have learnt from Jesus, and their stony hearts could have been changed. Some of the conventionally 'religious' establishment came with questions which were, to say the least, mischevious or worse. Jesus knew what was in their hearts as He uttered exactly the right words for each encounter. But how can we know? How can we have such wisdom when we have 'dialogue' with unbelievers? Quite simply, we need the Word and the Spirit. We must know and believe our Bible, accepting its divine inspiration; and we must go on being filled with the Holy Spirit, and constantly asking God for wisdom and discernment in *everything we say.* Of course this is true in the whole of life, but the need is especially obvious in the situations we have in mind here. We need to know, as Jesus did, where others are 'coming from' — what is in their spirit. Are they open to the truth? Are they truly seeking the one true God? The answer begins with guarding your own walk with the Lord, ensuring there is no unconfessed sin, letting your attitude to others be like that of Christ Jesus. Then: pray before meetings; pray before speaking; do not say what is not clearly testified in the Bible. Listen constantly to what the Holy Spirit is saying to you (which will only ever be words that glorify Jesus). Without the in-filling and the gifts of the Holy Spirit and the resources of a good knowledge of the written Word, you are going into situations of dialogue without essential equipping!

Turning now to the opportunities for dialogue today, one could say that it is ironic indeed that the so-called religious hatred legislation in the UK (and perhaps elsewhere) is likely to chill openness, make dialogue less likely and lead to greater misunderstanding. Truly, politicians can often achieve the exact reverse of what they purport to want. In the UK in their claimed attempt to prevent 'harassment' of minorities our politicians seem actively to want to chill open discussion between adherents of different faiths. There must be a residual suspicion in the UK that some politicians, at least, have deliberately framed legislation in an attempt to cut the UK further adrift from its Christian roots. In this they are surely, we would argue, aided and abetted by some of the media and in particular the BBC (see our Foreword).[6]

---

[6] In July 2008 the BBC screened a drama series called *Bonekickers* with a plot line in one episode of 'extremist Christians' beheading a moderate Muslim. A year later the BBC Trust, a group of 'independent' trustees supposedly working in the public interest, rejected public complaints. By implication this made Christianity fair game for this sort of treatment by the BBC. It is perhaps superfluous to add that other religions would never be treated in such a way.

Some religions, or at least their more vocal members, demand 'respect', and some politicians connive at this demand. The Oxford dictionary definition of respect is *deferential esteem*. This has to be a dangerous aspiration in an open society. Could it be said that Jesus 'respected' the scribes and Pharisees? Did Paul show 'respect' for the idolaters of Athens? Certainly Jesus and Paul (led by the Spirit) knew exactly where their hearers stood. Their words indicated that they had no intention of somehow using force to make their questioners or interlocutors change their minds; yet, needless to say, we can be certain that neither Jesus nor the apostle entertained any notion that man's idolatry itself could have the slightest scrap of validity. Again, needless to say, any true Christian today would hold precisely that position in his or her heart, mind and spirit. We can only ever see idolatry and the worship of other gods as abhorrent and deceptive, holding souls in darkness and captivity from which we know that the word of truth will bring release when there is a response of repentance and faith in Jesus Christ. We respect, as the Son of God did, and as the apostle did, the responsibility of the other human being to choose. We acknowledge their freedom to decide for themselves. We would be lying if we pretended to respect *beliefs* which we believe to be both false and dangerously misleading.

Respect, we remind ourselves, is something that has to be earned, it can never be a right. Certain politicians who are fond of demanding respect for what they see as 'victim groups', are themselves willing to be grossly disrespectful of other groups with which they disagree. We are hardly surprised that Christians are increasingly persecuted all around the world. Jesus foretold such persecution.

We believe that God has given men and women freewill,

including the freedom to accept or reject the claims of Christ. The New Testament certainly does not deny, cover up or gloss over the fact that there are differences between Christians and others. So we should not be beguiled by the 'respect' slogan into denying differences, especially as between *the religions*.

Returning to our discussion of dialogue, and bearing in mind the biblical material we have considered, it needs to be said that we should be realistic about the likelihood of disagreement. But disagreement does not have to mean that people part on bad terms. Disagreement is not, *ipso facto*, a bad thing. The right kind of respect (i.e. respecting others' right to choose) surely means that we should be able to disagree in an open and caring way, without undue fear of offence. People may be saddened or frustrated that they cannot agree, but should certainly not be offended. We really do need to be seen to set an example as we speak and relate to others.

A dialogue of ever closer union?

Freedom of religion is affirmed in the terms of the United Nations Universal Declaration of Human Rights, Article 18(b). That should inhibit governments from restricting our liberty to preach, teach and witness to everything in Scripture. Yet this freedom, as we have noted, is under real threat. Christians affirm this right. Do others? This right is enshrined in international law but is increasingly breached in various parts of the world.

In everything, we should exhibit a humble confidence in Jesus, noting carefully the words the apostle Peter uses: **Always be prepared to give an answer to everyone who asks you to give the reason for the hope that you have. But do this with gentleness and respect, keeping a clear**

conscience, so that those who speak maliciously against your good behavior in Christ may be ashamed of their slander. (1 Peter 3:15f, NIV).

The word rendered 'respect' is translated as reverence in the NRSV, as in the older RSV. A literal translation of the New Testament Greek for 'gentleness and respect' would be 'meekness and fear', but the NIV, GNB, RSV etc are surely closer to the mark in today's parlance. 'Meekness' can be misunderstood, and the word 'fear' may also be misunderstood in this context. But it is quite clear that we should have a humble confidence in the good news of Jesus.

The idea that all religions are true and equally valid is not as 'tolerant' as those who propound this philosophy like to think. It is actually rather arrogant, when the adherents of those religions all say something which (as we have shown) is very different. The biblical response to the syncretistic and/or Godist view has been examined at length in this book, but we affirm again that a correct scriptural response must inevitably be (a) Jesus is God (John 8:58f); (b) Jesus is Saviour (1 Timothy 2:5f; Acts 4:12); (c) Jesus is alive. Whilst all three points will be controversial as regards other religions, Christians see Jesus' resurrection (and consequently His being alive today) as His guarantee that our final enemy – death – has been defeated and trampled underfoot.

Dialogue leading towards ever closer religious union is an aim held by some Godists, but, unrealistic as that regrettable aim may be, it is nonetheless likely that pressure will build through the EU and the UN for *the religions* to align, in return for which there may be increasing levels of state support, direct and via NGOs,[7] as well as concessions

---

[7] EU = European Union; UN = United Nations; NGO = non governmental organisations

made at political level — especially in the UN, where some nations and religions are beginning to learn that they can pursue partisan religious agendas as well as partisan national agendas. The UN lent its name and support to the United Religions Initiative (URI), a pressure group, so as to support financially the URI's *International Year of Reconciliation* in 2009. In chapter 13 we noted that the Bible points towards a coming global religion under the Antichrist. Religions are likely to cooperate with these developments, either through coercion by the state or by the allure of worldly rewards.

A more likely scenario than *dialogue towards union*, surely, is suggested by 2 Timothy 4:4–6. Here the apostle tells Timothy plainly that he should be prepared 'in season and out of season' (or more prosaically *whether the time is right or not* in the words of the GNB translation) to share the good news of Jesus, and to make the most of the present opportunity because a time will come when people will reject sound doctrine:

I solemnly urge you to preach the message, to insist upon proclaiming it (whether the time is right or not), to convince, reproach, and encourage, as you teach with all patience. The time will come when people will not listen to sound doctrine, but will follow their own desires and will collect for themselves more and more teachers who will tell them what they are itching to hear. They will turn away from listening to the truth and give their attention to legends. (GNB).

Since Western society is today throwing off what it sees as the yoke of Christianity it will certainly want something of a religious nature to replace it. If *the religions* generally are facing political pressure as well as pressure from the average man (and woman) in the street, then perhaps the time will seem to many to be ripe for some new religion that appears to unite or absorb the world's older religions. But the key point made by Paul to Timothy is that people will 'gather around them' a 'great number' of teachers, who will tell them exactly what they want to hear.[8] Politicians will be all too ready to fall in line with this new religious teaching. Are they, even today, gathering around them just such 'teachers'? And if so, is this a case of the blind leading the blind? (Matthew 15:14).

Honesty: can Christianity interact with *the religions* outside of a multi-faith agenda?

In spite of the dangers suggested in the previous section, Christians should remain committed to spending time with non-Christians, listening to their questions and exercising spiritual wisdom and discernment. This leaves room and opportunity to bear witness to unbelievers, and our model should always be the manner in which Jesus and the apostles related to people (rather than some modern, secular models of dialogue). In chapter 1 we explored that popular and rather desperate idea that by aligning *the religions*, peace and compassion might prevail. Such an outcome will never emerge. Politicians are apt to announce 'peace' when it does not exist. In Britain we remember with sadness Prime Minister Neville Chamberlain returning to London from Munich in 1938 and waving a scrap of paper over his head with the fervent announcement of 'peace in our time' — on the eve of the Second World War. The duplicity of mankind in its quest for peace on its terms, whilst simultaneously denying that most basic cause of conflict — sin — is revealed

---

[8] The point is well made that the context in which Paul wrote his warnings to Timothy was that of the church itself. The world at large is always willing to gather to itself teachers who will tell them what they want to hear. It is a double tragedy when it is church people who eagerly gather teachers who refuse to preach 'sound doctrine'.

by the prophet Jeremiah, with acerbic accuracy:

> **From the least to the greatest,**
> **all are greedy for gain;**
> **prophets and priests alike,**
> **all practice deceit.**
> **They dress the wound of my people**
> **as though it were not serious.**
> **'Peace, peace,' they say,**
> **when there is no peace.**
>
> (Jeremiah 6:13–14)

This has ever been true. The love of gain is paramount in the hearts of ungodly men and women. Sometimes even prophets and priests practice deceit — and this was certainly true in the time of Jeremiah. All too often today we see even churchmen saying that sin is not sin 'as though it were not serious'. Sins today are explained away by circumstances and upbringing. And what was once thought of as sin is today celebrated. Alongside politicians, at least some clergy are wont to announce peace with the world, whether it is by finding peace with our sins, or in telling us that war will one day, through our own efforts, become a distant memory. They forget, perhaps, that it was Jesus Himself who warned of wars and rumours of wars (see Matthew 24:6–7) until the end comes. When warfare is absent, we are forever fearing the next war — and with some justification. Politicians will always be announcing peace, for in many respects that is part of their job description. For politicians to, as they see it, create peace between religions may for a short time enable them to announce 'peace, peace'. But they will create a peace of their imagining, just as so many people today create a God of their own imagining, which surely is the ultimate outcome of Godism.

In passing we note that it is rather sad to see encounters between *the religions* where children are involved as, for example, in multi-faith services or other multi-faith enterprises, for young children are easily swayed. The danger is that the 'difficult' parts of *the religions* are swept under the proverbial carpet, and the endeavour is always to find 'common ground' or some *golden rule* of compassion.

What Jesus requires of us

We have deployed many arguments in this book which challenge and question the Godist position. We have especially challenged the Godist philosophy where it is expounded from within the church. Readers will not be surprised to learn, perhaps, that we have only begun to explore the heart of God on this matter — the God so clearly revealed in the person of Jesus Christ. There are certainly many other 'arguments' that could be deployed, but there is a sense in which there comes a time when enough has been said. If people have neither understood nor accepted the position set out in this book, then in all probability they are unlikely to do so, and so further arguments are superfluous. The idea that all the (supposedly 'higher') religions are of God will not withstand the test of Christian Scripture. Jesus' comments in Mark 4:11–12 and 7:6 are both instructive and a clear warning to us today. In explaining the parable of the sower (Mark 4:1–20) Jesus affirmed that the secret of the Kingdom of God has been given to 'you'. He meant the twelve disciples but the comment is for all His disciples down through time. But to 'those on the outside', those with stiff necks who are determined not to yield to Him:

"... they may be ever seeing but never perceiving, and ever hearing but never understanding; otherwise they might turn and be forgiven!"

Jesus was quoting Isaiah 6:9–10.[9] There are religious people who 'search' for God, but ignore the great salvation that He has provided. They 'search' for Him in religions, but only frustrate themselves. They look in philosophy, in education, in the writings of non-Christian religions; they even convolute sex and religion, and search in the occult. People determined not to yield to Jesus will look directly at Him but not perceive Him, and they will hear the good message of salvation, but not understand. It is sad, but true.

The God-given task of Christians is to witness to others about our crucified, risen, living Lord Jesus Christ, and we are to pray fervently for people to hear and understand, repent, and believe in Him. We must do this faithfully and persistently in obedience to our Lord.

It is sometimes inside the church that great danger lies. We find people who have been exposed to teaching about Jesus,[10] but then say that He is only one of a number of paths. Is there is some unrepented sin, some area in which these people are unwilling to yield to Jesus?

Our primary responsibility is to cooperate with God in His saving work in us, but it is not a case of 'every man for himself' spiritually. In witnessing for Jesus we will encounter difficulty, opposition and persecution — even,

---

[9] The apostle Paul quoted the same passage in Acts 28:23–28.

[10] The point is fairly made that in some churches where, sadly, unsound doctrine is preached, there will be Christians who have not genuinely been exposed to all that Jesus has to offer. Nevertheless, even to Christians who have not been fed a good or nourishing spiritual diet, the claims of Jesus will generally ring loud and clear. They cannot easily shrug them off in their dalliance with Godism.

for some, to the point of death.[11] But witness we must, for that is what He has commanded, and indeed Christians love to do this, because He is so good and, no matter what the question, spiritually speaking, He is the answer.

The encounter with the rich young ruler is instructive (see Luke 18:18–30). Jesus recognized what was holding back this otherwise respectable man from becoming part of the Kingdom of God; it was his money, his wealth. Some are held back from entering the Kingdom of God because, rather than loving Jesus, they love 'religion' (or even religions). Unwilling to lay these aside, like the rich young ruler, they go away, sad. Knowing and quoting the Bible does not make a person a Christian. Even the devil quotes Scripture (see Luke 4:4–12). The devil's tactic is to lead us to query or doubt what God has said. ('Did God really say…?' has been the devil's lie throughout history, see Genesis 3:1.) And today there are people even in the church who doubt the claims of Jesus to be the way, the truth and the life. It is interesting that those who publicly doubt what Jesus said on this are also those most likely within the church to doubt what the Scriptures declare for example, on sexual ethics. The devil always offers us the mirage of being 'like God' in perceiving 'new' religious teachings at variance with what Scripture actually says. That many would be deceived in the end times is something about which Jesus Himself warned (see, for example, Matthew 7:15ff, Matthew 24:24f). That there is a stumbling block preventing people from yielding to Jesus is also made clear in scripture. It is man's hatred of Jesus (see John 15:18). Mankind, the apostle John noted, loved darkness (see John 3:19f); so many detest the Man who is the light of the world (see John 8:12 and John 12:46).

---

[11] Jesus was candid about what it would 'cost' to follow Him. See Matthew 8:18; 10:21–31 and 38. Also Matthew 16:24–28.

This world, as we have noted before, is not anti 'god'. This world is anti-Christ.

Drawing to a close

That Jesus was born to die from before the creation of the world is scripturally accepted (see Revelation 13:8). That God foresaw the need for a Saviour and gave His beloved Son, Jesus Christ, is also scripturally clear (see Hebrews 2:9–18). Sin must be atoned for, and Jesus is that atonement.[12] Normally kings expect their people to die for them, but King Jesus died for His people. To become part of His Kingdom, however, I need to have a relationship with *Him*, and one vital aspect of that relationship is that I become His disciple; He is my Teacher. As we go through life, Jesus teaches us how to live and sends His Holy Spirit to empower us. Repentance is vital. The call to repent of my sins and believe (and go on believing) in Jesus has always been an integral, essential part of the preaching and witness of Christians. God the Father welcomes into His Kingdom those who repent, believe in and love His Son, Jesus Christ, and follow Him obediently. Having turned from sin, they follow Him in His strength and not their own. They owe all to Him. *Christianity is not so much a religion as a relationship* —like a loving relationship of a child to parent. We recognise that this statement may bring some pain to those who have never enjoyed such a relationship. To such readers we would only say this: whatever you may

---

[12] The atonement is a huge subject. Readers may want to look at this as a separate study. In summary: atonement is an English composite word meaning reconciliation (i.e. at-one-ment, but this does not mean unified ontologically, there is always a distinction between man and God). The word atonement translates in the Old Testament from the word 'kaphar' – to cover. Meaning thereby that sins were covered by the blood of the sacrifice, and that the sinner and God had become reconciled. Today in theology, the word atonement has come to include the whole theme of redemption through the blood of Christ.

have missed out on in terms of earthly relationships, you *can* most certainly enjoy a loving relationship with God through Jesus, and with His Holy Spirit living in you. Taste and see that the Lord is good!

That the Christian church often does not look very Christ-like must be acknowledged. When we invite people to follow Jesus, or to 'convert', to use a slightly old fashioned word, we are not inviting them to convert from one religion to another 'religion'. Rather, as people respond in repentance and faith in Jesus, God converts sinners from their sin so that they can have the righteousness which comes from God, the righteousness of Jesus rather than depending on their own (supposed) 'righteousness'. Jesus converts people from their love of self (selfishness and self-centeredness) to love for Him, because of His work — His suffering and saving death for them on the Cross at Golgotha. Where people of *the religions*, and indeed of no religion whatsoever, have a genuine encounter with the risen Lord Jesus, and repent, believe and determine to faithfully follow Him as their Lord and Saviour, they are born again; and they find themselves to be part of His body, the church. Sometimes converts must exercise caution, and sometimes there will be physical danger, but sooner or later God will provide the opportunity for them to have fellowship with other true believers. Whether an institution or not, this fellowship becomes church. Public and faithful witness to Jesus must be done in the world at large, but also must be done in the context of a body of believers.[13]

The choice, then, for all people is basic and simple: eternal life (in Jesus Christ) or rejection of His offer of forgiveness and new life. Godism, that philosophy which

---

[13] Again the subject of the church is a huge one! Readers may want to look at this as a separate study.

holds that all religions are valid expressions of deity, might seem superficially to offer a promise, but the promise is a chimera. It is a false promise and indeed a promise broken before it is even expressed. People face many empty promises in this life, why should their hopes be raised with yet another one? God has made Himself known, through Jesus, and invites us to live — in Him.

Appendix 1

Some Implications Of Basic Godism:

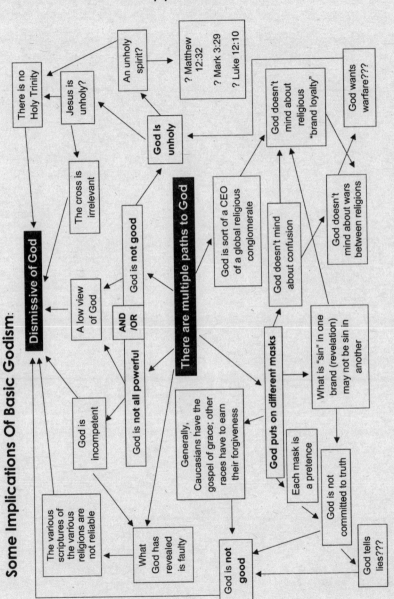

There is no Holy Trinity

An unholy spirit?

? Matthew 12:32
? Mark 3:29
? Luke 12:10

Jesus is unholy?

God is unholy

The cross is irrelevant

Dismissive of God

A low view of God

God is not good

AND /OR

God is not all powerful

There are multiple paths to God

God is sort of a CEO of a global religious conglomerate

God doesn't mind about confusion

God doesn't mind about religious "brand loyalty"

God wants warfare???

God doesn't mind about wars between religions

What is "sin" in one brand (revelation) may not be sin in another

God puts on different masks

Generally, Caucasians have the gospel of grace; other races have to earn their forgiveness

God is incompetent

The various scriptures of the various religions are not reliable

What God has revealed is faulty

Each mask is a pretence

God is not committed to truth

God is not good

God tells lies???

Appendix 2

Jesus' "I AM" statements

[The statements below marked ******** are those that are generally considered to be the key theological statements of Jesus, in revealing His Divine nature.]

John 4:26
"I who speak with you am he" – in answer to the Samaritan' woman's statement that the Messiah 'will come' and 'explain everything'.

John 6:48
the bread of Life ********

John 8:12
the light of the world ********

John 8:18
the one who testifies for myself

John 8:58
before Abraham was born, I AM (Matt 22:32) ********

John 10:7
the Gate ********

John 10:11
the Good Shepherd ********

John 10:36
God's Son ********

John 11:25
the Resurrection and the Life ********

John 13:13-4
your Lord and teacher

John 14:4
that you also may be where I am

John 14:6
the way, the truth and the life ********

John 14:10
in the Father and the Father is in me

John 14:20
in you

John 15:8
the true vine ********

John 17:16
They are not of the world, even as I am not of it.

John 18:5
I am he – in answer to the question, the guards looked for 'Jesus of Nazareth'. Met by Judas' kiss of betrayal.

Mark 12:26

quoting God (the Father) in God's revelation to Moses via the burning bush – and demonstrating an aspect of God's Lordship over time. 'God said ... 'I am the God of Abraham, the God of Isaac, and the God of Jacob.' He is not the God of the dead, but of the living.' [also Matt 22:32]

Mark 14:62

are you the Christ? – "I am"

[before the Sanhedrin – they all asked (Luke 22: 70) are you the Son of God?]

Matt 11:19

the Son of Man   ********

Matt 11:29

gentle and humble in heart, and you will find rest for your souls

Matt 28:20

with you always

Luke 22:70

[before the Council in Jerusalem] You are right in saying I am. [in answer to the question 'are you the son of God'?]

[see also Mark 14: 61-2]

Acts 9:5

"I am Jesus" – in answer to Saul's question "who are you Lord?"

Rev 1:17

the alpha and the omega

Rev 22:7 and 12

coming soon

Rev 22:16

the Root and Offspring of David, and the bright Morning Star

Appendix 3
(Cross refer to Chapter 11)

The Sheep and the Goats (Matthew 25:31–33)

"When the Son of Man comes in his glory, and all the angels with him, he will sit on the throne of his glory. All the nations will be gathered before him, and he will separate people one from another as a shepherd separates the sheep from the goats and he will put the sheep at his right hand and the goats at the left."

This passage, taken from the NRSV translation, is often referred to as the 'parable' of the sheep and the goats. But this is no parable. It is a factual statement of the future using picture language. A parable is a story with a meaning. Or to put is another way, a meaning .... with a story. But the passage in Matthew 25 has no hidden meaning. It is a very clear guide to Christians to understand the Lord's priorities for our lives. Jesus is teaching that how we treat our brothers and sisters in Christ, and whether or not we meet their basic needs, will form the basis of how *we* are judged by God.

The shepherd who separates the sheep from the goats in today's passage, is of course Jesus — the Son of Man. The sheep are the righteous and the goats the unrighteous. Sheep and goats is an allegory, or an illustration, that Jesus used a number of times. What Jesus is describing in this passage is the last judgement, with all the angels present and all the nations gathered. Matthew's gospel has been described as *pre-eminently the gospel of judgement* — and a number of other passages also speak of separation — so we have the separation of the wheat from the chaff, the sincere from the hypocrites, wise builders from foolish, good fish from bad and profitable from unprofitable servants. Each uses picture language, but tells of a sober and factual reality. One day there will be a judgement. One day there will be a separation.

The great misinterpretation of this passage is to assume that Jesus is teaching about our care for the great mass of humanity rather than, as Jesus says specifically, His own brothers and sisters. Remember, Jesus' body is today the church (see references at the foot of Appendix 3). The idea of **"the least of these brothers of mine"** has been controversial — especially in recent times — where church based people have used this as a justification for their so-called social gospel, Christianity's otherwise legitimate concern for wider society and especially the world's poor. Christians are certainly required to display a care for the wider world (Proverbs 19:17 – Proverbs 21:13). We are commanded by Jesus to love our neighbour as ourselves (Mark 12:31). Jesus elsewhere explained whom our neighbour is (Luke 10:30–37). Our neighbour is *not* our brother or sister in Christ, in whom we are to see the face of Jesus our Lord. We have a different relationship, and a different responsibility to our brethren, as Jesus stated quite clearly: **". . . the righteous will answer him, 'Lord, when was it that we saw you hungry and gave you food, or thirsty and give you something to drink? And when was it that we saw you a stranger and welcomed you, or naked and gave you clothing? And when was it that we saw you sick or in prison and visited you?'**

"And the King will answer them, 'Truly I tell you, just as you did it to one of the least of these who are members of my family, you did it to me.' (Matthew 25:37 — 40, NRSV.)

For non-Christians who have the wherewithal but consciously and with a stiff neck refuse to help — for example, worthy secular charities, rather than Christian ones, which may of course be a stumbling block to them — there will be a real and deserved judgement. They, along with Christians, have a responsibility to their neighbours. This is because people know that they should help the sick and the poor – and the needy in general. People know those things because ultimately their consciences tell them so. And their consciences tell them so because God has written his Law on their hearts. In Romans chapter 1 Paul explains that humans *are without excuse* because . . . **what may be known of God is manifest in them, for God has shown it to them. For since the creation of the world His invisible attributes are clearly seen, being understood by the things that are made, even His eternal power and Godhead, so that they are without excuse** (Romans 1:19–20, NKJV). And then he goes on (in 2:14) to add: **for when Gentiles, who do not have the law, by nature do the things in the law, these, although not having the law, are a law to themselves, who show the work of the law written in their hearts, their conscience also bearing witness, and between themselves their thoughts accusing or else excusing them.** (Romans 2:14–15, NKJV.) As the Lord Jesus quite clearly made this distinction between sheep and goats, Christians need to note that they have a special duty to their own brothers and sisters in Christ – to their own flesh and blood. The apostle Paul emphasised this same point in his great lesson likening the Church to a body with many parts (1 Corinthians 12:12–31). Jesus is especially concerned about those parts of His body that suffer:

God has combined the members of the body and has given greater honor to the parts that lacked it, so that there should be no division in the body, but that its parts should have equal concern for each other. If one part

suffers, every part suffers with it; if one part is honored, every part rejoices with it. Now you are the body of Christ, and each one of you is a part of it.

1 Corinthians 12:24–27

When people kneel before the judgement seat of God, as inevitably we all must do – one day – then if they have failed to do the basic things required by the law, things demanded by their own consciences, God will rightly and justly condemn them on that basis. There may of course be other things for which God will also condemn them. But the sober fact is that they will have, as Paul said, 'no excuse'. For Christians there will also be no excuse for failure to help their brethren over and above, in a real sense, their neighbours — where circumstances demand it. The apostle Paul wrote in this Galatians 6:10: **Therefore, as we have opportunity, let us do good to all people,** *especially* **to those who belong to the family of believers.** (My emphasis.) One day Christians should expect to give an account to God of how we have looked after our brothers and sisters in Christ.

Other scriptures concerning the Church being the body of Christ:

One body and each member belongs to the others. (See Romans 12:5.) The Holy Spirit works in each member. (See 1 Corinthians 12:27.) Christ is head over everything and the Church is his body. (See Ephesians 1:22–23.) The objective is to prepare Christians for works of service so that the Church may be built up. (See Ephesians 4:12.) Our sufferings are made for the sake of the Church. (See Colossians 1:24.) No Church will grow without help from God. (See Colossians 2:19.) There is one body . . . (See Ephesians 4:4.)

Appendix 4

THE GOSPEL

We have referred in this book several times to the *Gospel writers* and *gospel witnesses*, but what is this word 'Gospel' or 'gospel' exactly? Our English word has been linked with the old English *god* (good), and *spell* (news) or, 'good news', but in the original Greek language in Roman culture it had to do with victory. A 'Gospel' (one of the four canonical Gospels) is a true account of Christ's victory, which is God's victory over Satan (as David Pawson explains vividly in his recent book *Come with me through Mark*[1]). The 'gospel' as preached (e.g. in the Acts of the Apostles, and as described by Paul), is the good news of salvation in Christ, available to all who genuinely seek Him, and who turn to Him in faith and repentance. There are many good books and pamphlets which set out the gospel in a clear and concise manner. Rather than emulate these in the next few pages, the reader may wish to see what the Bible itself says about the gospel. This will take the form of a short Bible study to examine what God's word lays down on this vitally important matter. These are not, it should be added, 'proof texts', they are the author's own selection and ideally should be read as part of a wider reading of an entire Gospel. Many Christians think that the Gospel of Luke is a good one to start on.

The whole Bible, Old and New Testaments, shows how we humans were created for a relationship with our Creator God, which, frankly, we do not deserve. It shows how humans rebelled against God, something that is true for each individual as well as society as a whole. The Bible calls this rebellion 'sin'. Having given all mankind consciences, he also gave his chosen people a body of law (*torah*) which they were to observe.

---

[1] *Come with me through Mark* Terra Nova Publications ISBN 9781901949667

There is only one way to peace and a right relationship with God, and God proved to us that we cannot earn our way to a right relationship with Him. We are by nature rebels —sinners.

The Bible shows that God determined on a plan of salvation from the earliest of times. His plan would be most costly to Himself, as it involved surrendering His own greatly beloved Son to meet our deepest need. And as Jesus is one person of the 'godhead' it ultimately means that God *Himself* paid the price. Only by costly sacrifice could we humans begin to see the enormity of the crime of our rebellion against our Holy and spotless Creator. The only sacrifice that could possibly be acceptable to God was His own dear sinless Son. That is why Jesus had to die in our place (for the 'wages' of sin is death — see Romans 6:23). The cross of the Lord Jesus now stands between us and the wrath of God. By accepting the free gift of salvation earned for us by the Lord Jesus, we become part of His family - *saved from* the penalty of our sin and *saved to* a new life of worship and service as His own people.

A one verse 'Gospel'
Acts 16:31 — **"Believe in the Lord Jesus and you will be saved."** You cannot get more straightforward than that!

There are a few points to note about it:

1. An act of faith: "Believe in ...."
What is faith? It is not just saying that you believe. It is believing 'in' — an act of will, surrender, commitment and real trust. Other translations render this (perhaps more correctly) as 'believe on' which helps to double-emphasise this foundational aspect of believing.

2. **The object of faith — 'the Lord Jesus ...'**
To whom do we trust and commit our lives? — Jesus. He
was a human being and His name means Saviour. The Lord
— His title — is a divine title; He is God's Son.
3. **The outcome of faith: 'and you will be saved.'**
What does it mean to be saved?

NOW it means:
- forgiveness of all our sins and a clear conscience
- friendship instead of enmity with God
- being a member of God's kingdom and family, instead
  of being under Satan's dominion
- the gift of His Spirit and His power to be different

THEN it will mean:
- going to heaven instead of hell when we die
- having a new body in heaven like Christ's risen body
- being made perfect and full of glory
- seeing Christ, worshipping God face to face

ETERNAL LIFE is the term that links the NOW and the
THEN together.

Some key Bible Passages which explain the gospel
1. **Born again**
New life in Christ is so radical that it is not *like* being born
again, it *is* being spiritually reborn See John 3:1–21 (see
also Ephesians 4:22–24; 1 Peter 1:23; Colossians 3:3).
2. **Salvation**
We are 'saved' by God's gift — the Bible calls this grace —
and grace is God's free unmerited favour. It cannot be earned
in any way. This, frankly, is a stumbling block to many. Note
that grace cannot be effective *apart* from a seeker's personal
faith in Jesus Christ. (See Romans 3:21–26; Acts 2:38–41;
Acts 8:36; 1 Corinthians 11:29; Hebrews 4:2).

3. Atonement

To 'atone' for some wrong done to another means to make amends for that wrong. In the Christian sense the idea of atonement is that we humans have wronged God by sinning against Him, and it is the Lord Jesus who makes atonement for that sin by taking our guilt upon Himself. So, Jesus' death on the cross in our place is *the* atonement — the acceptable sacrifice to God. Once our sins are atoned for by Jesus, we become 'at-one' (by no means a definition of the word *atone*, but quite helpful, nevertheless!) with God (see Ephesians 2:1–10; 1 John 2:2; Colossians 1:13; Hebrews 9:24–29).

4. How to be Saved

No matter how sinful we have been, Jesus Christ, the Son of God, died for us and if we repent (i.e. genuinely turn away from our rebellion against God), God will forgive us. What do we need to do in order to accept God's free gift of salvation? As it has been said, we need to go through three simple steps, A, B and C: **(A)** Admit our need of salvation; **(B)** Believe in the Lord Jesus; **(C)** Commit our lives to Him. At a practical level, this means consciously praying to God, asking His forgiveness for past sins and His power to live a new life for Him.

Once we are saved, do we stop sinning? Sadly we do not completely stop sinning this side of heaven. The old sinful nature tries to reassert itself as God's enemy (and our enemy) the devil, tries to make us rebel against God. But being a Christian in the sense of John 3:18 does help us to *sin less*. As we go on in the Christian life, God graciously and patiently reveals to us areas of our lives where we need specifically to yield to Him. So God slowly and surely (and perceptibly) makes us more like Christ. When, after having become a Christian, we sin, we need to repent of (turn away from) that sin and ask His forgiveness. We might think of this in terms of a child and its parent — although a child might rebel against its parent, this does not alter the fact that the child is, and always will be, the child of its parent. This is, perhaps, a poor analogy (in that our sonship as Christians is by adoption and grace, and it relates in a special way to the concept of inheritance) but if we are truly of Jesus' flock, go on believing in Him and walking in obedience, we can have confidence that He will not lose us (cp. John 6:37). It may however be possible for those who have at some point professed faith in Jesus to simply walk away from Him and so to place themselves back the under judgement of God. This is a controversial debate within the church so we will not seek to be definitive about it, merely to observe what the Lord Jesus Himself said (Matthew 10:33), **"whoever disowns me before men, I will disown him before my Father in heaven."**

The Lord Jesus Himself referred to the fact that His followers would continue, from time to time, to sin (see John 13:10) and would therefore need to be 'washed' in respect of these later sins. Plainly, it is not His desire that Christians sin, but He has recognised that we are 'flesh' and therefore weak, and will sometimes yield to temptation. This is not the same, it should be added, as living in a state of complete and permanent rebellion against God. It is difficult to see how a true believer could continue to live in this way, but Christians can become misled, or have wrong notions. These deficiencies the Lord Jesus has made provision for. Once we have been saved (i.e. our whole being is 'clean' and does not need to be cleaned again, which is the meaning of John 13:10) which Jesus likens to having been bathed, we will continue to journey through life during which our 'feet' will become soiled (i.e. we occasionally sin). We do not need to be bathed again, but we do need to 'wash our feet' (repent of particular, known sins). Once we repent of such known sins, God has made wonderful provision for us to be restored (see Lamentations 3: 22–23; Gal 6:1; 1 John 1:9 and Proverbs 28:13).

Exactly how do we go through steps A, B and C? There is no 'approved' form of words for a prayer asking the Lord Jesus to save us and make us part of His family. God looks more on the heart than any precise words used. But the following prayer may be helpful to those who truly want to commit their lives to the Lord Jesus:

Dear Heavenly Father, I sadly recognise and acknowledge that I have rebelled against your right to be my God. I am a sinner.

I do believe that Jesus came to this world to be my Saviour and He has died in my place. Please forgive me for all my past sins. I turn from them to you, now. Please take me into your family and may Jesus now be my Lord, as well as my Saviour. Please fill me with your Holy Spirit so that I can live in His power for you, my Lord and my Saviour.

From now on I will acknowledge you publicly as my Lord and ask your strength to follow you each day. I thank you from the bottom of my heart for hearing my prayer and saving me. Please help me to remain close to you from this day forward. I humbly ask all these things in the Lord Jesus' name and for His sake. Amen.

Anyone who has prayed such a prayer for the first time (and it may be good, though by no means necessary, to do this with a trusted Christian friend) should immediately do two things. Firstly, find a good church, one that will help to build you up as you grow in the Christian faith. Ask God to help you find such a church, quickly. Second, let at least one other person know that you are now a Christian, preferably someone who will not be hostile to the idea! It is important that you learn to let other people know about your new life, and it will help to make the step more real to you. And don't feel overwhelmed by the step you have just taken, the God who planned from pre-history to bring His Son into the world to be our Saviour, is more than a match for any opposition you may face or any inadequacies you may feel!

Welcome to the family of Christ!

As soon as is reasonably practicable, a new believer should be baptised, so as to make a public confession of the change that has come upon them, but above all in order to respond in obedience to the call of Jesus. Part of His commission to His church is to baptise, so the call to baptism is part of the preached gospel.

In conclusion

In conclusion we might say that a true Christian is someone who has made a conscious decision to follow Christ and to become His true disciple. Such a person then walks through life with Jesus as their Lord and Saviour, as well as their teacher and friend (if they go on believing in Him, and walking in obedience). They will 'pick up their cross' daily, as they seek to follow Him, recognising that to be a true disciple will occasionally call for real sacrifices (in terms of time, money, relationships and, in some cases, life itself) but will daily require a struggle with what we sometimes call *the world, the flesh and the devil* — i.e. difficulties and temptations. These come from three different directions: (1) from this world, which tends to be anti-Christian in practice, if not in profession (and the word 'world' in this sense has to do with all that is opposed to God); (2) from 'the flesh'

— ourselves, and our own inclinations which all too often place ourselves at the helm of our lives, rather than allowing Jesus our Lord to take the helm; (3) from our real spiritual enemy, Satan, and his demons, who will from time to time seek to attack us, trying to make us doubt God, doubt our salvation and encourage us into sin. As regards Satan we should not be unduly afraid. He Who is in us (Jesus) is much greater than he who is in the world (the devil). What power the devil has is strictly limited, in spite of appearances to the contrary. The devil is more likely to cause us problems if we deliberately sin or deliberately turn our backs on Jesus.

Appendix 5

The Suffering Church
(cross refer to chapter 14)

When we talk about the suffering church we are talking about the persecuted church, in other words the church that suffers because it proclaims the name of Jesus Christ. It must be true that sometimes the church suffers for other reasons — perhaps because of its own rebellion against God; perhaps because of its own indifference to social or moral evil, which leads in turn to spiritual weakness. But we turn our attention for a moment to consider suffering in the context of persecution. Jesus said **"Blessed are you when people insult you, persecute you and falsely say all kinds of evil against you because of me. Rejoice and be glad, because great is your reward in heaven, for in the same way they persecuted the prophets who were before you."** (Matthew 5:11–12.)

In John chapter 15 (v. 18) Jesus said **"If the world hates you, keep in mind that it hated me first. If you belonged to the world, it would love you as its own. As it is you do not belong to the world, but I have chosen you out of the world. That is why the world hates you. Remember the words I spoke to you: 'No servant is greater than his master'. If they persecuted me, they will persecute you also. If they obeyed my teaching they will obey yours also. They will treat you this way because of my name . . . ."** And then in John 16:1, **"All this I have told you so that you will not go astray. They will put you out of the synagogue; in fact, a time is coming when anyone who kills you will think he is offering a service to God."** In saying that, Jesus was addressing the persecution that would afflict the immediate disciples and the early church. But He was also addressing all of those who would follow Him. What was true for the disciples of the Bible is true for us today, but not always in such extremes.

The people of God are no strangers to persecution. The entire Holy Bible is a testament not only to God's goodness, justice and mercy, but also to the devil's opposition to God, which manifests itself in opposition to God's people in particular, and to all mankind in general. Right back in the earliest parts of the Bible we see persecution of the righteous by the unrighteous. Righteousness is word that the world does not like. The real meaning of righteousness is being right with God (having been justified by Him, by grace through faith) and right living. Righteousness is in contrast to, and in opposition to, evil. Evil will not countenance righteousness. It will not look at righteousness, and so opposes it. Today a popular caricature of the church is that Christians are a lot of self-righteous people thinking how good we are and looking down on everyone else. Ironically, the world fails to understand that whatever righteousness Christians have is not self-righteousness, it is Christ's righteousness. We can only stand before a holy God as His children because our sinless Saviour (that is, our completely and utterly righteous Saviour) has accepted and paid the debt that belongs to us, the debt of our sins.

The earliest persecution we encounter in the Bible was of Abel by his brother Cain, in Genesis chapter 4. Abel's sacrifice was acceptable to God, whilst Cain's sacrifice was not. So Cain was very jealous of Abel and murdered him. In the church we too easily allegorise the account of Cain and Abel, tending to turn it into a sort of myth. It seems to the author to be literally true that as men try to build their own righteousness before God, whether through politics, or humanism, or religions, these same men are angered by the one sacrifice that is acceptable to God, the sacrifice of Jesus Christ, His Son. It seems to the author to be most likely that the account of Cain and Abel is literally true, that Cain murdered his brother on account of Abel's goodness compared to Cain's shabbiness. The Bible is replete with stories of those who suffered for doing right. We think of Daniel, thrown to the lions, yet protected by God. We think of Moses, opposed along with his people — the Hebrew slaves — by Pharaoh, the dictator of Egypt. We think of the prophets, many of whom were martyred for delivering God's message without fear or favour to people and to leaders who did not want to listen.

Our Lord Jesus repeatedly warned of persecution for those who follow him. Even within households — that brother would betray brother and children would betray parents. Jesus pointed out that even the Son of Man had nowhere to lay his head (Matt 8:20) — so His followers should not expect an easy ride. Jesus told us not to fear when arraigned before the courts. The Holy Spirit will give us the words we need to say in our defence, and just as pertinently, we might add, in Jesus' defence as well. Luke records Jesus as saying:

" . . . they will lay hands on you and persecute you. They will deliver you to synagogues and prisons, and you will be brought before kings and governors, and all on account of my name. This will result in your being witnesses to them. But make up your mind not to worry beforehand how you will defend yourselves. For I will give you words and wisdom that none of your adversaries will be able to resist or contradict." (Luke 21:12-15).

In Matthew chapter 10, Jesus also warns of persecutions to

come: "Brother will betray brother to death, and a father his child; children will rebel against their parents and have them put to death. All men will hate you because of me, but he who stands firm to the end will be saved. When you are persecuted in one place, flee to another. I tell you the truth, you will not finish going through the cities of Israel before the Son of Man comes.

"A student is not above his teacher, nor a servant above his master. It is enough for the student to be like his teacher, and the servant like his master. If the head of the house has been called Beelzebub, how much more the members of his household!

"So do not be afraid of them. There is nothing concealed that will not be disclosed, or hidden that will not be made known. What I tell you in the dark, speak in the daylight; what is whispered in your ear, proclaim from the roofs. Do not be afraid of those who kill the body but cannot kill the soul. Rather, be afraid of the One who can destroy both soul and body in hell. Are not two sparrows sold for a penny? Yet not one of them will fall to the ground apart from the will of your Father. And even the very hairs of your head are all numbered. So don't be afraid; you are worth more than many sparrows.

Whoever acknowledges me before men, I will also acknowledge him before my Father in heaven. But whoever disowns me before men, I will disown him before my Father in heaven. Do not suppose that I have come to bring peace to the earth. I did not come to bring peace, but a sword. For I have come to turn 'a man against his father, a daughter against her mother, a daughter-in-law against her mother in law' — a man's enemies will be the members of his own household."

Anyone who loves his father or mother more than me is not worthy of me; anyone who loves his son or daughter more than me is not worthy of me; and anyone who does not take his cross and follow me is not worthy of me. Whoever finds his life will lose it, and whoever loses his life for my sake will find it. (Matthew 10:21-39.)

Tough and uncomfortable teaching from our Lord. Every now and then we need to be jolted out of our soft, saccharin idea of 'gentle Jesus, meek and mild'. Here we encounter the awesome reality of the cost of following Jesus. The Lord Himself is the ultimate realist. He knew what his own death would be. He tells us plainly that to follow Him is no picnic — it never has been and it never will be easy. On account of Jesus, strife will emerge within societies, within friendships, and even within families. So, Jesus' call to discipleship includes frank warnings of danger, and of reviling, slander, accusation, floggings, arraignment before courts, hatred and death. There is a high cost to following Jesus. The Lord himself would be judicially murdered on the basis of false accusations. Each accusation was a lie, but this did not protect him. In the book of Acts we encounter the first persecutions against the fledgling church. But — and we need always to keep this very much in mind — God is in control. The early church was scattered by persecution and the gospel message of the crucifixion and resurrection of Jesus spread ever further. The whole epistle of First Peter is about preparing for suffering, preparing for persecution. Readers may want themselves to look up 1 Peter 4:12 – 19 in this regard.

So what do these persecutions have in common? Today, throughout the world, Christians are discriminated against. There is discrimination of society at large and even Britain is not immune from this. We have heard in recent years of Christian organisations that have state funding cut off because they refuse to toe the line on some politically correct issue. Throughout the world a favourite persecution tactic is to prevent Christians from building, or even repairing, church buildings. People are beginning to wonder how long it will be in Europe before local councils begin to use planning laws against Christians.

In Islamic countries, as in Hindu, there is an ever greater willingness to discriminate against Christians at an institutional level. So institutions such as the police and judiciary fail to protect minorities, and allow anti-Christian crime to go unpunished. Throughout the world today, another tactic of persecution is in the area of employment. Christians are routinely passed over for promotion. Christians will be dismissed on whatever pretext, and often find it difficult to gain alternative employment. There are also boycotts of Christian businesses, so making it harder for Christians to continue to live where they are. Whilst these persecutions may occasionally be extended to other minorities, it always seems to be most vehement against Christians. Persecution against Jews, that root-stock into which Christianity is in-grafted, requires separate study but, we note, it often accompanies persecution against Christians.

Framing laws to prevent conversion from one religion to another seems especially aimed at Christians. Under Sharia in Islamic societies, a male who converts to is supposed to be executed. And this sometimes happens. More often it is a case of murder — where Governments fear international outcry at the more fundamental aspects of their religious laws, they turn a blind eye when religious fanatics literally take the law into their own hands. In many counties, even where Christianity is theoretically tolerated, there can be real problems for those who want to worship openly. Limits on the numbers of people who can assemble, and on locations where they can assemble, are favoured tactics in some societies.

The words 'Christianity' and 'persecution' are almost synonymous. Jesus spoke clearly of the cost that would be incurred by becoming one of his disciples, and around the world today the body of Christ is experiencing great persecution. God commands us to remember our persecuted fellow believers and pray for them as if we were suffering right beside them (see, e.g. Hebrews 13:3).

God is not a loser: He will preserve for himself a Church and a holy nation in spite of persecution of His children. And martyred men, women and children — martyred as they have been down through history — will have a special place in the kingdom of heaven. Where do we find the end of this story? As we might expect, it is at the end of the Bible. We pick up the story in Revelation chapter 6, where John the apostle recounts his vision of heaven's seals being opened. The fifth seal reveals the souls of all those who 'had been slain because of the word of God and the testimony they had maintained'. They ask God openly how long it will be before their blood is avenged. They are told to wait a little longer, until the last of the martyrs are gathered to heaven. Then (in 7:13) we pick up the glorious climax. Those clothed in white robes: **. . . are those who have come out of the great tribulation; they have washed their robes and made them white, in the blood of the lamb. They are before the throne of God and serve him day and night in his temple. And he who sits in the temple will spread his tent over them. Never again will they hunger or thirst. The sun will not beat upon them, nor any scorching heat. For the lamb at the centre of the throne**

will be their shepherd, and he will lead them to springs of living water. And God will wipe away every tear from their eyes. (Revelation 7:13–17).

Finally, in Revelation 19, John recounts: **Then I heard what sounded like a great multitude, like the roar of rushing waters and like peals of thunder, shouting 'Hallelujah! For our Lord God Almighty reigns. Let us rejoice and be glad and give him the glory! For the wedding of the lamb has come, and his bride has made herself ready. Fine linen, bright and clean, was given her to wear'. (Fine linen stands for the righteous acts of the saints). Then the angel said to me 'Write: blessed are those who are invited to the wedding supper of the lamb'. And he added, "These are the true words of God."** (Revelation 19:6–8.)

Persecution today, as in generations past, ends in an eternal wedding feast and our Lord Jesus returning for his bride, the church. What an ending! Hallelujah indeed!

Other books by Glory to Glory Publications

KINGDOM SEEKERS *Mike Endicott*

What does it mean to seek first the kingdom of God? Mike Endicott encourages us to become kingdom seekers, and he sets out some exciting truths about God's kingdom, its attractiveness and centrality to the Christian life. Jesus affirmed that he is the way, the truth and the life, and the author explores some powerful implications of this. A prolific author, Mike lives in south Wales where, with others, he founded the first Well Centre as a place of ministry. He spends his life in prayer and the encouragement of others through ministry, teaching and writing.

THE HOPE *Mark Jones*

Unemployment is hitting people from all walks of life. Here is practical guidance for coping with the trauma, which affects our loved ones as well as ourselves. The clear message of this book is that with God-given hope there is no limit to what we can achieve for Him.

THE BIRTH OF CHRIST *Peter Sammons*

Did the nativity of the Lord Jesus happen in the way described in the Gospels? The author believes that the biblical account is true and has assembled impressive historical and biblical evidence to support this view. This book will both encourage believers and go a long way to convince skeptics.

LOVE NEVER FAILS *Adrian Rose*

Adrian suffered with serious illness from 1996 to 2003 which, at worst, caused him to be almost 100% disabled. This book tells the story of a young man's journey from sickness to health, and the huge part his Christian faith played in helping him to find peace, purpose and, eventually, miraculous healing.

MY GRACE IS SUFFICIENT *Linda Palmer*

Linda suffered for many years with M.E. (Chronic Fatigue Syndrome/ CFIDS). At her lowest point, Linda cried out to God for help. Nothing could have prepared her for the amazing way that He would graciously intervene in her situation . . . .

Forthcoming title

THE CASE FOR ENLARGEMENT THEOLOGY *Alex Jacob MA*

A response to the impasse within contemporary Jewish-Christian relations, arising from the inherent weaknesses of replacement theology and two covenant theology in the light of Romans 9–11. Any mature Christian understanding of Jewish-Christian relations needs to make allowance for the theological background and history within which these relations have developed. Alex Jacob provides this background, as well as introducing a biblically faithful way between the two theological poles.